MUSEUMS, PREJUDICE AND THE REFRAMING OF DIFFERENCE

D1581641

How, if at all, do museums shape the ways in which society understands difference?

In recent decades there has been growing international interest amongst practitioners, academics and policy makers, in the role that museums might play in confronting prejudice and promoting cross-cultural understanding. A small but growing number of museums articulate, as their primary purpose, the promotion of human rights and seek to engender support among audiences for notions of equality and social justice. Moreover, museums in many parts of the world are increasingly expected to construct exhibitions which represent, in more equitable ways, the culturally pluralist societies within which they operate, accommodating and engaging with differences on the basis of gender, race, ethnicity, class, religion, disability, sexuality and so on. Despite the ubiquity of these trends, there is nevertheless limited understanding of the social effects, and attendant political consequences, of these purposive representational strategies.

Richard Sandell combines interdisciplinary theoretical perspectives with in-depth empirical investigation to address a number of timely questions. How do audiences engage with and respond to exhibitions designed to contest, subvert and reconfigure prejudiced conceptions of different social groups? To what extent can museums be understood to shape, not simply reflect, normative understandings of difference, acceptability and tolerance? What are the challenges for museums which attempt to engage audiences in debating morally charged and contested contemporary social issues and how might these be addressed?

Drawing on in-depth case studies and a range of international examples, Sandell argues that museums frame, inform and enable the conversations which audiences, and society more broadly, have about difference and highlights the moral and political challenges, opportunities and responsibilities which accompany these constitutive qualities.

Richard Sandell is Deputy Head of the Department of Museum Studies at the University of Leicester. His research interests focus on the evolving social purposes, roles and agency of museums. His recent publications include *Museums, Society, Inequality* (2002).

MUSEUMS, PREJUDICE AND THE REFRAMING OF DIFFERENCE

Richard Sandell

Routledge
Taylor & Francis Group

LONDON AND NEW YORK

First published 2007
by Routledge
2 Park Square, Milton Park, Abingdon, Oxon OX14 4RN

Simultaneously published in the USA and Canada
by Routledge
270 Madison Avenue, New York, NY 10016

Reprinted 2007

Routledge is an imprint of the Taylor & Francis Group

© 2007 Richard Sandell

Typeset in Sabon by Saxon Graphics Ltd, Derby
Printed and bound in Great Britain by Antony Rowe Ltd,
Chippenham, Wiltshire

British Library Cataloguing in Publication Data
A catalogue record for this book is available from the British Library

Library of Congress Cataloging in Publication Data
A catalog record for this book has been requested

ISBN 10: 0-415-36748-4 (hbk)
ISBN 10: 0-415-36749-2 (pbk)
ISBN 13: 978-0-415-36748-6 (hbk)
ISBN 13: 978-0-415-36749-3 (pbk)
ISBN 13: 978-0-203-02003-6 (ebk)

Grateful acknowledgement is made to Weidenfeld & Nicolson, an
imprint of The Orion Publishing Group, for permission to reprint an
extract from *Birds of Heaven* by Ben Okri, 1996.

FOR CRAIG

Stories are the secret reservoir of values: change the stories individuals or nations live by and tell themselves, and you change the individuals and nations.

Ben Okri

CONTENTS

ILLUSTRATIONS

Figures

Illustrations 1.1, 1.3, 1.5, 3.2, 3.3, 3.7 and 5.3 appear by courtesy of the author.

Tables

PREFACE

Sociology, cultural studies, anthropology and museum studies have, over the past two decades, thoroughly positioned museums as sites in which social understandings of cultural difference are negotiated, constituted, and communicated. Although work within these disciplines has sometimes sought to acknowledge the complexities, contradictions and ambivalence involved in modes of cultural production (and, more rarely, those associated with processes of audience reception), analyses have very often highlighted the capacity for museums to function as instruments of power, generating discriminatory effects through the ways in which differences – in particular racial and gender variations – have been represented in hierarchical and otherwise negative, pernicious ways. The representational practices of the museum have frequently been characterised as excluding and oppressive through their capacity and their tendency to erase, marginalise or silence minority groups and identities.

In recent years, however, there has been a growing interest – especially amongst practitioners – in the potential which museums might hold to function as sites for the staging of liberatory interventions designed to contest or subvert dominant (oppressive, discriminatory) understandings of difference. Although relatively few museums have sought to develop exhibitions that *purposively* offer these alternative ways of seeing – which explicitly seek to communicate and engender support for concepts of equal human rights and social justice – there is nevertheless evidence of a much more widespread concern to represent different communities in more equitable and respectful ways. Museums of all kinds, and in many parts of the world, are increasingly expected to develop their displays in ways which reflect the diverse, culturally pluralist societies within which they are operating.

Although the concern to refashion museums as agencies with the capacity to counter prejudices and shape more egalitarian understandings of difference is more or less ubiquitous (Bennett 2005), limited attention has been given to exploring the social and cultural effects and consequences of newly emerging representational forms. In what ways do audiences engage with exhibitions designed to affirm differences, promote cross-community under-standing and respect, counter prejudice and intolerance and privilege ways of seeing underpinned by concepts of equity and social justice? What potential, if any, might museums hold to shape, not simply reflect, both individual and broader societal understandings of difference? What challenges and dilemmas are museum practitioners, involved in producing exhibitions and other public programmes that seek to confront different forms of prejudice, likely to encounter along the way? This book then draws on two distinct studies to address these largely neglected questions.

The first study, which focuses primarily on processes of audience reception – on the ways in which visitors respond to, interact with and make use of exhibitions purposefully intended to counter wide-ranging prejudices – informs the largest part of this book. By blending contemporary theoretical perspectives from a range of disciplines (primarily sociology, audience and media studies but also cultural studies, museum studies, discourse analysis and social psychology) and bringing these to bear on the analysis of empirical, in-depth visitor research, I aim to shed light on the social agency of museums; a term I use to refer to the capacity for museums to (in varied ways) shape, not simply reflect, social and political relations and realities. The second study I draw upon (principally in chapter 6) focuses not on processes of reception but on those associated with cultural production – on museum collections and displays and the opportunities and challenges bound up with their deployment in representational strategies designed to confront prejudices associated with disability.

In some senses, this investigation of social agency is in step with current museological thinking and practice. Although the conception of the museum as an agent of social change is sometimes fiercely contested, there is neverthe-less growing international interest in the adoption of purposes and functions which position museums as institutions which can be brought to bear on 'the social' in various ways. Consequently, one of my main aims is to develop a set of concepts, a language and a body of evidence with which to under-stand and explain these emerging trends and phenomena. Museums, I shall argue, can counter prejudice through their capacity to frame (and reframe), to inform and enable the conversations which visitors, and society more broadly, have about difference. However, in other ways, the arguments I develop in this book also serve to problematise these trends and to question some of the conventions in contemporary exhibitionary practice as well as current thinking within museum communication and representation. For example, some forms of prejudice emerge from my study as both more chal-lenging for audiences to engage with and more problematic for museums to confront. Through an exploration of the factors which account for this situation in which some forms of oppression and discrimination are univer-sally and unequivocally condemned whilst others remain either neglected or deemed to be negotiable and open to debate, I attempt to highlight the complex and dynamic relationship museums have with dominant social values and norms. My contention that museums might consider, in some circumstances, substituting their attempts to remain impartial and objective (by presenting diverse, sometimes opposing perspectives on particular issues and leaving visitors to come to their own conclusions) with approaches which privilege (and attempt to engender support for) a particular moral (non-prejudiced) standpoint is perhaps one with which many readers will be uncomfortable. A further purpose of this book then is to contribute to ongoing debates about the purpose, agency and concomitant social responsibilities of museums (and, indeed, other media engaged in the representation of minority or marginalised social groups).

Finally, it will be evident to readers that I have approached this study from a particular political and moral standpoint. However, although my investigations have been framed in various ways by aspects of my experience and identity and the views I have developed about the social role of museums, I did not set out to gather evidence with which to 'prove' a pre-determined conclusion and shore up my preformed ideas. Rather, my intention from the outset has been to discover how – *if at all* – museums might shape the ways in which audiences view, think and talk about difference.

Richard Sandell
June 2006

ACKNOWLEDGEMENTS

The ideas I discuss in this book have taken shape over many years and have grown out of a wide variety of experiences and opportunities. Although my interest in the social role of museums originates from my work as a practitioner, the opportunity to investigate the topic empirically came some years later when I began my doctoral research with the University of Sheffield's Department of Sociological Studies. I owe a particular debt of thanks to my supervisor Sharon Macdonald for her inspiration, guidance, insights and encouragement throughout the research process. I also wish to thank Jo Britton for her invaluable advice and for introducing me to new ways of approaching the topic of prejudice.

The time spent conducting fieldwork in the St Mungo Museum of Religious Life and Art and the Anne Frank House was both challenging and immensely enjoyable. I am grateful to the staff of both museums for providing me with access to such tremendously rich sites for investigation and for generously sharing their thoughts and ideas, in particular Harry Dunlop, Kiran Singh, Jan van Kooten, Frans van der Pieterman, Selwyn Eisden and Wouter van der Sluis. I thank also those many visitors who gave me their time and shared their reflections on the museum experience with me.

In 2004 I was awarded a Fellowship in Museum Practice at the Smithsonian Institution which enabled me, in the summer of the following year, to carry out additional fieldwork, to develop ideas that were emerging from my prior research in Europe, and to test these through engagement with other researchers and practitioners operating in very different social and political contexts. I am grateful to the many staff of the Smithsonian Institution who agreed to be interviewed for my research. I am especially indebted to Nancy Fuller at the Smithsonian's Center for Education and Museum Studies for her thoughts on my research as well as for sustaining me with her tremendous sense of humour. I must also thank the Smithsonian Institution's Women's Committee for their support of this unique programme. During the four months of my Fellowship I had the opportunity to visit and spend time in a number of different museums. In particular, I would like to thank the staff of the United States Holocaust Memorial Museum, the Lower East Side Tenement Museum, the Japanese American National Museum and the Museum of Tolerance for their willingness to engage in debate and share their resources.

There are many colleagues working in museums and universities who have generously given their time and assisted with this project in many different ways. I am especially grateful to Sarah Ogilvie, Ted Phillips, Katherine Ott, Beth Ziebarth, Robert Janes, Bruce Craig, John Suau, Margaret Lindauer, Christina Kreps, Joan Kanigan-Fairen and the late Stephen Weil.

Chapter 6 draws heavily on the findings of a project undertaken by the University of Leicester's Research Centre for Museums and Galleries. I am grateful to my colleagues with whom I collaborated on that project, especially Jocelyn Dodd, Annie Delin, Jackie Gay and Ceri Jones as well as the Arts and Humanities Research Board (now the Arts and Humanities Research Council) for their financial support through the Innovation Awards scheme.

This book would not have been completed without the research leave which the University of Leicester kindly granted me in 2005. I am grateful to all of my colleagues in the Department of Museum Studies for their support over the last nine years. In particular I must thank Jocelyn Dodd with whom I have collaborated on a number of research projects and whose insights have always enriched my work. I have greatly appreciated the support and guidance given to me by Simon Knell, Eilean Hooper-Greenhill and Suzanne MacLeod as well as their encouragement to press on when a finished manuscript seemed a million miles away.

For assistance with securing images I thank Barbara Lloyd, Gurpreet Ahluwalia, Alison Kelly, Nathalie Delorme, Karl-Heinz Steinle, Maren Read, Joan Headley, Andrew Chamberlain and for invaluable administrative support, Christine Cheesman. Thanks also to Matt Gibbons, Geraldine Martin, Katia Hamza and colleagues at Routledge for their ongoing assistance.

I owe a particular debt of thanks to Mark O'Neill for his interest in and support of my research over several years, for kindly agreeing to review an earlier draft of the book and for generously providing me with numerous insights and suggestions which have helped me to refine and clarify the arguments in this final version.

My parents, my sister Nicki and my friends have always been a source of encouragement and support. Lewis and Anna deserve a special mention for their capacity to provide most welcome distraction from the business of writing and at just the right moment. Finally, I thank my partner Craig – to whom this book is dedicated – for his unending patience and good humour over the many years it has taken me to complete this project.

1

MUSEUMS AND THE GOOD SOCIETY

At the St Mungo Museum of Religious Life and Art in Glasgow, Scotland, visitors find works of art, inspired by diverse religious beliefs, sharing a gallery space and presented alongside each other in ways designed to suggest their equal importance and value. Objects linked to the six most practised world religions – Buddhism, Christianity, Hinduism, Islam, Judaism and Sikhism – are displayed in ways which aim to highlight the commonalities between faiths as well as to show what is unique about each. Visitors are invited to share their reactions to the exhibitions and their views on the museum with others through written comments displayed within the galleries. These approaches to display are shaped by the museum's founding social purpose – to promote mutual understanding and respect between people of different faiths and of no faith (O'Neill 1994).

At the Anne Frank House in Amsterdam, visitors follow a prescribed route through the house and into the Secret Annex where the Frank family hid during the Second World War, learning more about the historical events surrounding the writing of the diaries that have become so widely known. Following their tour of the house, many of the museum's approximately one million visitors each year are surprised to encounter an exhibition exploring contemporary social situations in which human rights come into conflict. Visitors are encouraged to form and share their own opinions on such wide-ranging topics as homophobic hate crime, the controversial lyrics of rap artist Eminem, representations of disabled people in advertising and the rights of individuals and political groups to express their racist views. Although designed to encourage debate and to elicit audience responses in relation to challenging issues of prejudice and discrimination, the exhibition is nevertheless underpinned by, and aims to engender support for, the concept of equal human rights for all.

Although the purposive approaches to display embodied within exhibitions at the Anne Frank House and the St Mungo Museum are, in some ways, distinctive and experimental, they are nevertheless illustrative of much broader shifts in museological thinking and practice that have been taking place and which have become influential in shaping international museum rhetoric and policy. In recent years, museums have become increasingly confident in proclaiming their value as agents of social change and, in particular, articulating their capacity to promote cross-cultural understanding, to tackle prejudice and intolerance and to foster respect for difference. This confidence is reflected in both the mission statements of individual, socially purposive museums and in more broadly-framed policy and advocacy documents that articulate generic claims regarding the value of museums.

A relatively small, but growing, number of 'specialist' museums, whose primary purposes and rationales are concerned with combating prejudice and promoting human rights, have received increasing attention within the museum world. These include, for example, the Lower East Side Tenement Museum, the National Underground Railroad Freedom Center, the Japanese American National Museum and the Museum of Tolerance in the United States, the District Six Museum and Constitution Hill in South Africa, as well as the St Mungo Museum of Religious Life and Art in Scotland and the Anne Frank House in Holland. An ambitious new project, currently in planning – the Canadian Museum for Human Rights – claims it will be the largest centre for education around human rights in the world.[1]

Concern for these issues has not been confined solely to these, in some ways specialised, museums with explicitly social missions. The idea that museums of all kinds contribute, in varied ways, towards the creation of a less prejudiced society is increasingly reflected in the rhetoric from international museum agencies, professional associations and governments. The following statements, from the International Council of Museums, the American Association of Museums and the UK's Department for Culture, Media and Sport, are illustrative of the ways in which the roles, purposes and value of museums are increasingly being articulated:

> Museums have unique potential for addressing and fostering cultural understanding in interdisciplinary ways.
> (International Council of Museums 2005)[2]

> Museums perform their most fruitful public service by providing an educational experience in the broadest sense: by fostering the ability to live in a pluralistic society and to contribute to the resolution of the challenges we face as global citizens ... Museums can no longer confine themselves simply to preservation, scholarship, and exhibition independent of the social context in which they exist. They must recognize that the public dimension of museums leads them to perform the public service of education – a term that in its broadest sense includes exploration, study, observation, critical thinking, contemplation, and dialogue.
> (American Association of Museums 1992: 6–8)

[M]useums can help visitors reflect on their place in the world, their identity, their differences and similarities ... Museums can provide a tolerant space where difficult contemporary issues can be explored in safety and in the spirit of debate.

(Department for Culture, Media and Sport 2005: 11)

Although, as these statements suggest, contemporary conceptions of museums focus on their potential to operate as agents of positive (liberatory, empowering, inclusive) social change, sociological critiques of the ways museums function in society (especially, though not exclusively, drawing on historical examples) have often highlighted their tendency to represent cultures in hierarchical ways with oppressive and excluding consequences.

Wide-ranging studies – variously arguing from theory, from history and more rarely from empirical audience research – have attempted to show that museums of all kinds, including science museums that have made some of the strongest claims to objectivity, do not constitute 'neutral sheltering places for objects' (Duncan 1995: 1) but rather that they generate ideological effects by constructing and communicating a particular vision of society. For example, they have operated as instruments for the exercise of power and have been used to assert the legitimacy of the dominance of one group over others (Bennett 1988; Hooper-Greenhill 2000). They have functioned to engender feelings of belonging and worth in some and, in others, a sense of inferiority and exclusion. The museum's power to privilege particular forms of knowledge and to naturalise highly particularised sets of values has been deployed to invent and maintain national identities (Evans 1999; Macdonald 2003). By assembling objects and arranging them in ways that communicate specific messages, museums have been understood to privilege and promulgate certain ways of viewing and relating to difference, and to occlude or silence others (Macdonald 1998; Karp and Kratz 2000; Sandell 2005).

The particular discourses of difference that museums construct are socially, historically and culturally situated. They are informed by dominant social values and beliefs which become written into, concretised and rendered visible within exhibition narratives. Tony Bennett (1998, 2003), for example, has argued that public museums in the nineteenth century – though often created by individuals, liberal in inclination, who believed their work would contribute to a greater social good – were purposefully designed to highlight distinctions between groups in ways which reinforced and reproduced inequitable power relations. This approach is perhaps most clearly illustrated in typological methods of display, prevalent in nineteenth-century museums, which arranged objects in hierarchically structured ways intended to 'construct an evolutionary ordering of the relations between peoples' (2003: 6). These displays were intended to communicate racialised understandings of difference and to suggest the superiority – moral, cultural

3

and technological – of Western over non-Western peoples (Bennett 1988, Macdonald 2003).

Although critiques which highlight the museum's role in depicting cultures in pernicious ways (with injurious consequences) have been very influential in museum studies, they have nevertheless been criticised for focusing on *production* and neglecting processes of *consumption* (Mason 2006). Exhibitions may be constructed in ways that are *intended* to communicate particular understandings of difference, but limited consideration has been given to the ways in which visitors might engage with them. Audiences have often been disregarded or imagined as passive recipients of intended messages (ibid.).

This neglect of audiences and processes of reception is similarly evident in contemporary conceptions of the museum as a force for positive social change. Despite the increasingly insistent, confident and ubiquitous rhetoric, there remains both a paucity of empirical evidence and a lack of theoretical interrogation with which to inform and substantiate the claims that museums are making, and those being made on their behalf. Through a syncretic approach, combining in-depth field research with theoretical perspectives from a range of disciplines, this book seeks to enhance understanding of the agency of museums by investigating audience responses to exhibitions purposefully designed to 'combat prejudice'. I use this phrase to encompass efforts to enhance cross-cultural understanding and respect, to promote issues of equality, tolerance and human rights and to challenge negatively stereotypical representations of oppressed groups. For the most part, the arguments I shall develop are neither focused on specific social groups nor on particular manifestations of prejudice but are concerned, rather more broadly, with the museum's potential to (re)frame, enable and inform society's conversations[3] about difference.

My analysis focuses on the ways in which audiences engage with exhibitions where attempts have been made to 'write in' messages designed to promote equality and combat prejudice. What discourses or 'interpretative repertoires' (Potter and Wetherell 1987) are stimulated amongst visitors by the exhibition encounter? What cues, interpretive props or other factors within the museum's control might potentially influence the visitor's process of meaning-construction and how might these be deployed to combat prejudice? What role might audience perceptions of the museum's cultural authority play in influencing readings of exhibitions? In addressing these questions, I aim to develop a set of concepts which offer a way of understanding and describing, and a means of interrogating, the social agency of museums.

This first chapter outlines some of the key debates, tensions and challenges that are inherent within this project and outlines the critical framework through which my research questions are addressed. I set out the aims and objectives of the primary research which underpins the arguments developed throughout the book and introduce the methodological approach I deployed to investigate the role of museums in the combating of prejudice. The issues and topics I touch upon here are threaded throughout the book and are discussed in greater depth in subsequent chapters. They are, however, introduced here to establish a rationale and context for the approach I have taken.

Museums and the good society

Recent decades have seen a radical reassessment of museums' roles, purposes and responsibilities. No longer primarily inwardly focused on the steward-ship of their collections, museums are increasingly expected to direct their attention towards the needs of their visitors and communities through the provision of a range of educational and other services (Weil 1999). More recently, there has been a growing interest in the potential for museums to function as agents of social change, deploying their collections and other resources to contribute, in varied ways, towards a more just and equitable society (Sandell 1998, Sandell 2002a, Janes and Conarty 2005). Museums, then, have been required to develop new goals that respond to local and global social concerns, to articulate and justify their value in social terms, to demonstrate and measure their impact and to develop new working prac-tices to reflect these trends.

A review of recent museum literature highlights the diverse ways in which individual museums, shaped by their own local contexts, have responded to this widespread reorientation of museum functions and purposes. Viv Szekeres (2002), for example, offers an account of public programmes at the Migration Museum in Adelaide, Australia, intended to challenge racism experienced by local communities. Ruth Abram (2005) describes initia-tives at the Lower East Side Tenement Museum in New York designed to give support to newly arrived immigrants to the city including the provi-sion of English classes and development of a resource guide. Jocelyn Dodd (2002) discusses a series of initiatives at Nottingham Museums, England, which sought to tackle health inequalities in the region, including projects concerned with HIV and AIDS and high rates of teenage pregnancy. Lois Silverman (2002) describes projects in Bloomington, Indiana, which have explored the therapeutic use of museums through collaborative initiatives with a range of social service client groups. As these examples demon-strate, individual museums, responding to local contexts and imperatives, have engaged with social concerns and sought to address inequalities in varied ways. However, the refashioning of museums as organisations with the capacity to contribute towards a less prejudiced society – one in which cultural differences are affirmed, nurtured and celebrated – has been more or less universal (Bennett 2005).

Several factors have contributed to this reorientation of role and purpose and the widespread conception of museums as agencies with the potential to promote cross-cultural understanding and respect. These include the growing global influence of human rights discourses; the changing demographic composition of many Western societies; the 'new social movements' of the last fifty years that have led to a proliferation of previously marginalised voices; heightened international interest in multiculturalism, cultural diversity and an approach to the politics of difference which rejects assimilationist policies in favour of those which affirm cultural and ethnic differences; and the introduction of increased demands for accountability, in much of the Western industrialized world, that have increasingly required publicly funded institutions to demonstrate their value to society (Scott 2002). In some contexts, imperatives for the reshaping of museum roles and responsibilities have been galvanised by government policies, formulated at both national and local levels. In the UK, for example, the influence of government policy has been especially pronounced. In 2000 the Department for Culture, Media and Sport issued its policy guidance on publicly funded museums, galleries and archives in England making explicit the government's expectations that the cultural sector should play a part in the combating of social exclusion (DCMS 2000). At the same time, government policy in Scotland called for museums, alongside and in partnership with wide-ranging public and voluntary agencies, to play an active role in contributing to a social justice agenda (Scottish Museums Council 2000). The formulation of policies that have required museums to contribute to broader social objectives of government has frequently generated fierce debates around the instrumentalisation of culture. Such debates surrounding the intrinsic, economic and social value of culture and the nature of the relationships between arts institutions and the state, although important, have often tended to over-simplify the arguments on both sides and, in doing so, obscure some of the more fundamental questions surrounding the purposes and responsibilities of cultural organisations. I shall return to these important issues later in the book but, for the moment, shall simply point out that, whilst government intervention has very often played a significant role in shaping museum policy it would, however, be inaccurate to suggest that new approaches to more inclusive museum practice have only evolved in response to locally framed government policies. Indeed, it has been argued that, in some contexts, museums have pursued social goals that are out of step with the dominant priorities and position of government.[4]

Contemporary expectations, practices and debates

In response to these wide-ranging influences, museums have been increasingly expected to reform and revise their approaches to representing diverse groups. Tony Bennett has described a set of normative demands that have come to be placed on them:

> First, that, if not within each museum, then certainly across the relations between them, they should aim to address the interests of all sections of society; second, that museum exhibitions and displays should be respectful in their depiction of cultural differences, and accord equal value to the varied cultures they put on show; and third, that such exhibitions should be informed by the distinctive perspectives and knowledges of the particular social groups in question ...
>
> (Bennett 2003: 4)

These demands have translated into a series of questions that have challenged practitioners and continue to frame debates about the museum's social role. How can museums hope to represent all sections of society when group identities are increasingly conceived, not as singular and fixed, but rather as multiple and shifting? Which forms of difference are deemed authentic, valid and thereby privileged over others for inclusion, whilst others are left aside? Are there universal moral frameworks that should inform responses to these questions and, if so, should they take precedence over localised and situated norms of acceptability and tolerance? In response to these demands, expectations and questions, significant shifts in museum practice can be discerned. Over a period of many years, displays which – viewed from a contemporary perspective – have been perceived to be overtly racist have been revised or dismantled. In their place, more inclusive and equitable approaches to exhibition development have emerged as previously marginalised communities – especially women, minority ethnic communities and indigenous peoples – have questioned their exclusion from (or misrepresentation within) museum displays. These changes in display practice have very often been accompanied by strategies to broaden both the visitorships and staff of museums more accurately to reflect the composition of local communities.

Although widespread, the extent to which these changes have masked a deeper resistance to a more radical rethinking of notions of cultural and national heritage (and related understandings of difference, belonging and worth) remains open to debate.[5] Although some museums demonstrate a commitment to developing genuinely new approaches to representation and interpretation, and to engaging audiences in the challenge of addressing difficult questions of difference and equality, many others continue to produce displays and pursue practices which are perhaps more likely to enhance rather than combat prejudice.[6] Moreover, whilst progress has been made to represent some previously marginalised communities in more respectful and equitable ways, other social groups, it has been argued, remain neglected.

Figure 1.1: Brighton Museum in the south of England is one of relatively few that have represented lesbian and gay communities within their permanent displays

Klaus Müller (2001), Angela Vanegas (2002) and Mark Liddiard (2004), for example, have highlighted the paucity of exhibitions that include material relating to sexual minorities[7] (Fig. 1.1). Janice Majewski and Lonnie Bunch (1998), Annie Delin (2002) and Katherine Ott (2005a) have similarly drawn attention to the under-representation of disabled people within museum displays.

The fierce and often unhelpfully polarised debates surrounding the contemporary reorientation of museums' roles, purposes and responsibilities have tended to dwell on two principal questions. The first concerns the capacity that museums have to reinvent themselves as agents of empowering and liberatory social change. At one end of the spectrum of opinion, as Janet Marstine identifies, are the 'vocal minority of theorists who hold that museums, by definition, cannot change and that they are fast becoming obsolete' (2005: 27). At the other end are those theorists and practitioners who argue that it is unhelpful to view museums as necessarily complicit in maintaining inequitable relations of power. They acknowledge museums' histories and the part they have played in excluding and marginalising social groups but highlight a number of factors that have contributed to genuine change. Eilean Hooper-Greenhill (2000), for example, has described the emergence of a new form of museum, which she has called the 'post-museum'. As Marstine notes:

> Those who see a post-museum taking shape point to the example of some curators who are eager to share power by initiating open dialogue and forging new partnerships with groups previously disenfranchised. These theorists are also encouraged by the variety of institutions, from neighborhood museums to community centers to university galleries, that have recently been established or have been given new life and that take diverse approaches to the representation of race, ethnicity, class and gender.
>
> (2005: 27–28)

These more optimistic viewpoints also find support in shifting conceptions of the way power operates and is organised within modern society. They challenge conceptions of the museum's social role and purpose that are based upon theories which view power as hegemonic, monolithic, and exercised by a dominant or elite group against subordinates. Instead, they point to contemporary sociological analyses, heavily influenced by Foucault, in which view power is seen as fragmented, situated and dynamic (Abercrombie and Longhurst 1998). If power is understood in this way, then it becomes increasingly problematic to dismiss contemporary museum initiatives as manipulative, State-sponsored attempts to promote social order.

The second, and arguably more controversial, question concerns the extent to which (if at all) cultural institutions should be enlisted in attempts to effect social change. On the one hand are those who argue that museums should be free to pursue their 'core business' autonomously – preserving, documenting, displaying and studying cultural and natural heritage – in isolation from contemporary social or political concerns (Appleton 2001).

On the other are those who argue that museums have an obligation to deploy their agency in ways which respond to (and seek to influence) societal values. Situated between these polarised opinions, many practitioners remain ambivalent about the social roles and responsibilities of museums. This ambivalence is, for some, based on unease with the self-aggrandising character of claims that museums can 'change society'. For others, uncertainty is fuelled by an awareness of the problematic moral dilemmas and pitfalls bound up in attempts to deploy museums as agents of social change. The challenges and tensions inherent in the notion of the museum as an agency for countering prejudice are woven throughout the book and revisited, in the light of the research findings presented, in the concluding chapter.

Turning to the audience

Although conceptions of museums as agencies that are capable of reforming ways of viewing difference are widely supported, as I have previously stated, little is known about the *processes* through which this might be achieved. Indeed, developments in a range of disciplines which have seen a fundamental shift in focus from processes of cultural production to those associated with audience reception have helped to show that, whilst museums may have been *designed* to inculcate social values, to engender certain understandings of difference, their efficacy in doing so has been largely neglected. More particularly, whilst claims that museums can confront and counter prejudices, engender support for human rights and promote respect between communities have grown increasingly confident and explicit, there remains a paucity of evidence and understanding with which to substantiate these assertions.

The last twenty-five years have seen a radical reconceptualisation of museum–audience relations underpinned by the ground-breaking and highly influential work of Stuart Hall and others within the field of media and cultural studies. Audiences – traditionally imagined as passive recipients of media 'effects' – are now widely understood as themselves participating in the production process, constructing (and contributing to the distribution of) messages as part of the communicative circuit (Hall 1990a). Much of the early research into museum audiences was based on a 'conveyor-belt model' (Macdonald 2002: 219), which sought to measure the success of exhibitions by determining to what extent visitors had correctly absorbed the intended messages. These approaches have been increasingly criticised for failing to acknowledge the agency of the audience and, in response, 'a new wave of research has emerged which has begun from a premise of the audience as "active", as constructively appropriating cultural products in potentially myriad ways' (ibid.: 219).

Hall's encoding–decoding model (which I shall discuss more fully in chapter 6) led to a fundamental shift in emphasis from what media messages *do* to people, to what they *mean* to them (Ruddock 2001). Audiences are now widely viewed as active agents who do not simply absorb messages but are capable of constructing their own meanings that may radically differ from those intended at the point of production. This 'turn to the audience' clearly presents interesting opportunities as well as challenges to museums understood to be countering prejudice through the dissemination of purposively constructed social messages. Wide-ranging research has highlighted the potential for 'misunderstandings' (Hall 1990a) or for the occurrence of the 'boomerang effect' (Cooper and Dinerman 1951) where intended meanings are not simply resisted but turned around by audiences in ways which result in the construction of entirely oppositional meanings. Conceptions of the active audience therefore highlight the capacity for encounters between museum visitors and exhibitions designed to combat prejudice to result in wide-ranging (racist? sexist? heterosexist?)[8] meanings.

Current thinking within museum studies and, in particular, approaches to museum learning that are based on constructivist theories, might also be seen to challenge assumptions that museums can (or should attempt to) combat prejudice through effecting change in visitor attitudes and values. George Hein argues for the adoption within museum settings of a constructivist approach to learning which 'requires that the conclusions reached by the learner are *not* validated by whether or not they conform to some external standard of truth, but whether they "make sense" within the constructed reality of the learner'(1998: 34). Constructivist exhibitions for example, 'will present a range of points of view, will enable visitors to connect with objects (and ideas) through a range of activities and experiences that utilize their life experiences' (ibid.: 35). Such approaches encourage, facilitate and celebrate open-ended learning outcomes and are critical of more didactic approaches which legitimate and sanction only a limited range of responses and meanings created by the visitor. It might then be argued that these constructivist explanations of the ways in which visitors learn, challenge those museums seeking to engender non-prejudiced values and attitudes amongst visitors where alternative, oppositional readings of exhibitions (ones which reinforce or reproduce prejudice) are inevitably viewed as invalid, even aberrant. These various tensions and inconsistencies are threaded throughout the chapters in this book. As we shall see, the theoretical positions that might be seen to challenge the notion that museums have the capability to combat prejudice, simultaneously offer potentially fruitful ways forward for exploring how this might also be possible.

Audience responses to 'anti-prejudice messages'

Relatively limited research has been undertaken into the meanings audiences construct from media messages designed and encoded purposefully to counter prejudices. One notable example is Eunice Cooper and Helen Dinerman's (1951) study of audience responses to the 'anti-prejudice film', *Don't be a Sucker*. This twenty-minute film, produced by the US Army Signal Corps during the Second World War and subsequently widely shown (in a shortened form) both commercially and in educational settings, was designed to change audience attitudes by highlighting the futility of prejudice and the dangers of discrimination. Cooper and Dinerman's study of the reactions of high school and adult groups to the film found that, whilst some concepts were successfully communicated to some groups, there was nevertheless considerable potential for intended messages to 'boomerang', resulting in 'unexpected and undesired attitude changes' (1951: 27).

In museum contexts, despite the ubiquity and increasing confidence of claims regarding the role of museums in enhancing understanding, tolerance and respect for difference, there has been surprisingly limited research directed towards specifically investigating the ways in which audiences respond to exhibitions developed with these aims in mind. An early, and indeed still rare, study undertaken over fifty years ago usefully highlights many of the challenges inherent in attempts to investigate the agency of museums.

In January 1953, an exhibition of Japanese art opened in Washington DC and subsequently toured to museums in New York, Seattle, Chicago and finally Boston, where it closed in December the following year. The exhibition was sent to the United States by the Japanese government with two explicit aims: 'to acquaint the American people with the cultural and spiritual values and traditions of Japan and to help in some fashion to bring a sympathetic understanding of the Japanese' (Bower and Sharp 1956: 222). A large-scale study[9] of the 'effectiveness' of the project in achieving its stated aims was undertaken at three of the museums. To elicit information about reactions to the exhibition and, in particular, to investigate the 'effects' of the visit on opinions and attitudes relating to Japan and Japanese people, the study employed a range of research methods. The primary source of data came from interviews conducted with respondents in their homes, after they had visited the exhibition, where they were asked to 'tell of their reactions and opinion changes in retrospect' (ibid.: 223). Other methods included a small experimental study with a group of university students in Boston who were asked to complete questionnaires both before and after visiting the exhibition.

Publishing their findings in 1956, Robert Bower and Laure Sharp concluded that 'by and large the exhibit did not appear quickly to convert large numbers of Americans to a pro-Japanese attitude' (ibid.: 228). Within their interview data, however, they found some evidence of learning and opinion change in both 'favorable' and 'unfavorable' directions. Many respondents believed that they had learned something new and positive about Japanese people and could point to specific areas in which their knowledge had increased. 'Appreciation of beauty, religious spirit, the place of tradition in Japanese life, high standards of craftsmanship, patience and sense of humor were qualities most often discovered' (ibid.: 227). Moreover, some interviews contained statements which suggested to the researchers 'that derogatory stereotypes of the Japanese had at least been challenged – respondents saying, for instance, "I didn't realize they had such a sense of humor," or "I had no idea their religion was so like ours" ' (ibid.: 228). The findings from the 'before and after' questionnaires, used with students, were also presented as evidence of opinion change. The group were asked to express their agreement or disagreement with a series of statements about Japanese people.

> Fifty-nine percent agreed *before* seeing the exhibit with the state-ment "The Japanese place a low value on human life" and only 49 percent *after* the exhibit. The statement "Most of the Japanese culture has been borrowed from other peoples" received 31 per cent agreement before the exhibit and 22 per cent after.
>
> (ibid.)

Interestingly, there was also some evidence of audience responses which ran counter to the intentions of the exhibition. A few visitors had come away with 'unfavorable' ideas about Japanese people that, the researchers argued, had been newly acquired or strengthened as a result of the visit. 'These [visitors] were apt to say that the exhibit had suggested or reinforced the idea that the Japanese were fierce, warlike, or cruel ...' (ibid.: 227).

Although, in reporting their findings, Bower and Sharpe say nothing of the broader social and political context within which this attempt to shape the attitudes of American audiences occurred, the project is very clearly shaped by the particular exigencies of the post-war period. Moreover, the language and research design deployed both in this study, and in the one conducted by Cooper and Dinerman, are reflective of models of communication which, though dominant in the 1950s, have come to be widely refuted. (I shall discuss the ways in which theories of media–audience relations and interactions have evolved in more detail in chapter 5.)

More recent discussions of the potential for museum exhibitions to influence audience perceptions of difference similarly suggest the potential for appar-ently 'aberrant', 'deviant' or oppositional constructions of meaning such as those found in the 1950s studies. For example, an exhibition at Nottingham Castle Museum and Art Gallery in 2000 declared, in an introductory panel, its intentions in the words of the artist, Alison Lapper (Fig. 1.2):

Figure 1.2: Untitled photograph by Alison Lapper

Source: By kind permission of the artist

> My work reflects and responds to other people's attitudes to me.
> I hope to question and change society's attitudes about physical
> beauty, normality, disability and sexuality. As a disabled person,
> I am generally perceived as ugly, sexless, inert, helpless and miser-
> able.
>
> I know I am not.
>
> My work gives me the opportunity to represent myself to the world
> on my own terms ...
>
> (Sandell 2002a: 16)

Despite the explicitly stated nature of the exhibition's aims, one visitor's letter of complaint provides a powerful illustration of the potential for the construction of oppositional meanings. A woman from Nottingham, who came across the exhibition whilst visiting the museum with friends, wrote:

> We were particularly offended by the display of photographs of a disabled woman and her baby, which I can only compare to the old 'freak show'. I know we live in the age of 'political correctness' but I do not think that the Castle was the place to display such items of so called modern art.
>
> (ibid.: 16)

Similarly, an article by Philip Gourevitch concerning audience reactions to the United States Holocaust Memorial Museum in Washington DC, found that visitors' 'diverse reactions reflect the beliefs and attitudes they brought to the museum as much as anything they discovered within its walls' (1995: 45). Whilst these brief examples offer little in the way of conclusive evidence, they nevertheless serve to problematise museums' claims concerning the combating of prejudice and highlight the need for further, in-depth (and differently framed) investigations.

Shaping the unpredictable?

What then are the implications of these findings for an investigation of museums' roles in tackling prejudice? If individual visitors are understood to generate and actualise their own highly personalised and variable meanings from the same exhibition encounter, what role, if any, might museums play in facilitating the generation of meanings that counter, rather than reinforce, prejudice? Despite the variability and unpredictability that has often been found in audience responses to various media, there is nevertheless both theoretical support and empirical evidence to suggest a degree of influence on the part of cultural producers. As Stuart Hall has argued, there must be some relationship between the preferred message inscribed at the point of production and those decoded by audiences, 'otherwise we could not speak of an effective communicative exchange at all' (1990b: 515). This suggests that we need to look more closely at the audience–exhibition encounter to explore the parameters museums might place on audience meaning and the interpretive frameworks, props and cues they might offer to visitors in their attempts to ameliorate prejudice.

Cultural authority versus reader resistance

Media theorists argue that audiences are increasingly beset by a potentially bewildering array of media messages which compete for their attention.

These messages, emitted through a variety of media – television, newspapers, theatre, film, museums and so on – are differentially perceived by audiences. Some are noticed, taken up and used, whilst others are ignored or discarded (Silverstone 1994, Abercrombie and Longhurst 1998). This suggests that we must also consider the specific and unique properties that museums, in comparison with other forms of media, might bring to the communicative process. In particular, might the museum's status as an authoritative knowledge-provider lend weight to the argument that museums have an especially significant role to play in combating prejudice? Sharon Macdonald's research at the Science Museum in London, for example, provides empirical evidence to support the view that museum exhibitions are often read in ways which reflect their perceived cultural authority. Many visitors came with an expectation that the museum would give 'clear-cut "right answers"' (2002: 241). Though the scientific subject matter of the exhibition in question is likely to have a bearing on visitor perceptions, it nevertheless usefully points to an area for further investigation.

Moreover, the cultural authority of the museum – its capacity to determine and authoritatively communicate meaning – is evolving. New approaches to framing exhibitions (for example, the use of interpretive devices which attempt to reveal to visitors the 'constructedness' and inevitable partiality of displays, and the deployment of techniques which explicitly co-opt visitors into a shared process of establishing meaning) are transforming museum–visitor relations and creating new forms of authority. I return to these important issues more fully in chapter 6 but, for the moment, it is perhaps fair to say that there exists a degree of tension between the notion of the active or resistant audience (an analysis that gives primacy to the agency of the visitor in constructing meaning) and the conception of the museum as an authoritative and trustworthy knowledge-provider (a view which might suggest that audiences defer to the museum in determining meaning).

My interest here is in exploring the potential for museums to deploy their cultural status and authority to frame society's conversations about difference in ways which privilege a particular and unequivocal moral standpoint, one based on concepts of social justice. The suggestion, that museums might adopt and attempt to generate support for a particular (non-negotiable) moral position is, I am aware, somewhat unfashionable in contemporary museological practice. In recent years there has been growing support for the replacement of the authoritative curatorial voice with diverse perspectives, a strategy designed to enable visitors to see that the decisions and judgements made by exhibition makers are contingent and open to interpretation and debate (Karp and Kratz 2000). Of course, such an approach still involves a process of selection as some viewpoints are deemed appropriate and given voice through their inclusion within the museum whilst others are silenced through their omission. Whilst acknowledging the value of presenting plural perspectives, I shall nevertheless argue throughout the following chapters that this interpretive strategy also enables museums to avoid taking a stand on controversial issues and thereby potentially constrains their capacity to challenge prejudices. In other words, by including different viewpoints but failing to arbitrate between them museums imply that they are of equal value, an implication which, in some instances, might be undesirable.

Investigating audience responses

This review of key theoretical issues and tensions inherent in this project also serves to highlight some of the challenges involved in investigating the role of museums in (re)framing social understandings of difference. It suggests key questions and issues to be addressed and begins to establish coordinates within which a research design that is theoretically and practically suited to the investigation of the role that museums might play in combating prejudice can be developed.

Socio-cultural perspectives on prejudice

When I first began to think about how I might investigate the 'impact' of museums on audiences' prejudiced attitudes and behaviour, I envisaged a 'conveyor belt' model (similar to that described by Sharon Macdonald earlier). This would require me to 'measure' audience attitudes, both before and after visiting exhibitions, to determine the 'effects' of the museum experience. As I began to develop a critical theoretical framework within which this research could take place, this approach was soon revealed to be unhelpful and poorly suited for the purpose.

Adopting a socio-cultural, discursive understanding of prejudice proved critical in helping to shape a more appropriate research design. Discursive approaches, as we shall see in chapter 2, view prejudice not as an individual, 'personal pathology' (Wetherell and Potter 1992: 208) but as a structural feature of societies which are 'organized around the oppression of one group and the dominance of another group' (ibid.: 198). Rather than attempting to 'measure' prejudice and changes in individuals' attitudes, this discursive approach led me to locate my research within a qualitative paradigm and to explore the constitutive nature of everyday talk and text in constructing and reproducing prejudice. So, instead of utilising attitude measurement scales in questionnaires, issued before and after an exhibition visit (such as those used in Bower and Sharp's 1950s study of visitor reactions to the exhibition of Japanese art described earlier), I used open-ended, in-depth interviews to generate and capture the conversations and accounts of visitors, stimulated by and generated through a museum visit (see Appendix 1). In addition, I used written comments that visitors made in response to their experience through comments books and cards. With the aid of qualitative research software, I analysed these accounts to investigate the ways in which people talked about difference and related issues of inequality, discrimination and rights and looked for repertoires and interpretations that might be considered egalitarian and tolerant, prejudiced and discriminatory or even contradictory. I also looked for patterns within these highly individual, personalised accounts that might suggest that visitors' 'linguistic performances' (LeCouteur and Augoustinos 2001) were shaped or framed in some way by the exhibition encounter. Whilst accepting that my own experiences and values inevitably retain a strong influence on the research process, I would also argue that the research design I eventually developed enabled me to adopt a much more critical and exploratory stance than that with which I had originally approached the topic.

Throughout the research process I have been aware that the term 'prejudice' is rather unfashionable outside of social psychology and is undoubtedly very rarely used in the fields of sociological and cultural studies within which much of the enquiry into the politics of museums and their representational practices has been conducted. In sociological approaches to understanding relations between different groups, as we shall see in the following chapter, the term 'prejudice' is tainted by its association with overly individualist, cognitivist and behaviourist explanations of social conflict. Nevertheless, I have chosen to retain the term partly, no doubt, because it is one to which I have grown accustomed (and which I am accustomed to defending) but more importantly because the 'combating of prejudice' most accurately and concisely describes the roles and practices which, I shall argue, museums can fulfil. Moreover, 'combating prejudice' implies a purposeful, explicit and political goal – one that suggests the active removal of something that is socially undesirable. Related terms such as 'tolerance', 'inclusion' and 'recognition', though widely used in the museum sector, are rather less satisfactory for this project, a point I shall return to in chapter 2.

The primary research undertaken for this book addresses three main areas. The first is concerned with the intentions, aims and strategies of museums that articulate goals around the combating of prejudice and is investigated through interviews with staff at two case studies and through analysis of museum documents (policies, reports, websites and publicity material). The second and largest part of the study focuses on questions of audience reception and response. Drawing on data generated through observation of visitors, in-depth interviews and written comments on exhibitions, I explore the ways in which audiences engage with displays intended to tackle prejudice. Interviews are also the primary source of data for probing visitors' experiences of museum consumption and for eliciting attitudes towards museums as knowledge-providers. The third area I aim to address concerns the implications which the findings of my audience research might hold for museum practice more broadly, in settings beyond those used as case studies. With this final goal in mind, I draw on a number of illustrative examples to

Figure 1.3: The Anne Frank House, Amsterdam

contextualise the particular practices of the museums that have served as the focus of my empirical audience investigations.

The sites in which in-depth audience research was carried out were the Anne Frank House in Amsterdam, Holland (Fig. 1.3) and the St Mungo Museum of Religious Life and Art in Glasgow, Scotland (Fig. 1.4). Selecting suitable case studies is always of critical importance in any research project and the extent to which the chosen sites are deemed to be typical or atypical of museums at large was deemed to be especially significant. With this in mind, these two sites were chosen for very specific reasons. Although claims that museums can operate as agents of cross-cultural understanding are increasingly made by, or on behalf of, museums of all kinds there are still relatively few in which the combating of prejudice is articulated as their central raison d'être. In many ways these specialised forms of museum offer the most suitable place in which the 'effects' on audiences can be investigated. Rather than typical or representative, they can be viewed as suitable case studies because they represent 'extreme instances'. In case studies of this kind, 'a specified factor is seen in relief – highlighted in its effect' (Denscombe 1998: 33). Nevertheless, though 'extreme' in one sense (the extent to which they view the combating of prejudice as central to their mission and purpose), the case studies are, in other ways, much more typical of museums

Figure 1.4: The St Mungo Museum of Religious Life and Art, Glasgow

Source: Photograph by kind permission of Glasgow Museums

in general and this has implications for the generalisability of the research findings. For example, like most museums, both the Anne Frank House and St Mungo Museum utilise exhibitions and other public programmes to communicate with their audiences. The interpretive devices they deploy within their displays are increasingly found in a wide variety of museums. Moreover, the majority of visitors to these sites are unaware of their relatively unusual, socially-driven, missions viewing them as, in many ways, similar to other museums which they might visit. These factors, relating to issues of generalisability, are important since my study is underpinned by a desire not simply to understand processes of audience reception within the two specific sites but rather to consider the implications of the research findings (in terms of role and responsibility) for museums more broadly. What potential exists within wide-ranging museums operating in different social contexts to contribute towards the creation of a less prejudiced, inequitable society?

A further factor that influenced my selection of research sites is the differentiating characteristics of each museum. Though both case studies articulate goals linked to the combating of prejudice they differ in terms of the specific forms of prejudice with which they are concerned and the interpretive strategies and devices they adopt to realise their goals. The Anne Frank House is dedicated to 'combating present-day forms of Nazism, anti-Semitism, racism and xenophobia [and] contributing to the realization of

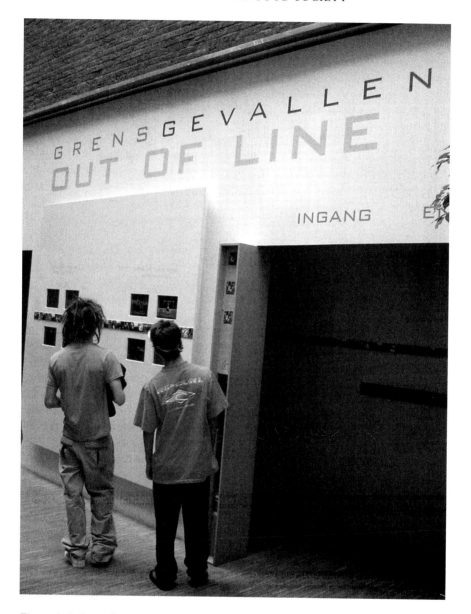

Figure 1.5: *Out of Line*, the Anne Frank House

a pluralistic democratic society in which every human being is seen as a unique individual and treated equally under the law' (Anne Frank House 2004: 24). One of the main ways in which it seeks to do this is through temporary exhibitions and through interpretive techniques which demand visitor interaction and response. Positioned at the end of the museum visit,

21

Figure 1.6: South Indian bronze statue of the Hindu deity, Shiva Nataraja

Source: Photograph by kind permission of Glasgow Museums

temporary exhibitions are designed to explore contemporary issues that relate to prejudice and discrimination. The exhibition showing during this research project, *Grensgevallen* (translated by the museum as *Out of Line*) (Fig. 1.5), is especially relevant as it is not only concerned with racism but also seeks to address prejudice based on sexuality, disability, religious faith and so on. *Out of Line* makes use of interactive, multimedia presentations to invite visitors to respond to contemporary, 'real-life' dilemmas where basic human rights (specifically, the right to freedom of expression and the right to protection from discrimination) come into conflict with each other. The St Mungo Museum of Religious Life and Art, one of the sites run by the local authority service, Glasgow Museums, explores the importance of religion in people's everyday lives across the world and across time, aiming to promote mutual understanding and respect between people of different faiths, and of none (O'Neill 1994). This museum was chosen especially because, in contrast to the temporary exhibitions at the Anne Frank House, St Mungo's makes central use of museum collections – the ways in which objects are positioned in relation to each other and the ways in which they are interpreted – to achieve its aims (Fig. 1.6).

Although in-depth audience research was confined to these two sites, I draw on a range of museum examples, especially in the penultimate and concluding chapters, to contextualise the findings from St Mungo's and the Anne Frank House, to explore their broader applicability and the

22

implications they might hold for museums operating in different social and political contexts. My aim has been to build a theory of museum–audience engagement which, whilst generated out of highly localised investigations, has relevance to a much broader range of settings.

Research methods and data sources

An advantage of case study research is that it fosters the use of both multiple sources of data and multiple methods of data collection and generation. As Robert Yin states, 'any finding or conclusion in a case study is likely to be much more convincing and accurate if it is based on several different sources of information, following a corroboratory mode' (1994: 92). Accordingly, although the main source of data that is used to address my research questions is generated from in-depth interviews with visitors, I have also made use of other data sources (especially visitors' written comments and interviews with museum staff) and methods (observation of visitors within exhibition galleries) to contextualise and enrich this material.

Since the ways in which individual visitors approach the museum experience, and what they take away from it, are undoubtedly influenced by factors including age, gender, ethnicity and so on, a conscious attempt was made to include as broad a range of research participants as possible. I did not, however, attempt to gain a sample that was entirely representative of the museum's overall visitor profile; an approach that might, for example, be expected in quantitative studies which attempt to determine the ways in which responses are influenced by the social characteristics of respondents.

Structure of the book

This first chapter has sought to provide a rationale for the study as a whole by identifying and reviewing emerging trends in museological thinking and practice and highlighting the paucity of research that has been undertaken to investigate the efficacy of museums in relation to the countering of prejudice. I have also attempted to introduce the key issues and themes with which this study engages and, in doing so, to highlight both the theoretical tensions and methodological challenges that are inherent in analyses of the museum's social agency.

Chapter 2 is where I seek to blend theoretical perspectives from a range of disciplines (principally audience and media studies, discourse analysis and social psychology) to develop a theoretical framework that is both robust and also sufficiently flexible to accommodate the challenges posed by the study. Whilst much of the research into prejudice to date has emerged from the discipline of psychology, this chapter proposes a socio-cultural approach to the phenomenon; one which explores the constitutive nature of everyday talk and text in constructing and reproducing prejudice. This chapter further argues for an understanding of prejudice which acknowledges its highly politicised and contextualised nature. Museums, I argue, are sites in which individuals can make, articulate and practise accounts of society that can be prejudiced, non-prejudiced or contradictory. This approach requires an analysis of language, both that of the museum and that of the visitor, to examine how it is used in constitutive ways.

In chapter 3 I consider, in greater detail, the missions, aims and contexts of the St Mungo Museum of Religious Life and Art and the Anne Frank House. I describe the exhibitions visitors encountered during the period of the study and begin to consider the ways in which they approached and perceived their museum experiences. I also explore the interpretive strategies through which both sites seek to construct particular understandings of equality, the approaches that are used to communicate their preferred messages of cross-cultural appreciation and respect, and the devices they deploy both to engage audiences in debating challenging issues and to elicit their views.

Engaging with contemporary theories of media–audience relations, chapter 4 examines the complex, often contradictory, ways in which visitors engaged with the exhibitions and encoded messages they encountered. Visitors were undoubtedly influenced by what they found within both the Anne Frank House and St Mungo's – though often in surprising and unpredictable ways. The conceptual framework I deploy to analyse the diverse visitor responses generated in my study builds on a theory of media audiences proposed by sociologists Nicholas Abercrombie and Brian Longhurst (1998). Drawing on their approach to conceptualising audiences, I argue in this chapter that textual analyses, which attempt to determine the relative agency of media (museum) and audience (museum visitor) in the determination of meaning, are limited in their power to explain the complex ways in which audiences view, respond to and engage with museums. Instead, exhibitions and displays are more appropriately conceived of as *resources* (not simply as *texts*) that exist alongside others in the broader mediascape. These resources may be taken up, utilised and endorsed, they may be appropriated and recoded or, indeed, they may ignored, resisted, challenged or wholly rejected.

Visitors may be highly active (as is demonstrated in their ability to play with, challenge and resist, as well as to take up and confirm the messages they encounter) but that is not to deny the capacity for museums also, though in complex ways, to shape and inform the meanings generated out of the museum experience. Chapter 5 explores this capacity in greater depth by investigating the museum's distinctive, potentially unique, contribution to the combating of prejudice. Again, drawing on data from the audience study, I analyse audience perceptions of the museum as medium and the characteristics of the museum visit compared to other forms of media consumption. My interests here concern the ways in which the museum is perceived by audiences in relation to other media (for example, newspapers, television documentaries and so on) that might also contribute to normative understandings of cultural difference. What role might the museum's cultural authority play in influencing the ways in which audiences read, respond to and 'filter' the resources they encounter in exhibitions? This chapter also explores which interpretive devices and exhibitionary cues and props might be considered most effective in communicating (and garnering support for) the museum's intended messages.

Chapter 6 takes discussion of the social agency of museums in rather a different direction. While the previous chapters have focused predominantly on audiences and issues of reception, chapter 6 turns attention to questions of production – the poetics and politics of exhibition making and representation. To explore the particular challenges and dilemmas practitioners might face in developing displays which attempt to contest or subvert prejudiced ways of seeing, I focus here on disability (and associated prejudice based on perceptions of physical difference). This chapter draws on the findings from a project, recently undertaken by the Research Centre for Museums and Galleries,[10] which sought to uncover the hidden history of disability within wide-ranging museum and gallery collections and to examine the attitudes curators held towards the interpretation of this material. The chapter presents the often surprising findings of this investigation and, drawing on examples of disability-related representation in museums and in other media, discusses the opportunities and the dilemmas inherent in attempts to address the cultural invisibility of disabled people.

Finally, in the concluding chapter, I attempt to pull together the key arguments set out in the book and consider the overarching implications of this study both for museum practice and for future research agendas. To assist me in this task I draw on a range of different museums to explore the broader applicability and relevance of the ideas and themes that emerge from my case studies. Here I connect discussion of the museum's potential to counter prejudice with broader debates about the purposes and responsibilities of cultural organisations. My intention is not to provide a definitive set of answers but rather to pose questions and offer suggestions which, I hope, will encourage further debate as well as stimulate further experimentation in museum practice.

The museum's agency in combating prejudice is not as straightforward as many rhetorical claims may suggest. Rather, as this book aims to show, the means by which this potential can be realised are multifarious and the ways in which audiences respond to interventions designed to offer non-prejudiced ways of seeing are both complex and, to an extent, unpredictable. 'Capturing' the influence of a museum exhibition on visitors' understandings of difference – and unravelling this from the many other influences that shape the ways in which individuals construct meaning – is far from straightforward. Nevertheless, I shall argue that the interpretivist,

25

qualitative research methods I have deployed in my audience study offer a fruitful way to explore the social effects and consequences of museum displays, even though these are inevitably entangled with and disguised amongst other sources of influence. Drawing on the rich data generated through this study, I intend to show that museums have a role to play in contributing towards a less prejudiced, more equitable society. Museums can enable and facilitate conversations about difference, providing a forum (and one with unique qualities) in which disputes, arising from the conflicting values held by different communities, can be addressed and explored. They can inform and (re)frame the character and substance of these conversations by offering resources – material and conceptual – which privilege concepts of social justice, which nurture respect for difference and challenge prejudice and discrimination, opening up opportunities for mutual understanding and respect.

2

ON PREJUDICE

Visitors to the Museum of Tolerance in Los Angeles, California are invited to enter the main exhibition space through one of two entrances – the first marked 'Prejudiced' and the second, 'Unprejudiced' (Fig. 2.1). Those attempting to enter through the second doorway find that it is locked, a device designed to frame the ways in which visitors approach the interactive exhibits they subsequently encounter. Visitors progress (through the 'Prejudiced' doorway) into 'The Tolerancenter' with wide-ranging interactive exhibits designed to highlight the causes and consequences of prejudice and discrimination, to reveal the power of words and images to shape lives, to promote respect for difference and to assert the significance of personal responsibility and individual choices (Geft 2005). Prejudice, the museum's approach suggests, is not simply a fixed characteristic of a few disagreeable or deviant individuals but rather a pervasive feature of all societies and one in which, in varied and dynamic ways, we are all implicated. This, as we shall see, represents one amongst many competing ways of conceptualising prejudice.

Though the conception of prejudice as a social problem – as an issue that has demanded widespread debate, research and action – has only emerged in the twentieth century[1] the phenomenon has come to be viewed, in many countries, as one of the most pressing contemporary social concerns (Duckitt 2001). Prejudice is, today, a familiar and widely used term perhaps most commonly taken to refer, in a pejorative sense, to socially undesirable attitudes or behaviours towards individuals or groups that are marked by difference. The targets of prejudice vary according to context but frequently include groups defined as different from a dominant majority in terms of gender, race and ethnicity, class, sexuality, nationality, disability, religion, age, health, economic status and so on.

The familiarity of the term 'prejudice', however, obfuscates the polarities that have characterised attempts to define, understand and research the phenomenon. The last century (and especially the last five decades) has produced a vast body of research shaped by both the socio-political exigencies of particular contexts[2] as well as by theoretical trends and developments within a range of disciplines. This has resulted in diverse – sometimes

Figure 2.1: The entrance to the Tolerancenter, Museum of Tolerance, Los Angeles

Source: Photograph by kind permission of the Simon Wiesenthal Center

conflicting – approaches to conceptualising and investigating prejudice. My intention in this chapter is not to provide a detailed survey of developments and trends within this body of research but rather to highlight some of the key positions that have been taken up by research constituencies and which hold particularly significant implications (epistemological, political, methodological) for investigation of the museum as a site for the combating of prejudice. Drawing on theoretical perspectives from discourse studies, social psychology and audience studies, this chapter seeks to address the following questions: What constitutes prejudice and which of the competing conceptions of the phenomenon can be taken up most advantageously, to investigate the agency of museums? Towards which groups is prejudice directed and for what reasons and purposes? What role have the media and other forms of public discourse been understood to play in reproducing and reinforcing prejudice? How might the *combating* of prejudice by museums be recognised, investigated and evidenced?

Defining and conceptualising prejudice

Prejudice is a complex subject that has been approached from a variety of epistemological, theoretical and methodological perspectives within the arts and social sciences. Disciplines including history, politics, economics and sociology have all contributed to the topic (Brown 1995), though it is social psychology that has generated much of the research and discussion around prejudice, especially in the second half of the twentieth century. Social psychological research has been largely dominated by approaches which locate prejudice at an *individual* level, deploying cognition-based methods to understand 'the prejudiced mind'. These approaches are, I shall argue here, largely unhelpful in exploring the potential agency of museums in tackling prejudice, not least because they very often seek to analyse and understand the phenomenon in a social and political vacuum, ignoring both the contexts within which institutions and individual actors operate and the lived experiences of minority groups that are commonly the targets of intolerance and hatred. Discursive analyses have, in recent years, increasingly challenged individualist and cognitivist perspectives by arguing that prejudice is a social phenomenon concerned with maintaining and reproducing power relations within an inequitable society; a phenomenon which cannot be fully understood by focusing solely on the contents and processes of the individual mind. These discursive perspectives, I suggest, offer a more appropriate way of conceptualising and investigating the role of museums in combating prejudice.

Politicised versus neutral definitions of prejudice

Many definitions contain explicit assumptions and value judgements which position prejudice negatively, as something that is both innately 'bad' and socially undesirable. Though many researchers have employed these pejorative definitions of prejudice, others have sought to develop more neutral or value-free approaches which downplay the negative connotations most often associated with the term. As Martha Augoustinos and Katherine Reynolds state, 'the move towards less pejorative definitions has been associated with the rise of cognitive models ... that have come to view prejudice as a natural and inevitable consequence of inherent cognitive processes such as categorization and stereotyping' (2001: 3). Attempts to adopt these more neutral definitions have been heavily criticised for their potential to deny, or at least to underplay, the social and political consequences of prejudice and the extent to which localised expressions (and the everyday lived experiences of individuals against whom they are directed) are imbricated with wider processes of oppression, exclusion and discrimination. Mark Rapley, for example, highlights the inadequacy of investigating prejudice in a purely atomistic and mentalistic way which views individuals as operating autonomously and asocially, arguing that these explanations, through rhetorical means, effectively release individuals from moral responsibility for their actions:

We should, on the evidence of mainstream psychology, feel rather sorry for Adolf Hitler. He was most probably born with an unfortunate personality (a genetic endowment about which he could do little) and, in later life, was nothing but the victim of an unconscious, automatic, and cognitive miserliness which drove him (and the rest of the presumably similarly afflicted German nation) to categorize the Jews as 'parasites'.

(2001: 233–234)

The political implications of Rapley's scathing comments are clear. If the problem of prejudice is conceived of as a 'state of mind' then solutions will be sought in terms of education, training and other interventions at an individual level. This has the effect, as Le Couteur and Augoustinos state, of 'deflecting attention from the political necessity of societal and structural change' (2001: 229). These critiques then helpfully steer us away from depoliticised definitions which privilege cognitive inevitability and which tend to pathologise prejudice, towards those which view the phenomenon in the context of its locally contingent, political expediency and consequences. However, these politicised conceptions also highlight the dynamic, relativistic and uneven character of prejudice practices and pose challenges – philosophical and methodological – around identifying which manifestations are, in a given context, considered most undesirable and socially unacceptable and how the boundaries which separate these from 'tolerated' and socially sanctioned forms of prejudice are fluid and shifting.

Prejudice towards whom?

Understood in *social*, rather than *individual* terms, prejudice is concerned with the maintenance, justification and legitimation of power relations – relations which serve to oppress, disempower and marginalise those who are perceived to be different from the dominant group. Difference is conceived of in hierarchical terms – prejudice is directed against members of those communities who are believed to be not only *different* from but also *inferior* to the dominant group. This approach to understanding prejudice therefore acknowledges that the particular targets of prejudice will inevitably vary from context to context and over time to suit locally situated political and social ends.

The ubiquity of matters of 'race', national identity, immigration and multiculturalism has ensured that the myriad causes and consequences of racism have received the greatest attention, both in the literature on prejudice and in terms of policy and practice aimed at tackling the problem. There is a substantial body of research, for example, concerned with prejudice experienced by Indigenous communities in postcolonial contexts[3] and by minority ethnic communities in Western societies.[4] However, in different places and at different times, prejudice on the basis of gender, disability, class, sexual orientation, faith, age, health and so on have all been highlighted as causes for concern. Various social movements that marked the second part of the twentieth century – including feminism, multiculturalism, lesbian and gay rights and disability rights – have, with varying degrees of success, been influential in locating particular forms of prejudice as unjust, socially undesirable, and deserving of attention. Legislative frameworks also play a part in shaping prejudice practices although they are by no means wholly determining. Indeed, even when the political and social climate in a particular context dictates that certain forms of prejudice are deemed unacceptable – and very often that unacceptability is embodied within legislation and government policy – they do not necessarily disappear but often evolve to assume more subtle and covert forms. The capacity for prejudice practices to evolve in response to changing normative values is most clearly illustrated in the emergence of what has come to be termed 'modern racism'. Various studies have highlighted the replacement of 'old-fashioned racism', characterised by overtly expressed and extremist views based on White supremacism, with 'modern racism' which sees the appropriation and use of apparently egalitarian and liberal arguments to argue for discriminatory and racist ends (LeCouteur and Augoustinos 2001, Walker 2001).[5]

Different forms of prejudice will emerge as especially salient in different contexts and at different times. For example, recent research undertaken by Gill Valentine and Ian McDonald (2004) highlights the shifting and uneven character of prejudice directed towards a range of groups in the UK. Based on focus groups with white majority Britons, the study considers attitudes towards women, minority ethnic groups, lesbians and gay men, disabled people, transsexuals and transgendered people, gypsies and travellers and asylum seekers. The research found that, whilst it is generally deemed socially unacceptable to be prejudiced against a group for 'no good reason', many felt it was acceptable to feel less positive towards some because this standpoint, they believed, could be justified and was therefore considered 'rational'. The report, entitled 'Understanding Prejudice: Attitudes Towards Minorities', identifies asylum seekers as the group towards which prejudiced views were, at the time of the study, most openly and powerfully directed. The report's authors conclude that, 'It is generally socially acceptable to express such views and there appears to be little social sanction against this form of prejudice' (2004: 11). These findings echo the views expressed by John Richardson in his examination of the role that British newspapers have played in the production and reproduction of racism. Richardson argues that, in recent years:

> An anti-refugee discourse has emerged in popular media culture, in which it has become common place and to a greater extent

accepted for impoverished individuals and groups (who frequently are *white*) to be demonised, verbally and physically attacked and to be excluded – if not from Our shores entirely then at least from social resources, employment and therefore from an acceptable standard of living.

(2004: xv)

The fluid and contingent character of prejudice also emerged from my research into museum audiences. Some visitors, as we shall see in chapter 4, fervently expressed their support for concepts of equality, human rights and tolerance at an abstract, generalised level but subsequently qualified their statements by identifying specific groups to whom, they believed, such concepts should not apply.

The shifting and situated character of prejudice, that I have so far outlined, poses particularly vexing questions for exhibition-makers. Which forms of prejudice – directed towards which social groups – might museums decide to confront and which, conversely, are ignored (or perhaps condoned) through inaction? What kinds of framework, what sources of influence and authority, might museums draw upon to assist them in making these decisions? How might museums negotiate conflicts that will inevitably arise between universalist claims to equality for all groups and the particularities of locally contingent manifestations of prejudice?

Some museums have responded to the challenges presented by the shifting landscape of prejudice in interesting ways. For example, Irene Hirano, Director of the Japanese American National Museum, describes the ways in which the organisation responded to the events and aftermath of September 11, 2001 and the emerging prejudiced and discriminatory actions directed against US citizens who were perceived to be of Muslim or of Arab origin.

Because Japanese Americans had experienced discrimination following the outbreak of World War II – which ultimately led to the incarceration of 120,000 people – the ethnic tensions related to Arab Americans and Muslims after Sept. 11 resonated with us and were of great concern. We saw a responsibility to provide a forum that would enable people to talk about these issues and enable us to share our historical knowledge, mostly through personal stories ... We looked at our public programs schedule and considered what we'd like to do. At the same time, we saw this as part of the ongoing work of our museum. An important role that we can play is to be a place for that kind of dialogue.

(Hirano 2002: 77–78)

The museum subsequently instigated a 'town hall meeting' with input from a range of relevant parties including an Arab American community leader, a Japanese American who talked about his experiences and those of his family at the start of the Second World War and a representative from the Federal Bureau of Investigation who spoke about racial profiling. The meeting was aired on a public radio station on 11 October 2001 and later repeated due to demand from the station's audience.

An understanding of prejudice as both relational and as geographically, culturally and historically situated, presents museums with challenges as well as opportunities. In particular, the relationship which museums have with normative social understandings of difference, tolerance and acceptability is, as we shall see, a complex one. These issues resurface at different points throughout the book and, since they emerge from my analysis as especially salient, their implications are explored in greater depth in the concluding chapter.

Discursive analyses of prejudice

Challenges to mainstream social psychological approaches that conceptualise prejudice in predominantly individualistic and cognitivist terms as a 'personal pathology' (Wetherell and Potter 1992: 208) have been made not only on political and moral grounds but also more fundamentally in terms of their capacity to explain and explore prejudice as a social phenomenon. Since the 1980s, discursive analyses – which represent a significant departure from earlier strands of prejudice research – have gained increasing recognition (although within social psychology they nevertheless remain relatively marginalised). These approaches focus not on what is 'going on inside the head' but rather on the purposive nature and constitutive force of language.

> Social psychology has been concerned, predominantly, with examining the 'cognitive' contents of the mind; making use of notions such as attitudes, stereotypes, and representations, and has focused on how such cognitions are generated by cognitive mechanisms and processes. From this perspective, cognition is conceptualized as prior to language.
>
> (LeCouteur and Augoustinos 2001: 216)

In contrast, discursive approaches view prejudice, 'as both interactive and communicative and as located within the language practices and discourses of a society. It is through everyday language practices, both in formal and informal talk that relations of power, dominance and exploitation become reproduced and legitimated' (Augoustinos and Reynolds 2001: 10). Discursive approaches view these ways of talking not as the output of a prejudiced mind but rather, at a societal level, as the products of a prejudiced society. 'The analytic site therefore is not the "prejudiced" or "racist" individual,

but the discursive and linguistic resources that are available within an inequitable society' (ibid.: 10). Within a discursive approach, how then might
researchers empirically investigate prejudice?

Discourse analysis advocates the detailed examination of text and talk
– what is actually being said both in everyday conversation and in formal,
institutional contexts – in order to understand the constitutive force
of language. That is not to say that prejudice is necessarily confined to
language; some discourse analysts acknowledge that prejudice can manifest
itself in many different forms. It is generally argued, however, that discourse
plays a significant role in the social manufacture and reproduction of many
discriminatory practices (van Dijk 1993).

Amongst those who propose discursive explanations of prejudice, there
are nevertheless significant philosophical differences in approach. Some
argue that textual accounts and conversations reflect underlying cognitions
in individuals. For Teun van Dijk:

> the structural properties of text and talk are assumed to be moni-
> tored (and explained) by underlying *cognitions* of language users,
> that is, by memory processes and representations such as mental
> models of specific events, knowledge, attitudes, norms, values and
> ideologies. At the same time these discourses, interpreted as situated
> forms of action, as well as their underlying cognitions, are acquired
> and used in *sociocultural contexts*, such as those of politics, educa-
> tion, scholarship, the media, and corporate business.
>
> (1993: 13)

Others have adopted a more radical, non-cognitivist position. For
example, Jonathan Potter and Margaret Wetherell

> challenge the epistemological status of the 'attitude' concept itself.
> For them, the theoretical notion of an attitude, and the assumption
> that it can be encapsulated by the way a person responds to a ques-
> tionnaire scale, assumes the existence of internal cognitive entities
> that are relatively enduring.
>
> (LeCouteur and Augoustinos 2001: 218)

Rather they argue that individuals will make different evaluations at different
times and in different contexts. Instead of 'attitudes', they prefer the notion
of 'interpretative repertoires', defined as 'sets of metaphors, arguments, and
terms that are used recurrently in people's discourse to describe actions and
events' (ibid.: 218). In more traditional approaches to prejudice research,
researchers have tended to look for consistency in people's 'attitudes' and
accounts, viewing language as an indicator of relatively stable internal

mental representations (ibid.). In contrast, an important characteristic in much of the discursive research is the *variability* of discourse.

> What people say depends on the particular context in which they are speaking and the function(s) that the talk may serve. In the ebb and flow of everyday life, the context within which talk occurs and its accompanying function continually shift and change.
>
> (ibid.: 217)

Text and talk is therefore *functional, purposeful, constitutive* – it is directed to accomplish certain social tasks.

The purpose and function of text and talk

This functionality and purposiveness of language can be detected in visitors' responses to exhibitions at the St Mungo Museum and the Anne Frank House. Many visitors explicitly declared their support for concepts they identified in the museum's displays, such as 'equality', 'tolerance' and 'the importance of learning from the past'. In both their interview responses and in the written comments in visitors' books and comments cards, many seemed eager to condemn discrimination, to 'perform' their own tolerance. The four examples below were taken from visitors' written comments:

> What a very interesting exhibition excellently displayed with just enough information for an introduction. I am particularly impressed by the equality and tolerance throughout for people of different faiths. Thank you.
>
> (St Mungo Museum, 17 March 2003)

> This museum is truly a testimony against discrimination, against persecution based on race, gender, religion, creed, sexual orientation or any other constructed difference. It stands for human rights and dignity.
>
> (Anne Frank House, 24 July 2002)

> Absolutely favourite spot in the city. Not only do you get to view the magnificent Dali, but all religions are treated with honour. Peace in our world depends on sharing this open view.
>
> (St Mungo Museum, 13 January 2003)

> Very well done. I liked the intermingling of religious artefacts, it gives a very balanced view on religion which I think we all need now and in the future as well.
>
> (St Mungo Museum, 9 April 2003)

Drawing on these comments, it might be argued that visitors use discursive practices to reaffirm their own identities as open-minded, non-prejudiced citizens. These confirmatory statements perhaps enable visitors to reassure themselves that their personal views and values are closely aligned with those that they perceive to be represented within the museums.

Moreover, the functionality of language can be seen in attempts by some visitors not only to reaffirm their non-prejudiced position to *themselves* but also to present themselves to *others* in a positive light. Some visitors, for example, appeared comfortable with discursively locating themselves within the museum's intended audience through use of the first person: 'I' or 'Us'. These visitors, as the written comments below illustrate, positioned themselves as recipients of the exhibition's messages of tolerance and mutual understanding, perhaps as 'flawed' individuals who believed they had something to learn from their visit:

> I am extremely impressed by this exhibit and how it helps me see the similar need for belief, devotion and worship among all humans. Though the expression of faith is different around the world, the need of some to know God is universal. Thank you.
>
> (St Mungo Museum, 16 September 2001)

> An exhibition that can teach us all something. Definitely worth seeing.
>
> (Anne Frank House, 3 November 2002)

> I think the videos at the end on free speech versus discrimination are an excellent addition. They make us pause to reflect on our own personal values and hopefully on how many decisions we make affect other people.
>
> (Anne Frank House, 8 November 2002)

Many others, however, took the opportunity to position themselves rather differently, casting themselves as *already* tolerant and liberal. In doing so, they sometimes invoked, in opposition, an imagined, prejudiced audience for the museum. Joan,[6] a teacher from Colorado visiting the Anne Frank House with her friend, commented:

> I really think that what the Netherlands has done as a community, being so free and open, I respect, so I wanted to visit. My view, I'm really against people who are racist or prejudiced in any way so I think my coming to this house is a different experience than somebody who is racist or prejudiced.

Similarly, a retired secretary[7] visiting the St Mungo Museum with her husband, a foundry worker, told the following story:

> I've a friend who married an Indian chap and at the beginning, that was forty years ago, and her family disowned her and his family disowned him … They went to America and they did very well but he didn't get the chances here and I was very interested because he has still kept his religion. Not in your face, but he's kept it and I was quite interested in it. He also had pictures about Sikh things and I said 'what is your religion' and he was telling me and it was totally different from what I'd thought. I'd classed all Eastern religions the same and they're not, I mean the Sikhs were the noble men, they were the ones with very high ideals and I didn't know anything about that and they tell you a bit about that here. Anyway I saw what people did to those two and I just thought it was terrible and yet in our village, we had a black boy and everyone loved him and they all played with him and everything. And he grew up and became a footballer and what he suffered on the field because he was black … and yet in our village he didn't.[8]

Categories and stereotypes

A further way in which text and talk are purposefully deployed is through the categorisation and stereotyping of others. Cognitivist theories have tended to view these processes of generalisation and distinction as inevitable, natural, cognitively-helpful ways of enabling us to make sense of the world around us. Discursive analyses, however, approach the subject entirely differently.

> Although discursive psychology does not deny that people use social categories to talk about the world (clearly they do, and in very interesting and strategic ways), it does challenge the view that social categories are rigid internal entities that are applied inflexibly. Furthermore, categories are not treated as cognitive phenomena that are located in people's heads – as preformed static structures that are organized around prototypical representations of the category. Rather, discursive psychology emphasizes that people constitute categories discursively in order to do things.
>
> (LeCouteur and Augoustinos 2001: 219)

From a discursive perspective, categorisation is therefore seen as 'a complex and subtle social accomplishment' (Potter and Wetherell 1987: 116) – used for certain ends such as blaming, justifying, refuting, accusing, excusing or persuading (LeCouteur and Augoustinos 2001).

Stereotyping is a particular form of categorisation, one which involves not only generalising about social groups but also differentiating between them in hierarchical ways. By highlighting, exaggerating and fixing a few readily recognised traits, stereotypes offer reductive and essentialising interpretations of particular groups at the expense of heterogeneity and complexity (Hall 1997). They operate as a 'short cut' providing distinctive, readily recognisable ways of marking difference which, despite their apparent simplicity, are nevertheless suffused with complex and very often pejorative meanings and associations (Dyer 1993). The functions and purposes of stereotyping have been explored, not only in social psychology but in a range of disciplines. In cultural and media studies, for example, Stuart Hall (1997) has explored stereotyping as a signifying practice, closely bound up with the exercise of symbolic power, which is purposefully used to achieve certain outcomes. As Hall explains, the practice of stereotyping:

> sets up a symbolic frontier between the 'normal' and the 'deviant', the 'normal' and the 'pathological', the 'acceptable' and the 'unacceptable', what 'belongs' and what does not or is 'Other', between 'insiders' and 'outsiders', Us and Them. It facilitates the 'binding' or bonding together of all of Us who are 'normal' into one 'imagined community'; and it sends into symbolic exile all of Them – 'the Others' – who are in some way different – 'beyond the pale'.
>
> (1997: 258)

Stereotypes are strategically deployed both in everyday conversations and in wide-ranging media to support and legitimate prejudiced understandings of certain groups. The ubiquity of stereotypes and their recurrent use in diverse settings makes them especially resilient and resistant to challenge (Kratz 2002).

Museums are, of course, one of many settings in which stereotypical representations of social groups may be encountered, reinforced and reproduced but also, potentially, resisted and challenged. Recent research into the representation of disabled people in British museums and galleries has highlighted the presence of objects, descriptions and images which support largely demeaning and pejorative stereotypes. Although the study found that disabled people were very often absent from (or invisible within) exhibitions, it also revealed the presence of commonly recurring stereotypes which emphasised passivity, dependence and freakishness or alternatively heroism, through which individuals transcended their disability. These stereotypical representations of disabled people have been found to be commonplace in other media – especially literature (Kriegel 1987), broadcast media (Barnes 1992) and photography (Hevey 1992). The challenges bound up in attempts to contest or undermine these stereotypes through critical interventions are explored more fully in chapter 6.

The opposite of prejudice

For the purposes of this study, then, prejudice can usefully be understood as a discursive practice that is strategically deployed to accomplish certain tasks – to inferiorise particular social groups, to constitute difference as 'otherness' and in doing so to maintain inequitable power relations. But what terms and concepts are most appropriate to describe the outcome of initiatives designed to ameliorate prejudice? If prejudice is diminished or removed, what emerges in its place?

Tolerance, though widely used as a convenient shorthand term to refer to the opposite of prejudice is, I suggest, somewhat problematic. Michael Walzer helpfully identifies a continuum of different scenarios, 'attitudes' or 'states of mind' that are described by tolerance (the attitude) and toleration (the practice).

> The first of these ... is simply a resigned acceptance of difference for the sake of peace ... A second possible attitude is passive, relaxed, benignly indifferent to difference ... A third follows from a kind of moral stoicism: a principled recognition that the 'others' have rights even if they exercise those rights in unattractive ways. A fourth expresses openness to the others; curiosity; perhaps even respect, a willingness to listen and learn. And furthest along the continuum, there is the enthusiastic endorsement of difference ...
>
> (1997: 11)

Walzer continues by questioning whether this final state of mind – the valuing and affirmation of difference – in fact falls outside of the definition of toleration. 'If I want the others to be here, in this society, among us, then I don't tolerate otherness – I support it' (ibid.: 11). At least in some contexts, then, tolerance (or the practice of toleration) can suggest a somewhat grudging acceptance of difference by a mainstream dominant majority – an acceptance that is often conditional upon groups conforming, assimilating or simply 'keeping a low profile'. I wish to suggest that the goal that museums might more appropriately aim for, though more ambitious, is to contribute to a society based on recognition of the equal moral worth of different individuals and in which there is mutual respect between groups. This respect encompasses an expanded view of equal human rights; one which includes the right to maintain a differentiated group identity and resists the assimilationist associations that can stem from goals that focus primarily on the promotion of tolerance.

Investigating the combating of prejudice

The discursive analytical approach that we have so far focused on begins to suggest an appropriate methodology for research into the role that museums might play in combating prejudice. The conversations, accounts and 'linguistic performances' (LeCouteur and Augoustinos 2001) of visitors can be analysed to investigate the ways in which people talk about cultural difference, those perceived as 'other' and related issues of social inequality. Might these discursive accounts be considered egalitarian and respectful of difference, prejudiced and discriminatory or even contradictory? However, the questions that are central to this book remain. To what extent can visitors' text and talk be said to have been *influenced* or *shaped* by the museum or indeed by other forms of public discourse? How, and in what ways, might a museum visit affect the content, intonation and constitutive purpose of visitors' accounts?

Though the questions I pose here are museum-specific, they are nevertheless versions of more generalised lines of enquiry that have been addressed elsewhere. Discourse analysis (applied to the investigation of prejudice) has sought to explain the relationships between the formal, institutional, dominant (or 'elite') text and talk emanating from the realms of politics, education, business and the media (through, for example, government policy and parliamentary debate, newspapers and television and educational curricula) and the informal conversations and prejudicial utterances of everyday life. The field of media and audience studies has addressed somewhat related issues, though these have generally been couched in rather different terms. Over the past few decades, research in this discipline has been preoccupied by investigation of the relationship between media and audiences with considerable attention focused on the extent to which media influence the ways in which audiences think, behave and talk. Though little research has been conducted specifically into the role of the media in constituting, reinforcing or combating prejudice, the field of audience studies has nevertheless generated an especially rich source of theory with which to investigate and understand the agency of museums. These theoretical tools will be explored in much greater detail in chapter 4. However, for now, it is helpful to recognise that researchers within the discipline of audience and media studies have been influenced by trends in discourse analysis and have been increasingly open to the investigation of media influence through analyses of conversations amongst audiences (Alasuutari 1999).

This highlights the potential complementarity and integrative possibilities between approaches from the two distinct but related fields of discourse analysis and audience studies. I wish to argue that a syncretic perspective, drawing on and combining approaches from both these fields, will serve to illuminate the media–audience relationship within the specific context of the museum and to suggest a way forward for addressing the research questions with which this book is concerned.

Connecting the structural and the everyday

Several writers have argued for an integration of macro (structural) and micro (everyday) levels of discourse analysis in order better to explain and understand processes and manifestations of prejudice. For example, Philomena Essed (1991) is critical of exclusively macro sociological perspectives which view prejudice (and racism in particular) primarily in a structural way, arguing that such approaches neglect the everyday experiences of those who experience discrimination. Her concept of 'everyday racism', an integrated approach that sees individuals, and the ways in which they deploy language, as actors within a power structure is perhaps helpful here. For Essed, the concept of everyday racism 'connects structural forces of racism with routine situations in everyday life. It links ideological dimensions of racism with daily attitudes and interprets the reproduction of racism in terms of the experience of it in everyday life' (ibid.: 2). Similarly Teun van Dijk's work on elite discourse and racism integrates the

> societal and structural nature of racism as a system of social inequality, including shared ethnic prejudices or racist ideologies of white groups, on the one hand, with individual group members and their opinions and discourses as well as their contextual and personal variations, on the other hand.
>
> (1993: 14)

According to van Dijk, the ways in which individuals talk about prejudice in everyday life are framed and shaped by elite[9] discourses at a macro, structural level. Although he recognises that the relationship between macro (societal, structural) and micro (individual) manifestations of prejudice is dialectical,[10] his work is nevertheless based on an assumption that elites 'have a leading role in shaping the production and interpretation framework' (ibid.: 10) underlying the conversations which take place at an individual, interpersonal level. He states that,

> The leading elites in politics, the media, scholarship, education, corporate business, and many other social domains control the access to valued social resources and privileges, and thus are mainly responsible for inequality between majority and minority groups. Among many other actions, elite discourse is one of the important means that establishes, enacts, maintains, expresses, and legitimates such dominance.
>
> (ibid.: 17)

In this analysis, media texts are characterised as not only *influential* but, importantly, as *purposeful*. van Dijk argues that the *purpose* of elite discourse is to persuade ordinary non-elites to share the views of the elite:

> The major functions of such discourse about minorities are persuasive, that is, speakers aim to influence the minds of their listeners or readers in such a way that the opinions or attitudes of the audience either become or remain close(r) to those of the speakers or writer. In this way, speakers or writers may justify or legitimate specific cognitions or actions of themselves or other in-group members, or derogate those of out-group members.
>
> (ibid.: 30)

Though focusing specifically on racism (which, it must be acknowledged, has specific and distinguishing characteristics in comparison with other forms of prejudice), Essed's and van Dijk's overarching theoretical approach nevertheless contains elements which might usefully be widened to encompass other forms of prejudice and also applied to understand the relationship between the discourse of the museum and the text and talk of visitors.

These discursive approaches to understanding prejudice can be seen as both helpful and flawed (or at least problematic). Perhaps most helpfully, this approach serves to locate prejudice as a socially constructed phenomenon rather than as a 'personal pathology' (Wetherell and Potter 1992), challenging the notion that museum visitors are inherently either 'prejudiced' or 'unprejudiced'. The political potentials and obligations of the museum are therefore recognised rather than obscured by a cognitive focus on 'the prejudiced individual'. More problematically however, this approach is based on two (largely unquestioned) assumptions. Firstly, the elite discourse of the media is portrayed almost exclusively as *purposefully* and *necessarily* prejudiced. Though it is acknowledged that discourse can be designed to counter as well as promulgate prejudice[11] these possibilities have received very little empirical attention. Within discourse analysis it seems that little room is left for the possibility of anti-prejudice media discourses. Perhaps most importantly, where these are acknowledged, they are seen as necessarily oppositional or dissident (van Dijk 1993) – as acting against a single, dominant centre of power. These analyses are increasingly open to challenge from theoretical arguments, to which I referred in chapter 1, which view power as fragmented and dynamic. If power is understood in this way then it becomes more problematic to identify and talk of oppositional or dissident discourses. Similarly, it becomes problematic to conceive of museums as either wholly and straightforwardly complicit in the manufacture and reproduction of prejudice or wholly opposed to it. The categorisation of discourses and representations embodied within museum displays as either prejudiced and oppressive or – in binary opposition – non-prejudiced and

liberatory, obscures the ambivalence and contradiction inherent in all processes of cultural production and reception.

The second major difficulty with these discourse analytic approaches is
their tendency to assume passivity and acquiescence on the part of audiences. Consideration of potential audience responses to elite discourse is
largely absent from these perspectives although audiences are generally
imagined as relatively compliant. For example van Dijk states:

> Ordinary people are more or less passive participants in the many
> discourse types and communicative events controlled by the elites,
> such as those of the mass media, politics, education, scholarship,
> business corporations, the churches, the unions and the welfare
> offices among many other domains and organizations of society.
> We assume that since the elites dominate these means of symbolic
> reproduction, they also control the communicative conditions in the
> formation of the popular mind and hence, the ethnic consensus.
>
> (1993: 9–10)

Similarly, though perhaps less explicitly and directly, the discursive approach
within social psychology tends to underplay the agency of the individual.
LeCouteur and Augoustinos claim that, 'Individuals utilize whatever ideological resources a society makes available in order to justify and legitimate
racist outcomes, but this is always viewed primarily within the context
of oppressive structural arrangements which need continually to be justified and legitimated for their maintenance and reproduction' (2001: 229).
These approaches therefore can be seen to share a determinist, hegemonic
approach to discourse. At a localised, individual level, the discourses of
everyday life are assumed to be framed by formal institutional discourses
and little consideration is given to the extent to which individuals might
reinterpret, resist or directly oppose the messages they contain.

This is where it is especially helpful to be mindful of, and to draw upon,
developments within sociological and cultural studies-based approaches
to understanding audiences and processes of reception. Within these disciplines, researchers have increasingly turned to the audience and found
that they very often respond to media discourse in diverse, unpredictable
and frequently surprising ways. The theoretical understandings of audiences which these disciplines have generated – as active rather than passive
consumers of media messages and other forms of public discourse – help to
problematise discursive approaches to understanding prejudice which, as
we have seen, tend to assume passivity and acquiescence.

In chapter 4 I shall describe, in some detail, the protean ways in which
museum audiences respond to and engage with the messages inscribed
and embodied within the exhibitions that they encounter. Interpreting
the data generated from in-depth interviews with visitors, I shall discuss

the significance that these variable responses hold for understanding and explaining the agency of museums in combating prejudice.

In the next chapter, however, the focus turns to the sites in which these audience investigations took place – the St Mungo Museum of Religious Life and Art and the Anne Frank House.

3

PURPOSE, MEDIA AND MESSAGE

The St Mungo Museum of Religious Life and Art and the Anne Frank House

In December 1999, the leaders of ten historic sites including the Lower East Side Tenement Museum (United States), the Workhouse (England), the Gulag Museum (Russia), the Slave House (Senegal) and the District Six Museum (South Africa) signed and issued a statement which read:

> We are historic site museums in many different parts of the world, at many stages of development, presenting and interpreting a wide variety of historic issues, events and people. We hold in common the belief that it is the obligation of historic sites to assist the public in drawing connections between the history of our sites and its contemporary implications. We view stimulating dialogue on pressing social issues and promoting humanitarian and democratic values as a primary function. To advance this concept, we have formed an International Coalition of Historic Site Museums of Conscience to work with one another.
>
> (Abram 2002: 125)

The formation of the Coalition (and, indeed, its subsequent increased membership and profile) is reflective of a growing international interest in the potential for museums, and their agential capacities, to be brought to bear on wide-ranging social issues and concerns. This interest is evidenced in a number of trends: through widespread initiatives intended to broaden museum visitorships to include previously excluded or underrepresented communities; increasing professional debate around the social purpose and value of cultural organisations; the espousal of policies which position museums as agents of cross-cultural understanding; and demands for representation and for more inclusive and democratic museum practices from diverse constituencies.

The idea of the museum as an agent of social change and, more particularly, as a 'reformatory apparatus' (Bennett 2003) capable of shaping ways of seeing, thinking and behaving, is by no means new. Tony Bennett's historical analyses of museum policies and practices highlight the connections that can be drawn between nineteenth-century uses of museums and their contemporary conceptions as 'differencing machines' (2005) with the capacity to function as agents of cross-cultural understanding. For example, nineteenth-century ethnology exhibitions, he argues:

> were meant to demonstrate hierarchically organised relations of inequality between different people by exhibiting them as racial types, leading from the primitive to the civilised. Such exhibitions were also meant to display the power of western nations over colonised peoples: the power to command cultural material and frequently bodies too, and to exhibit these without any regard to the sensibilities or opinions of the peoples from whom they were taken.
>
> (ibid.: 4)

Nevertheless, in recent years, the idea of the museum as a technology for (democratising, empowering, liberatory) social change has become a powerful determinant of contemporary international museum rhetoric and policy. Moreover, the rise of business managerialism within the publicly funded cultural sector since the late 1970s has encouraged many museums to seek more clearly to define their purpose and to communicate this more widely to constituencies. These statements of purpose or mission vary immensely but increasingly reflect a belief in the museum's social (as well as economic and intrinsic cultural) value.

Although inevitably rooted in their own histories which account for their unique circumstances, the St Mungo Museum of Religious Life and Art and the Anne Frank House – the sites in which I chose to investigate the ways in which audiences responded to exhibitions designed to counter prejudice – can be seen as part of this broader trend towards articulating the purpose of museums in social terms. This chapter provides some background on the establishment, missions and strategic goals of these two organisations and describes the exhibitions and displays which visitors encounter there. The visiting agenda and motivations of the individuals and small groups that I interviewed there are also considered.

The St Mungo Museum of Religious Life and Art

> St Mungo's is not an objective museum. It exists explicitly to promote a set of values: respect for the diversity of human beliefs.
>
> (O'Neill 1995: 50)

> In terms of interpreting and inspiring society afresh, the St Mungo
> Museum is probably the most important museum to have opened
> in Britain since the V & A.
>
> (Artley 1993: 51)

Background

When the St Mungo Museum first opened on 1 April 1993 it attracted
considerable interest from the media, wide-ranging groups in Glasgow,
the visiting public and the international museum community. The museum
attracted controversy and criticism as well as considerable praise and recognition for its groundbreaking and innovative approach to displaying objects
with religious significance.

The museum grew out of opportunism rather than long term planning,
a factor which had considerable influence, much of it positive, on the way
the museum project subsequently took shape. The building which now
houses St Mungo's was originally intended to be a visitor centre for the
adjacent cathedral, a project led by Glasgow's Friends of the Cathedral.
However, when the project ran into financial difficulties the local government, Glasgow City Council, stepped in and began to consider a range of
uses for the building. The idea for a museum of religious life and art gathered momentum as the Council realised its potential to address a number of
strategic priorities for both the museum service and the city.

A range of social, political and economic factors can be seen to have
shaped the decision to develop a museum of religious life and art with a
specific, socially driven purpose based on the promotion of understanding
between different faith groups. The City Council saw that the museum had
the potential to be a unique, 'world class' tourist attraction, to complement other museums in the service and to support Glasgow's ambitions to
develop its cultural facilities for the international tourism market. It was
also felt that the museum could be an important resource for local people,
'for all of whom religion was part of their cultural background, even though
many were no longer believers' (O'Neill 1995: 50). Moreover, the idea of a
museum of religious life and art provided a means of developing more inclusive cultural services that would better reflect the multicultural nature of
Glasgow. As Mark O'Neill, the leader of the team that created the museum
stated, 'One of the things that was most noticeably missing [from the
existing galleries and museums within the service] was that Glasgow was a
multicultural society. Religion seemed an interesting way of approaching the
problem' (O'Neill cited in Gledhill 1993: 29). More specifically, the project
was viewed from the outset as an opportunity to contribute to the combating
of racism and religious sectarianism in the city. As Jem Fraser observes,
'St Mungo's Museum was a brave step in a city whose image has never

47

been helped by the depth of animosity between its two rival football teams traditionally associated with the two largest denominations of Christianity – the Catholic Celtic and the protestant Rangers – whose warring armies of fans clash with monotonous regularity' (2005: 92). This goal can be seen to mesh with broader strategic imperatives which were emerging at a national government level. In the 1990s, the Scottish Office and since 1998 the Scottish Executive, have introduced a number of initiatives aimed at combating racism in Scotland. The *One Scotland Many Cultures* campaign continues today to highlight the Scottish Executive's concern for social cohesion.[1]

Mission and purpose

The museum's mission statement was developed early on in the project and has not subsequently been changed.

> The St Mungo Museum of Religious Life and Art, Glasgow Museums, explores the importance of religion in people's everyday lives across the world and across time, aiming to promote mutual understanding and respect between people of different faiths, and of none.

This statement of purpose is prominently displayed to visitors in the entrance to the building and appears on the museum's website and on most promotional materials. Soon after the museum opened, O'Neill stated in an interview in *The Times* newspaper, 'Our aim is to promote mutual respect and understanding of different religions. We are trying to get rid of prejudice, on the grounds that it is mostly based on ignorance' (Gledhill 1993: 29).

Although the museum's purpose and social goals can be seen to have been shaped by a range of socio-political factors at local and national levels, it is nonetheless important to recognise the significance of individual actors in shaping this project. Mark O'Neill, who led the St Mungo's development team, came to the project with considerable experience of community based museum projects and held strong views about the potential for museums to address social concerns. Indeed, soon after the museum opened in 1993, O'Neill explicitly acknowledged the significance of the personal values and opinions held by individual contributors in shaping the final museum, stating that 'Many of the staff shared a conviction that if people understood more about each other's beliefs, mutual respect would be more possible' (1994: 28). This belief in the potential for museums to engage with contemporary social issues (whilst also fulfilling roles in relation to tourism development and other agendas) underpinned the way in which the museum developed, its mission statement and the shape and tone of the displays which were finally installed.

Figure 3.1: The *Gallery of Religious Art*, St Mungo Museum

Source: Photograph by kind permission of Glasgow Museums

The displays

The museum is composed of three main permanent galleries and a temporary exhibitions space, each with a distinctive atmosphere and appearance. The *Gallery of Religious Art* is generally the first gallery that visitors encounter and it displays objects that communicate 'something of the meaning of the religions they represent directly through their aesthetic power' (O'Neill 1995: 50). Unusually, objects linked to a range of religions are displayed alongside each other within a shared gallery space (Fig. 3.1). As O'Neill explains:

> This created startling juxtapositions, with Salvador Dali's *Christ of St John of the Cross* in the same room as an ancestral screen from the Kalibari people of Nigeria, a seventeenth-century Turkish

Figure 3.2: Thematic cases within the *Gallery of Religious Life* juxtapose objects and images from different faiths to examine the ways in which religion pervades many aspects of daily life

Source: Photograph by kind permission of Glasgow Museums

> prayer rug and an Australian Aboriginal dreamtime painting. The room was shaped by the architects so that, even though the objects were of greatly differing scales and visual qualities, all were seen to be treated with equal respect.
>
> (ibid.: 50–51)

The *Gallery of Religious Life*, situated through a doorway off the art gallery, offers a very different visual experience. In contrast with the relatively bright, spacious and open room that houses the art objects, visitors to this gallery are directed along a U-shaped route in a dimly lit room to view cases densely filled with objects (Fig. 3.2). Objects here are displayed in two main ways. Thematic cases located around the edge of the gallery juxtapose objects and images from different faiths to examine the ways in which religion pervades many aspects of daily life. In keeping with the museum's purpose, these thematic cases can be understood to privilege concepts of sameness between different religions. As curator Harry Dunlop explains, 'The gallery attempts to communicate what people believe and share in common (such as Rites of Passage) and what is unique and special in each cultural tradition' (2002: 8).

Differences between the practices and beliefs of the main faith groups are largely highlighted in ways which avoid controversy or the apportioning of criticism to specific religions. However, negative or controversial aspects of religion more generally are by no means neglected. Rather, as O'Neill explains, the interdisciplinary and thematic approach enabled the museum to more readily tackle controversial topics without compromising the mission to promote mutual understanding and respect. 'Displays on Birth, through Coming of Age and Marriage to Death and the Afterlife, gave a structure within which we could also deal with Missionaries, Divine Rule, Peace, War and Persecution' (1993: 11). Whilst questions of balance and parity are inevitably critical in a museum of this kind, they are most clearly rendered visible to the public in this particular gallery. While the thematic cases attempt to maintain a broad balance in representing the main religions, the centre of the gallery houses six equally sized display cases, each of which is devoted to one of the six most practised world religions – Buddhism, Christianity, Hinduism, Islam, Judaism and Sikhism.

The *Gallery of Religious Life* also features what the museum refers to as 'talkback boards' which, though increasingly used in museums today, were far less widespread when St Mungo's first opened. As Harry Dunlop explains, 'we included a talkback board in the *Gallery of Religious Life* which invites visitors to add their own opinion to the displays. Since most people have an opinion on at least some aspect of religion, these have proved extremely successful. Visitors love having a good read and an argument with each other' (Dunlop 2003). One reviewer of the museum, shortly after it opened, commented on the effectiveness of this particular interpretive device:

> To deflect possible vandalism in this gallery, the curators have wisely provided notice-boards which encourage visitors to pin up their own reactions to the exhibits. I found it almost impossible to get near the boards. 'Religion should be shown for what it is – garbage. Show the wars, famines, in the name of spurious Gods' wrote William Walsh of Kelvinside Gardens. 'Lovely painting by Dali showing Jesus as he is – "I am the Way, the Truth and the Life",' enthused another visitor. 'Moving and inspiring – another first for Glasgow,' said a third. I have never seen people so absorbed and excited by a museum exhibition.
>
> (Artley 1993: 51)

The third main gallery on the top floor of the museum looks more closely at religion in Scotland. The *Scottish Gallery* takes a thematic approach addressing such topics as 'Keeping the Faith' (how religion is maintained across generations), 'People and Places' (how Scottish people have connections with a range of holy places in other parts of the world), the role of missionaries and the sensitive subject of ongoing conflict between Protestants and Catholics in Scotland.

The fourth main gallery is used for changing exhibitions. Significantly, this provides an opportunity for the museum both to address specific themes and issues and to include particular faiths which are not

Figure 3.3: *Faithfully Yours*, a temporary exhibition, which marked the museum's ten-year anniversary

represented in the permanent galleries. During the period in which fieldwork was undertaken, the exhibition on display was *Faithfully Yours* (Fig. 3.3). This exhibition, which marked the museum's ten-year anniversary, comprised photographs by Glasgow Museums' photographer, Jim Dunn, who had been commissioned to capture the rich diversity of faith and religious practice across Glasgow.

In addition to the main galleries, the museum also has an introductory video featuring testimonials from people of different faiths, a small Education gallery (situated off the Scottish Gallery, which provides children's activities), and, outside, Britain's first Zen garden.

Collaboration and consultation

The project had to be developed very quickly with St Mungo's opening just two and a half years after its conception. Though this presented many logistical challenges it also freed the curatorial team to take more risks than might otherwise have been possible if there had been time for a full feasibility study and long term planning (O'Neill 1994). Despite the time constraints, it was recognised early on that consultation with a range of stakeholder groups, though time consuming, was necessary if the museum was to have widespread credibility and if it was to achieve its mission of promoting respect between different faith communities. Mark O'Neill explains the importance of community collaboration in bringing the project to fruition:

> If the aim was to communicate something of the meaning of the objects, we had to reverse the usual process in museums of draining them of their dangerous meanings to render them safely aesthetic, historical or anthropological. In the case of religion, 'meaning' has an emotional or spiritual dimension that can be described much more powerfully by those who experience it than those who have simply studied it. Some sort of consultation or collaboration with believers was therefore required.
>
> (1994: 28)

This process achieved a number of important outcomes. Not only did it help to garner support for the museum from wide-ranging constituencies but it also generated oral testimonies which were used to provide both written quotations and audio commentaries alongside the exhibits. 'We included these diverse responses and opinions as injections of human emotion,' explains Harry Dunlop, 'in an attempt to allow visitors to empathise with the issues being raised in a deeply personal way' (2003). (This particular interpretive device, as we shall see in due course, plays a significant role in enabling visitors to make connections with the subjects on display.)

The process of collaboration continues to be important in the way the museum develops its programmes today. *Meet your Neighbour*, a series of public events programmed by St Mungo's each year, is organised in partnership with a range of organisations which share the museum's overarching goals. The fieldwork undertaken for this study coincided with the *Meet Your Neighbour* festival in 2003 – a programme of workshops, musical performances and discussions for visitors and school groups that was organised in conjunction with a range of inter-faith agencies including the Churches Agency for Interfaith Relations in Scotland, Glasgow Sharing of Faiths, the Jewish Representative Council, and Sense over Sectarianism.

Admission to St Mungo's (and indeed to all of the museums within the Glasgow Museums service) is free to all visitors and the museum attracts approximately 150,000 visits each year. Visitors' written comments on the cards displayed in the *Gallery of Religious Life* are collected and recorded in a database by the museum and these show that responses to the museum are 'overwhelmingly positive' (Glasgow City Council 2001). Whilst most critical visitor responses have generally taken a written form, using comments cards in the gallery or complaint letters sent to the museum, it is nevertheless worth noting that the displays have also prompted rather more visceral hostile responses. Just a few months after the museum opened in 1993 a member of the public attacked the large nineteenth-century South Indian

Figure 3.4: Just a few months after St Mungo's Museum opened, a member of the public attacked the nineteenth-century South Indian bronze statue of the Hindu deity Shiva Nataraja

Source: Photograph by kind permission of Glasgow Museums

bronze statue of the Hindu deity, Shiva Nataraja; a powerful illustration of the potential for visitors to respond in ways which are directly counter to those intended by the museum (Fig. 3.4). As Mark O'Neill explains:

> He pulled this bronze object, weighing about 500 kilos over onto its face, severely damaging its arm. When asked by the member of staff who detained him why he did this he said he did it for Christ. This confirmed our conviction that a museum like St Mungo's was necessary.
>
> (1994: 31)

The Anne Frank House

> [T]he visitors to the Anne Frank House should not be left with the sad but comforting feeling that it was 'all over' in 1945 with the end of the Nazi era. They should have the uneasy feeling that what happened to Anne Frank might happen just as easily and unreasonably to themselves; that the only way to prevent this is to take an active and serious stand for equality and democracy.
>
> (van der Wal 1985: 56)

When the house on Prinsengracht, Amsterdam, in which Anne Frank wrote her diary was threatened with demolition in 1957, the Anne Frank House organisation was established to secure its future. The original charter set out the dual purposes of the House which continue to guide the organisation's mission today.

> The Anne Frank House is dedicated to the preservation of the property at 263 Prinsengracht in Amsterdam, and especially of the attached Annex, as well as to the propagation of the ideals left as legacy to the world in 'The Diary of Anne Frank'. The House endeavours to further advance these goals by combating prejudice, discrimination and oppression and by striving for a democratic society, both in form and content, as described in the 'Universal Declaration of Human Rights.'
>
> (Anne Frank House 2000: 25)

Whilst the dual purposes of the organisation have remained broadly constant, the ways in which it seeks to fulfil its mission have evolved to meet shifting social and political conditions (van der Wal 1985). Today, the Anne Frank House manages a number of activities alongside the museum including the mounting of international travelling exhibitions and development of a resource-rich website, ongoing research into manifestations of Right-wing extremism and racism in the Netherlands, wide-ranging educational projects including resources for schools, anti-discrimination training for police and other professional groups, and initiatives in partnership with a range of employers, aimed at promoting equality of opportunity for minority ethnic communities in the Dutch labour market.

The Anne Frank House opened as a museum to the public on 3 May 1960. The museum includes the Secret Annex where Anne Frank wrote her diary and where she and seven others hid from the Nazis during the Second World War. In its first year, admission to the museum was free and it attracted 9,000 visitors. Ten years later the annual attendance had risen to 180,000, forcing the museum to close for several months in 1970 to undertake essential maintenance and repairs to the building. When the museum reopened in 1971, despite the introduction of an admission charge, visitation continued to increase and the organisation expanded its educational activities beyond the museum.

In 1990, when the number of visitors per year exceeded 600,000, the museum decided to redevelop the site to increase floor space for improved museum facilities whilst also undertaking restoration work to return the front of the building at 263 Prinsengracht to its original condition. The new museum finally opened in 1999. The Secret Annex where Anne Frank was in hiding during the war remains at the heart of the museum but there are also expanded museum facilities including changing exhibitions and event spaces, a shop and café.

Mission and purpose

On 10 October 1998, Matthew Shepard is buried in Caspar, Wyoming, in the United States. Matthew was a young homosexual who was a victim of a shocking crime, committed out of hatred. He was assaulted and murdered because of his sexual nature. At Matthew's funeral, Fred Phelps, a minister of a Baptist church in Kansas holds a demonstration. He and a number of his followers want to express their view that homosexuality should be opposed. The demonstrators at Matthew's funeral carry signs with the words 'Matthew burns in hell' and 'Aids cures faggots'. What's more important?

Freedom of speech: *In this case, Minister Phelps' freedom to freely deplore homosexuals in direct confrontation with them or:*

The right to be protected from discrimination. *In this case the right of family and friends of the victim to be spared such discrimination. It's your choice.*

This statement is taken from the interpretive booklet which accompanied the temporary exhibition, *Grensgevallen* (translated by the museum as *Out of Line*), which was showing at the museum during the period in which fieldwork for this study was conducted.

On my first visit to the Anne Frank House in 2002 I was intrigued to find this exhibition which invited visitors to engage with a series of real-life contemporary scenarios concerned with wide-ranging forms of prejudice and discrimination, to make decisions relating to these, and to share their personal opinions with other visitors. I recall the mixed emotions, the considerable discomfort as well as intrigue which I felt at the realisation that – of the ten visitors in the exhibition at that time – I was alone in expressing the opinion that protection from discrimination should prevail over freedom of speech when the far-right religious group carried offensive banners at the funeral of Matthew Shepard.

Most of the nearly one million visitors to the Anne Frank House each year are similarly surprised (some are intrigued, some delighted and others angered) to encounter temporary exhibitions such as *Out of Line* which invite them to share their views on such wide-ranging topics as neo-Nazis on the internet, the lyrics of Eminem and Ku Klux Klan demonstrations in Texas. So well known is the story of Anne Frank that most visitors have at least some idea in mind of what they will encounter during their visit to the House. For many, having read the diary often many years earlier, the opportunity to visit the Secret Annex where Anne Frank and seven others hid during the Nazi occupation of Holland in World War II is something of a secular pilgrimage. Visitors anticipate that the House will provide an opportunity to learn more about the events of the time and perhaps the chance to reflect, through the relative safety and comfort provided by historical distance, on the life and experiences of the young Jewish girl whose diaries have become known worldwide.

The House certainly fulfils these expectations but there is little in the way of advance warning, from guide books or clues from the outside of the building itself, to suggest that the museum is committed not only to preserving, presenting and interpreting the building where Anne Frank and her family hid but also to disrupting visitors' sense of distance and detachment and to challenging them to make connections with their own lives. As Jan van Kooten (2003), Head of the Educational Department, explains:

> There is a danger that people, however emotionally charged their visit, may simply feel pity for Anne and sadness for the circumstances which led to her death. We don't want people to leave without being triggered to realise that her story is also about today. We want to challenge people's indifference to contemporary prejudice and intolerance.

The museum designed the exhibition *Out of Line*, situated towards the end of the visit, specifically with this purpose in mind. Having followed a prescribed route through the rooms inhabited by the Frank family while in hiding, the visitors emerge from the house itself and enter a distinctly contemporary space. This contrasts sharply with the intimate and historic character of the earlier part of the visit to the Annex, signalling a return to the present day. The accompanying booklet, made available to visitors at the entrance to the exhibition, explains its premise.

> *Out of Line* is an interactive exhibition that deals with contemporary issues. The exhibition focuses on two basic rights: freedom of expression and the right to be protected against discrimination. In western democracies these are now regarded as fundamental rights most citizens take for granted. But what happens when these two basic rights clash? Which right carries the most weight? The visitors to the exhibition will have a chance to speak out on this topic.

Examples of these clashing rights, featured in the exhibition, are wide ranging. Alongside scenarios that relate to contemporary racism and anti-Semitism are others that consider prejudice and discrimination on the basis of disability,

Figure 3.5: The interactive exhibition *Out of Line* at the Anne Frank House

Source: Photographer: Klaas Fopma. By kind permission of the Anne Frank Stichtung

faith, gender and sexual orientation. I felt this was especially significant for my study because, while most visitors to the House might reasonably be assumed to be (at least partially) receptive to anti-racist sentiments, they may nevertheless find themselves facing issues around other forms of prejudice with which they are less comfortable and on which their views are less resolved.

The exhibition occupied a stark, dimly lit room with a metal floor and bare walls and visitors could choose either to take a seat or stand to face two large screens that covered much of the far wall (Fig. 3.5). A mixture of news footage and other material for each scenario was provided through an audio-visual presentation, accompanied by narration that argued alternately for 'freedom of expression' (shown on the left hand screen with accompanying red graphics) and 'protection from discrimination' (shown on the right in green graphics). Each scenario lasted for approximately three to four minutes during which time visitors heard the case for both points of view. A few visitors, perhaps inevitably, found the arguments too brief and simplistic to do justice to the complex issues in question. However, given the location of the exhibition after the physically and emotionally tiring experience of the House, the relatively speedy turnover of examples appeared to work well in engaging the diverse audience (especially in terms of age and nationality) and in overcoming the considerable challenges of accommodating the high number of visitors.

In 2005, *Out of Line* was replaced with *Free2Choose*, an exhibition which similarly invites visitors to make choices concerning contemporary social issues. The presentation of opposing points of view on the same issue provides an opportunity for the Anne Frank House to dispense with the measured, 'impartial', curatorial voice that most museums strive for. This device certainly succeeds in provoking responses from visitors. In *Out of Line*, after both sides of the issue had been presented, those who were seated (with access to a console in front of them) were asked to make a choice – to press the red button if they believed that, in this particular situation, the right to freedom of expression outweighed the right to protection from discrimination, or vice versa by pressing the green button. The results of the vote were displayed through red and green neon bars on the ceiling that lit up according to the number of votes cast.

Though the message of the Anne Frank House is one that aims to promote equal human rights and to challenge prejudice, there are, of course, a whole range of factors that are likely to impact upon the extent to which this message is accepted, rejected or turned around by visitors. Not surprisingly, as we shall see in the following chapters, reactions are extremely diverse. However, whilst visitors are inevitably free to articulate prejudiced remarks to other members of their group or may even choose to write them in the visitors' book, the opportunities for expressing these views through the exhibition itself are, in effect, prohibited by the museum through the voting format. In *Out of Line*, visitors had only two choices – both of which were predicated upon notions of equal human rights for all. The voting format of the exhibition did not enable visitors to express their support or endorsement of, for example, racist or homophobic viewpoints – only for the right of individuals and groups to express those opinions. (The significance of this framing device and the issue of choice is discussed more fully in chapter 5.) Encouraging visitors to respond by casting a vote for one of two neatly categorised, opposing options might, at first glance, appear to be reductive and limiting. However, the strength of this format lay in the invitation to visitors to consider a range of scenarios and to explore the particular situations in which they might feel compelled to switch positions – for example, to understand the conditions and circumstances which might lead them to move from support for 'freedom of expression' to support for 'protection from discrimination'.

Although some visitors commented that, in some scenarios, the content was biased, this may say as much about their own values, attitudes and life experiences as it does about the bias of the exhibition's creators. *Out of Line* was not intended to lead towards one particular conclusion – the right to freedom of expression and the right to protection from discrimination were presented as equally important, though frequently conflicting, features of a democratic society. Indeed, new, updated examples were only included in the exhibition when, having been trialled with the staff of the museum, they succeeded in dividing opinion (van Kooten 2003). The museum's Director, Hans Westra, explains the shift in intention that has occurred within the organisation and which is embodied within its approach to temporary exhibitions such as *Out of Line*. 'Until five years ago we wanted people to leave taking on board a number of statements – the world according to the Anne Frank House. Now we put questions at the centre. The aim is to develop both compassion and critical thinking' (Vallely 2002: 6).

It is also interesting to consider the extent to which responses to *Out of Line* and *Free2Choose* are framed by the emotionally charged visit to the Secret Annex. Many visitors make a connection between the message offered by the first part of their visit to the House and the contemporary issues in the exhibition, illustrating the museum's potential to provoke, and perhaps to inform, discussion and reflection. For example, Freddie, a web developer from England in his late forties, said:

> I think what the museum is trying to do is to give the whole picture, both political, historical, emotional. And the last section, where we went in and it was asking you to vote, I think is a good way of expressing that, in fact, this is one pebble dropped in a stream in 1945 but it's ongoing, it's still with us. We've still got prejudice, we've still got war, look at Ireland, it's still here, we're still living through it. Although we don't suffer from it, other people do. I think it's a good conscience pricker, you come away thinking 'how should I feel, how should I react if that happened to me?'

It is interesting to note that, after the fieldwork for this study was undertaken, the House continued to update the exhibition introducing new content including some especially controversial examples which turn the spotlight directly on recent high-profile events in Holland and on increasingly apparent tensions in Dutch society. Whilst some researchers have argued that the Dutch reputation for tolerance masks a rather different reality,[2] the image of Holland as a harmonious and accepting society, at ease with its multicultural demography, has nevertheless endured until relatively recently. In the last few years, events that have received high-profile international media coverage have undoubtedly damaged this reputation and sparked national debates around immigration, integration and freedom of speech. In 2004, the Anne Frank House introduced a scenario into *Out of Line* that focused on Pim Fortuyn, the Dutch politician, murdered in 2001, who believed that Article 1 of the Dutch Constitution which concerns anti-discrimination, needed to be abolished. A further scenario considers the controversial attacks on Islam and, in particular, its treatment of women, by a Dutch member of parliament, Ayaan Hirsi Ali. As the Anne Frank House later noted in its 2004 Annual Report, 'This particular addition to the exhibition became startlingly timely in November when Dutch filmmaker Theo van Gogh was murdered and politician Ayaan Hirsi Ali had to go into hiding because of her controversial statements' (Anne Frank House 2005: 13).

While many visitors enjoy these exhibitions, spending some considerable time working through each of the examples, the museum acknowledges that not all visitors feel that they complement the experience of visiting the Secret Annex (van Kooten 2003). Indeed some visitors, as we shall see, feel that the Anne Frank House (and indeed museums in general) are no place to address contentious contemporary issues.

Getting the message?

Visitors at both sites, interviewed at the end of their visit, were asked – 'Do you feel the museum is trying to communicate any particular message? If so, what would you say that is?' Responses to this question took two main forms. For some visitors, the presence of a 'message' implied partiality, intentionality and manipulation, characteristics which they did not generally associate with the idea of the museum. Although perceptions that the museum was not attempting to convey a particular message were evident in the data from visitor interviews at both sites, they were most frequently and forcefully expressed at the Anne Frank House. For example, Clive, a teacher in his late forties from Middlesex, commented:

> I saw it as information rather than a particular message. It was saying something about what it was like to be in these streets, looking out on that canal as a child, not being able to speak, not being able to flush the toilets, no fresh air, so it does bring about what tyranny and oppression might be like; occupation by another group of people bringing their ideas, what it might be like to be dominated, oppressed. Those kinds of things.

Nigel, a retired school principal visiting from Australia, similarly questioned the idea that the museum attempted to influence visitors in a purposive manner:

> I didn't think that it was trying to say anything to us. I felt it was presenting things as they were and then, especially with the last bit, getting people to make up their own mind. I don't think there was any sort of brainwashing, it was just presented as it is or as it was.

And Nathalie, a computer technician from Germany, stated:

> No. I think it's pretty neutral. You can make up your own mind. It really only shows how it was. Maybe you're led to a certain opinion, but you're not influenced really, you're just told the facts.

At St Mungo's, although visitors were more likely to identify the presence of a particular message, some nevertheless expressed sentiments which echoed those above. Anna, a young student from Finland, stated:

> Maybe the whole idea of this museum is, in my point of view, to offer people information and maybe stop people for a little while – you know to understand other people's point of view because they come from a different background and different religions and wars have been happening for religious reasons. I don't know, I didn't catch a particular message. I can't say one thing.

Further on in the interview, visitors were asked about their perceptions of museums (in general and in comparison with other forms of media) as providers of knowledge and information. Here, the idea that museums are generally viewed as unbiased and reliable (especially in comparison with other media sources) resurfaced. I return to this particular issue, and the implications it holds for understanding the role of museums in countering prejudice, more fully in chapter 5.

In contrast with the responses which questioned the existence of a particular message, many other visitors (at both sites) appeared comfortable with the idea that the museums were attempting to put forward particular viewpoints. Many visitors readily identified at least some key features of the intended messages. Typical responses at the Anne Frank House included:

> I think the message is that the smallest things may lead to big things, like, who would have imagined a small thing of just discriminating against people would lead to a whole of bunch of people dying because of it. I guess that's what the message is, that small things can lead to big things.

> Don't repeat what's happened. I think that's an important message. You can't let it happen again. Be aware of the kind of society you want to live in.

> I think possibly there's an anti-discrimination message that runs through the whole exhibition.

And at St Mungo's, many visitors similarly identified themes linked to the museum's intended message of mutual understanding and respect, although these were often inflected in different ways:

> Glasgow is a multicultural society and having it all under one roof is kind of saying we're all neighbours and should all try and get on even though we're all from different backgrounds and religions.

It's a multicultural country. We actually spoke about it earlier on. We used to say Great Britain is a Christian country and, to a degree, I believe that but because there's that much different cultures within it, I think this place is trying to learn people about other cultures, other religions.

Well, I suppose it's trying to say we should all live in harmony, you know, there are all these religions in the world. Yeah, just express yourself and people try and express themselves in different ways and there's not a wrong way or a right way, just try and get on together. We shouldn't be pushing against each other. I think that's what it's trying to say.

Whilst many visitors may have recognised and acknowledged at least some of the main features of the museums' intended messages, it would be naïve to equate this with audience compliance or consensus or to suggest that these messages were internalized or appropriated as their own. As we shall see in due course, textual determinism cannot simply be read off from widespread audience recognition of the key elements inscribed within the exhibitions. Indeed, the discussion in chapter 4 reveals how visitors engaged with the messages they recognised in variable, complex and unpredictable ways.

The visiting agenda

I was initially surprised at the ease with which many visitors 'correctly' identified the main features of the museums' intended messages, not because I questioned the capacity for audiences to understand and interpret what they saw but because, as the interviews unfolded, it became clear that most had approached their visit with little or no awareness of the sites' atypical, socially driven purposes.

Most interviewees linked their motivation for visiting to leisure-based agendas – the opportunity to see a particular painting, simply somewhere to spend free time or somewhere to share with visiting friends or relatives – rather than a conscious desire to learn more about different cultures or to engage with issues of prejudice. Significantly, most approached their visit to the Anne Frank House or St Mungo's in much the same way as they would a visit to any other museum.[3] At St Mungo's Museum, the allure of the famous Salvador Dali painting, 'Christ of St John of the Cross' (Fig. 3.6), proved especially powerful.[4]

I'm visiting with my parents, they're up to visit Glasgow for a week. We knew about the Salvador Dali painting and my Dad wanted to

Figure 3.6: 'Christ of St John of the Cross' by Salvador Dali

Source: By kind permission of Glasgow Museums

see it and my Mum and I wanted to look round the museum and visit the cathedral

> (Ruth, a housewife from Glasgow).

Jim, an accountant on holiday with his wife, said:

> We were on the tour bus and were going to come back and see the cathedral but I remembered a friend had mentioned the Salvador Dali. They said it was in here so we wanted to come and see it.

Several visitors were less purposive, more casual in their decision to visit St Mungo's:

> The receptionist at the hotel ... we asked what was interesting to go and have a look at and she suggested coming here. It was well worth it.

> (Valerie, visiting with her daughter)

Eunice, a woman who worked in the catering industry and lived in Bradford, England, was visiting Glasgow by herself:

> I didn't know the museum was here, I came to look at the cathedral so it was a shock to find this here.

Many first-time visitors to St Mungo's appeared to come with rather inchoate expectations, with a considerable degree of uncertainty about what a museum of religious life and art might contain. In contrast, visitors to the Anne Frank House tended to have very clear expectations of what they would encounter. These expectations, no doubt, were drawn from wide-ranging sources – the diaries which many visitors mentioned that they had read, conversations with acquaintances who had previously visited and a multitude of documentaries and dramatic productions based on Anne Frank's life. Whilst a significant proportion of visitors to St Mungo's had made a relatively spontaneous decision to 'drop in', visitors to the Anne Frank House had generally made a more purposeful and conscious decision to visit and many had gone to considerable efforts to do so (Fig. 3.7). This difference is, in all likelihood, a function of the sites' different circumstances. While St Mungo's is free of charge and visitors are unlikely to be required to queue to gain admission, the Anne Frank House is a charging museum which generally requires standing in line for a significant amount of time to gain entry. The iconic status of Anne Frank can account for most visitors' decisions to visit the House:

Figure 3.7: Visitors very often queue around the building to gain admission to the Anne Frank House

> I've always wanted to come here after reading the book ... just amazing and when I found out that the house was here and there was an exhibition, I was very interested to come and see.
>
> > (Lindsey, a carer from Sydney, visiting with friends)

> It's well publicised. To be honest, that's all there is to it. We got the 'Amsterdam Pass' and there's lots of other museums that I've never heard of that are probably just as interesting but this is the one that's publicised worldwide. We've got the Diary, so ... and that's all there is to it.
>
> > (Robert, from Derby, visiting with his family)

In some ways, its unrivalled status on the tourist map of Amsterdam can sometimes mean that people feel almost obliged to visit the House. Betty, a retired schoolteacher from Colorado, visiting with her friend, explained:

> It's part of history. You come to Amsterdam and you go to Anne Frank's. Everybody goes to Anne Frank's house.

Similarly, Simon, a teacher from Germany, commented:

> Anne Frank is well known and maybe it's a duty to visit this house.
> I read about her and I'm also a history teacher so maybe for me it's
> just absolutely necessary.

Encountering the unexpected

Visitors, then, approached their museum experiences with wide-ranging
motivations and intentions. Only a very small minority of interviewees
(to whom I shall return in chapter 5) offered reasons for visiting which
suggested a purposive desire to gain a better understanding of cultural
differences. Despite this, many appeared receptive to unanticipated, even
unsettling aspects of the visit. Deborah, an office manager from Tyneside,
England, visiting with her daughter, stated:

> I just came to look at the [Salvador Dali] painting so that was the
> main reason, but I quite enjoyed looking at the different religions,
> at different perceptions of life, death and marriage and everything
> on the same floor as the painting, that was quite interesting.

Similarly Michael, a community worker in his fifties visiting the Anne Frank
House from the United States, observed:

> You come out of here uneasy and I think that's good. People don't
> ordinarily like to go to places where you come out uneasy but I think
> there's something attractive about this little girl, young woman, that
> draws you in, seduces you in and then you say, 'I can't leave now
> I've got to face something that I maybe don't want to.'

However, some other visitors were distinctly uncomfortable with some
aspects of the exhibition encounter which were at odds with their expectations and their views on what was appropriate in the museum context. Tom,
a telecommunications engineer in his fifties and his wife, Lynette, an educational administrator, discussed their reactions to the *Out of Line* exhibition:

> TOM: Clearly there's a greater freedom or acceptance over here in Hol-
> land of gays and lesbians and their rights under the law. I don't know if
> that's progressive and the rest of the world is catching up or not but...
> LYNETTE (*interjecting*): I thought it was out of place. I suppose it was
> a shock, it was out of context of having gone round in a sombre at-
> mosphere, the lighting and all that keeps it low key and then suddenly
> you're sat in a theatre and you're seeing a discussion on the rights and

wrongs of gays and lesbians in the context of the Muslim religions. I thought it was out of context.

At St Mungo's, the section of the *Gallery of Religious Life* that deals with the 'Coming of Age' includes a photograph depicting a young girl accompanied by the following text:

> Ritual removal of the clitoris, Cairo, Egypt, 1980s. Female genital mutilation affects over 70 million in Africa and the Middle East. The World Health Organisation has condemned the practice, and it has recently been outlawed by many governments including those of Egypt and Mali.

This particular exhibit has consistently provoked responses from visitors, many of whom are uncomfortable with discovering it in the museum. One visitor pinned their comments to the gallery's 'talkback boards' on 20 April 2003.

> What purpose does the exhibition of the picture of a sexually mutilated girl in the 'coming of age' section serve? How would you like to be tortured, photographed while it all happens and then being publicly displayed? Would you like to see your face up there? It totally destroys the credibility of the whole exhibition. It's bad enough that these things happen. Do you have to display them and condone them? I am disgusted.

A number of interviewees also commented on the photograph but opinion as to whether this was an appropriate topic for the museum to include was, not surprisingly, divided. Comments made by Eleanor, a retired anthropologist from Leicester, England, suggest support for the museum's decision to address this disturbing issue:

> I mean that, to me, will be a lasting image. Do you know the photograph I'm referring to? I have always just thought that was the most appalling event in a girl's life and to actually see a photograph of it happening ... is even more shocking than reading about it and that it still goes on and there must be terrible infection and death caused by it quite apart from the horrible event ... but I mean it's a good thing to see isn't it?

In contrast, a number of responses revealed some visitors' discomfort at unexpectedly encountering difficult or painful subjects within the museum. These responses, collected during the period of my study, were not unusual. In an article in the *Museums Journal* less than a year after the museum opened, Mark O'Neill (1994: 31) highlighted the photograph as an especially provocative and controversial element of the displays:

> [A] major controversy associated with the museum was the way it handled the issue of female genital mutilation. Two local feminist groups issued a press release saying that this was a gender not a religious issue and that the museum was trivialising it by treating it in the section of the museum dealing with coming of age. They picketed the museum the next day, and argued that we should remove a photograph showing a young girl immediately after a clitoridectomy had been performed, her face full of pain, puzzlement and betrayal. Of the many drafts of the label, the final version used the term circumcision and did not condemn the practice; the photograph spoke volumes. After an hour-long discussion on the steps of the museum the protestors agreed to meet with museum staff more formally. While the staff were prepared to revise the label, they were certain that they had the right, indeed the duty, to deal with the issue.

Conclusion

The St Mungo Museum and the Anne Frank House present ambitious missions that reflect a shared belief in the idea of the museum as a force for positive societal change. Although the topics they address and the interpretive devices they employ are in many ways distinctive, both sites present exhibitions that confront highly emotive and politicised issues. As a consequence they are perhaps more likely to attract criticism than other museums which very often side-step difficult issues, especially where these relate to topics which continue to provoke divided public opinion.

The exhibitions they present, while stimulating debate (and, indeed, explicitly inviting visitors to articulate and contribute their own opinions), are nevertheless underpinned by (and attempt to privilege and engender support for) concepts of social justice and equal human rights. While the museums are unapologetically uncompromising in their adoption of particular moral standpoints, at the same time, they also appear appropriately cautious of claiming that the values and positions that they espouse are straightforwardly communicated to, and adopted by, audiences. Rather, they are concerned to engage visitors in dialogue and to challenge them to think about complex and challenging questions.

The exhibition encounter, as we shall see, generates wide-ranging reactions among visitors but to what extent, if at all, might these responses constitute the combating of prejudice? In the next two chapters I address this central question through detailed analysis and interpretation of the conversations and written comments of visitors, stimulated by their engagement with the exhibitions I have described. I draw, in particular, on theories that have emerged from sociology and cultural studies to interrogate processes of reception and to understand the relationship between diverse media forms and their audiences. In doing so, my intention is to explore the social consequences and effects, as they relate to questions of prejudice, of visitors' engagement with museums.

4

THE VISITOR–EXHIBITION ENCOUNTER
Reconciling and rethinking museum– audience agency

> As people visit an exhibition, with all its parts and communicative possibilities, they might take off from any number of details, devise their own questions and answers, focus on particular portions or pieces, skip labels altogether, and see an exhibition through interests and experiences not anticipated by exhibition developers.
>
> (Kratz 2002: 94)

In her account of a travelling exhibition of photographs of the Okiek people of Kenya, an exhibition that set out to challenge essentialised and totalising representations of its subject, Corinne Kratz discusses what she calls the 'double-sided nature' of exhibition experience. Her analysis highlights the complexity of the interpretive processes generated out of the visitor–exhibition encounter and the interactions between 'what visitors bring to the exhibition and … what exhibitions bring to visitors' (ibid.: 94). Visitor experiences may be intense or relatively superficial, fleeting or extended, purposive or casual, each encounter involving variable degrees of attention, engagement and emotional intensity. However, although the ways in which visitors might engage with exhibitions are wide-ranging, uneven and unpredictable, they are not entirely unpatterned. The challenges of capturing (and making sense of) the character of these processes as they are actuated and the meanings they contain might account, at least partially, for the relative paucity of research into the agency of museums in the combating of prejudice.

Contemporary understandings of audiences – as agents active in the construction of meaning – present a significant challenge to museums that seek to combat prejudice. The traditional transmission or dominant text model of communication, in which audiences passively and uncritically absorb the messages they are exposed to, is no longer widely supported. Rather, research suggests that museum audiences can construct wide-ranging meanings from a museum visit, mediated, shaped and informed by a range of personal and socio-cultural factors. Potentially, these meanings might be entirely oppositional to those intended by the museum, exhibiting not tolerant or egalitarian attributes but rather prejudiced (for example, homophobic, racist or sexist) ones. Moreover, some proponents of the constructivist model of learning which predominates in much of the contemporary museum studies literature suggest that museums should seek, not to dictate or prescribe the nature of 'valid' learning outcomes but rather to value those myriad, personalised meanings that can be made from a museum visit (Hein 1998). Given this context, how then can we better understand the role and agency of the museum that seeks to confront prejudice? How can the relative agency of media and audience (often conceived of in terms of a conflict or a struggle for primacy) be understood and reconciled?

To address these questions I analyse visitor responses (written and spoken) to exhibitions at the Anne Frank House and the St Mungo Museum of Religious Life and Art, identifying themes and patterns within the data generated by this study. Whilst this chapter focuses on the ways in which visitors engaged with the museums' preferred and implied messages, producing their own articulations of cultural difference, the following chapter considers the character of the museum experience itself and discusses its significance for framing audience responses. I begin by outlining broad shifts in approaches to the investigation of media–audience relations. This mapping serves to identify and develop a theoretical framework for addressing these issues and locates the study within the broader field of audience studies. Drawing on empirical data from the case studies, I then focus on the ways in which audiences engage with messages encoded by museums that seek to challenge prejudice. The chapter concludes by reviewing the appropriateness of prevalent theories of audience reception for this study. I shall posit a modified approach that attempts to provide a more nuanced and flexible understanding of the role of museums in enabling visitors to engage with, make sense of and negotiate difference, in ways which privilege concepts of equality, cross-cultural understanding and mutual respect.

Determinant texts and active audiences

Throughout the twentieth century there has been a sustained interest amongst academic researchers in the mass media and, in particular, in the potential they may (or, indeed, may not) hold to persuade and cajole, to manipulate and inform the public mind. Although media research has taken many forms, deploying different theoretical perspectives that have resulted in divergent approaches to investigation, most studies have in common 'some form of anxiety about some form of influence' (Corner et al. 1997: 2).

The use I make of sociological theories (that have been developed within media and audience studies) to explore the roles that museums might play in countering prejudice serves to highlight assumptions that have underlain many of these investigations into the 'influencability' (Ruddock 2001) of the media. Studies have often, either implicitly or explicitly, assumed that media institutions are attempting to wield iniquitous or otherwise undesirable influence – to achieve self-serving outcomes which conflict with the interests of their audiences and society at large.[1] This assumption is reflected in the use of language – media 'influence' is often characterised as 'manipulative' or 'pernicious' and audiences are cast as 'hapless and helpless' (ibid.: 141) or perhaps 'heroically resistant' to the intended manipulation. In these contexts, the articulation by consumers of meanings which undermine, resist or directly oppose those intended by media producers is often celebrated as evidence of the capacity for audiences to resist the powers of the (malevolent and self-serving) media. This celebration of audience agency and autonomy, however, sits rather less comfortably in the context of museums that are attempting to promote cross-cultural respect and understanding. The amelioration of prejudice and intolerance is a strategy which is likely to be welcomed by most constituencies and to be beneficial to many marginalised groups. And yet, at the same time, it is also necessary to remain critical of the motivations and intentions underlying such strategies. Derek McGhee's study of intolerance in Britain, for example, alerts us to the possibility that the construction of prejudice and hatred as social problems can potentially be used by governmental institutions to detract attention from wider socio-economic inequalities which can account for their emergence. What might, on the surface, appear progressive and desirable, he suggests, can nevertheless simultaneously be coercive and oppressive. I have argued earlier that, whilst some remain critical of museums with socially driven goals, characterising them as agents of social control and manipulation, engineering social change in ways which serve the interests of government,[2] such analyses no longer satisfactorily explain the wide-ranging projects and developing practices of museums internationally that are directed towards tackling prejudice and enhancing cross-cultural understanding. In some contexts, for example, museum interventions designed to confront and undermine prejudices have been both instigated and shaped by marginalised communities and sometimes in the face of unsympathetic government policies. Whilst these ideas are discussed elsewhere in the book I raise them again here since I wish to suggest that the assumptions that underlie many studies of media influence (with concomitant effects on the language used to describe them) are potentially challenged by the notion of a museum that attempts to wield 'influence' to generate positive social 'effects'.

Although many studies over the previous fifty years have shared common concerns over media influence, the field has experienced paradigmatic shifts in the ways in which media/text and audience/reader relations have been conceptualised. Many reviews of the field have generated classifications of traditions of audience research.[3] Though these conceptual mappings vary in the terms used and the specific ways in which different research phases are classified, there is nevertheless considerable consensus amongst them. Nicholas Abercrombie and Brian Longhurst's (1998) account is especially helpful. They identify three main phases of audience research that represent different ways of conceptualising and investigating forms of media influence – 'effects', 'uses and gratifications' and 'encoding/decoding'.

'The effects tradition'

Research in what has come to be known as 'the effects tradition' is characterised by the notion that audiences are prone to manipulation and influence by media consumption. This has been a pervading theme in research and, whilst it has increasingly been challenged within the field of audience studies, it has nevertheless endured in the public consciousness, in particular through debates about censorship and the effects on viewers of portrayals of television violence or sex (ibid.). Abercrombie and Longhurst outline the key characteristics of early work in the field:

> In the earliest versions of effects research the effects of the media on the bare individuals of mass society were held to be fairly direct and unmediated … the essential model here is of the media as a narcotic where messages are injected into the mass audience as if from a hypodermic syringe. The audience in turn responds to this stimulus in a fairly direct manner.
>
> (ibid.: 5)

Research within the effects tradition then has taken media agency for granted and casts audiences as uncritical, innocent dupes. This is not entirely surprising given that many of the research questions being addressed within this tradition have been formulated from the perspective of the media (rather than audience). Investigations have been undertaken for the benefit of media institutions; research effort has been directed towards identifying the media 'reach' – the size and composition of a given audience – which is then used as the basis for judging effects and measuring media success (McQuail 1997).

The characteristics of media research in the effects tradition can also be detected in research specifically into museum audiences. As Sharon Macdonald highlights, much of the research into museum audiences in the past has exhibited:

> [a] cognitive emphasis on 'what visitors have learned' or whether they have 'got' or 'not got' the 'messages' intended … Such an approach characterises the audience as relatively 'passive'. It is

based on a conveyor-belt model … in which information does or does not succeed in being effectively 'transmitted' to the public, and in which the emphasis is often on discovering barriers (which might include, say, educational ability or pre-existing 'false' ideas) that might impede this process.

(2002: 219)

Uses and gratifications research

In the second phase identified by Abercrombie and Longhurst, the emphasis has switched from the *influence* of the media to the *uses* which audiences make of it. Research within this phase 'reversed the question posed by effects studies – asking "what people do with the media" instead of "what the media do to people"' (Moores 1993: 6–7). This approach emphasises:

(1) the social and psychological origins of (2) *needs*, which generate (3) expectations of (4) the mass media or other sources, which lead to (5) differential patterns of media exposure (or engagement in other activities), resulting in (6) need *gratifications* and (7) other consequences, perhaps mostly unintended ones.

(Katz et al. 1974: 20)

Though elements of the uses and gratifications approach have endured and can be detected in more recent work (in particular, the conceptualisation of the audience as active) research in this tradition has been heavily criticised. Highlighting the common ground between the 'effects' and 'uses and gratifications' phases, Abercrombie and Longhurst categorise both approaches within a single paradigm (which they label 'behavioural') and usefully summarise the three key criticisms which research in this paradigm has attracted.

First, the audience tends to be characterized on an essentially individualistic or society-wide level and there is a relative neglect of concrete social groups and their interactions. Thus, individuals are affected by media or use them, or society is led in particular directions. Second, the audience is affected by, or uses and responds to, a stimulus and there is relative neglect of the analysis of texts and meanings, with the associated emphasis on the complexity of meaning and textual structure. Third, there is an emphasis on the functions of the media, in terms of propaganda and influence in campaigns for effects, or for the individual in terms of the satisfaction of needs for uses and gratifications.

(1998: 9)

Stuart Hall subsequently addressed these criticisms, based for the most part on the behaviourist characteristics of both approaches, in his development of the encoding and decoding model. This model not only represents the third main phase of audience research highlighted in Abercrombie and Longhurst's analysis but also marks a paradigmatic shift in the ways in which media–audience relations have been conceptualised and investigated. The encoding and decoding model sought to take account of '[l]arger historical shifts, questions of political process and formation before and beyond the ballot box, issues of social and political power, of social structure and economic relations' (Hall 1982: 59) which had been largely omitted from research in the two prior phases.

Encoding–decoding research: from 'effects' to 'appropriation'

Stuart Hall's analysis of media communication, in which he blurs the distinctions between processes of production and consumption, has contributed to a radical reconceptualisation of media–audience relations. Audience members – traditionally imagined as recipients of media 'effects' – have come to be understood as themselves participating in the production process, constructing (and contributing to the distribution of) messages as part of the communicative circuit (Hall 1990a). The encoding–decoding model provided a starting point for an entirely new body of research which focuses primarily on issues of reception. According to Hall, messages are encoded at the point of production but:

> before this message can have an 'effect' (however defined), satisfy a 'need' or be put to a 'use', it must first be appropriated as a meaningful discourse and be meaningfully decoded. It is this set of decoded meanings which 'have an effect', influence, entertain, instruct or persuade, with very complex perceptual, cognitive, emotional, ideological or behavioural consequences.
>
> (1990b: 509)

Following Hall's analysis, if we wish to investigate the 'effects' of museum communication encoded with the aim of combating prejudice, we must look at the ways in which those messages are received, decoded, appropriated by audiences. Audiences then emerge as active agents who, rather than obediently absorbing messages carefully produced for their consumption, are capable of constructing their own meanings, of not only decoding but 'recoding' (Macdonald 2002: 219) the message and reproducing meanings that may radically differ from those intended at the point of production.

In Abercrombie and Longhurst's typology of approaches to audience research, Hall's encoding–decoding model represented a significant departure

Table 4.1 Paradigms of audience research

	Behavioural Paradigm	*Incorporation/Resistance Paradigm*
Audience	Individuals (in social context)	Socially structured (e.g. by class, gender, race)
Medium	Stimulus (message)	Text
Social consequence(s)	Functions/dysfunctions, propaganda, influence, use, effects	Ideological incorporation and resistance
Approaches	• 'Effects' • Uses and gratifications	Encoding and decoding

Source: Taken from Abercrombie and Longhurst 1998: 37).

from earlier behaviourally-based studies. Indeed, they suggest it marked the start of what they term the Incorporation/Resistance Paradigm (IRP) which, in contrast to research in the Behavioural Paradigm, 'defines the *problem* of audience research as whether audience members are incorporated into the dominant ideology by their participation in media activity or whether, to the contrary, they are resistant to that incorporation'. They further stress that 'the paradigm is defined by the *debate* between these two positions and not necessarily by the *endorsement* of one of them' (1998: 15). The key elements of these two paradigms can be seen in Table 4.1.

Many of the most influential audience studies widely cited in the literature (for example, David Morley's (1980) study of viewers' responses to the *Nationwide* television programme and Janice Radway's (1984) research into romance readers) can be viewed as conducted within the IRP. These and many other empirical studies over the past twenty years have sought to understand and explain media/text–audience/reader relationships in the context of the distribution of power and have variously argued for the primacy of text or audience in the construction of meaning, depending on the context being researched. Broadly speaking, within the paradigm, there has been a shift away from mediation theories – which give primacy to the text and medium and their influence on passive audiences – to reception theories which view audiences as active, constructing their own individualised and socially mediated meanings from a range of media (Silverstone 1994).[4] Abercrombie and Longhurst discuss this shift in terms of a continuum of research.

> No theorist of the audience has completely endorsed either the Dominant Text or the Dominant Audience model … these positions represent the ends of a continuum and, over the past twenty or thirty years, media research has see-sawed between them, sometimes emphasizing the activity of the audience and sometimes the powers of the text.
>
> (1998: 29)

Although wide-ranging empirical studies looking at different kinds of media and diverse forms of audience have oscillated between these positions, there has, in broad terms, been a growing support for the Dominant Audience model.

Constructivist understandings of museum learning

This 'turn to the audience' is also evident in the literature specifically concerned with museum audiences. Current thinking within museum studies (and theoretical approaches to museum learning in particular) argues for a constructivist explanation of the ways in which meaning is made within museums. Constructivism sees a move away from the traditional transmission model of communication (whereby, in museum terms, information is transmitted from an exhibition to the visitor) to one in which the visitor (their agenda, prior knowledge, motivation and so on) plays a much more critical role in the construction of meaning. Constructivists suggest that the visitor should be enabled to bring their life experiences to bear in creating a meaningful encounter with the museum's displays. This approach, based on an understanding of audiences as active, can be understood to pose a challenge to the conception of museums as agencies capable of countering prejudice, by highlighting the potential naïvety of claims that particular ways of seeing, thinking and behaving can straightforwardly and successfully be transmitted to audiences (thereby effecting change in visitors).

Other features of constructivist approaches to museum learning pose additional challenges to museums that attempt to promote particular values and viewpoints. George Hein (1998), for example, argues for the adoption within museum settings of a constructivist approach to learning which eschews the notion that there is a single, 'correct' message to be taken away from an exhibition. Constructivist exhibitions avoid didactic approaches which offer narrow and fixed ways of approaching the topic in hand and which legitimate and sanction only a limited range of responses amongst the visitors. Instead, they provide a range of perspectives and viewpoints, facilitate open-ended learning outcomes and offer ways of validating the diverse conclusions that visitors reach, even when they do not correspond with those of the exhibition makers. This approach is clearly problematic in the context of museums that seek to counter prejudice where, although debate and other forms of engagement may be encouraged, lines will inevitably be drawn to distinguish between those responses which are validated (which fall somewhere on the 'tolerance–respect' spectrum) and those which are viewed as undesirable, invalid, even deviant (those which to a greater or lesser degree exhibit prejudice).

In what circumstances then might museums wish to substitute modes of interpretation which aim to stimulate and legitimate wide-ranging responses for those which enable them to enunciate a singular moral standpoint that unequivocally condemns prejudice? How might advocates of constructivist approaches to exhibition development distinguish between issues around which there is legitimate controversy (which visitors should be enabled to debate and relate to in diverse ways framed by their own life experiences) and the underlying (non-negotiable) social values which might be deployed to resolve those controversies? The issues highlighted here will resurface at various points throughout the discussions that follow and, in the concluding chapter, I shall attempt to draw together and address some of the difficult questions they raise.

Media–audience agency in the museum context

I now turn to the findings from audience research undertaken at the Anne Frank House and the St Mungo Museum of Religious Life and Art, and explore them in light of the theoretical developments outlined above. The discussion is built around data (from both visitor interviews and analyses of written responses produced by visitors and extracted from comments cards and books) which offer insights into the distribution of agency between text (museum/exhibition) and audience (museum visitor) in relation to issues of cultural difference. It seeks to offer an understanding of the interpretive processes generated out of the audience–exhibition encounter, taking account of both the capacity for audiences actively to construct their own meanings in socially-mediated ways and the textual power of museum exhibitions, the possible constraints or cues which might enable or privilege preferred (non-prejudiced) readings.

It is necessary at this point to highlight the fact that the audience responses discussed below were *spontaneous*, as far as this is possible within the context of any audience study. By this, I mean that they were stimulated primarily by the exhibition and by interaction with other visitors. Interview questions were kept open and exploratory and none explicitly asked visitors for their views on issues of difference, prejudice or equality (see appendix 1 for interview protocols). Significantly, these topics incidentally emerged in visitors' responses and with quite considerable frequency.

Variability in responses

Unsurprisingly, there was tremendous variability across visitors' spoken and written responses. In the early stages of analysing the interview and comments data, this variability was sometimes frustrating. It could seem as if the extremely diverse and wide-ranging backgrounds, perspectives and experiences of visitors were capable of producing an infinite range of reactions to the exhibitions, making it difficult to identify and unravel significance and meaning in individual comments. In response to the same interview question – for example, 'Do you feel the museum is trying to communicate any particular message?' – entirely different responses might be generated. Tom, a telecommunications engineer from Chesterfield in England, for example, was adamant that the message of the Anne Frank House was:

> Dislike of the Germans! That certainly comes through, I mean I don't know what German people feel as they go through the building but there's clear condemnation of their way of life at that time.

Alternatively, Harold, a retired teacher visiting from Newfoundland, suggested:

> It could have been a lot nastier, it could have been, you know, 'these bad, bad Germans' but you don't get that, I didn't get that here.

Similar variability and contradiction can be seen amongst the following comments cards from St Mungo's:

> Your museum is playing down Christianity and giving place to false cultures. The highest standard of living in the world are where Christianity thrives (best treatment for women).
>
> (5 May 2003)

> Very informative on the major religions of the world although the exhibits seem to favour Christianity.
>
> (30 May 2003)

Despite such variability in visitors' talk and text, further analysis revealed recurrent themes and modes of response within the data.

Confirmation, opposition, negotiation

How did audiences 'receive' and engage with the museum's various preferred messages of cross-cultural understanding, mutual respect and equal human rights? Many visitors' accounts contained responses which could readily be classified in ways that echoed those found in other studies of media audiences. These studies, heavily influenced by Hall's theory of encoding and decoding, have very often deployed a tripartite structure of audience positions or readings consisting of responses which are either *confirmatory* (those which accept and endorse the preferred message encoded at the point of production), *oppositional* (those that could be said to be antonymous to those intended by the producer) or *negotiated* (those containing contradictory elements). This structure proved helpful in under-standing and interpreting many visitors' responses although it is important to stress that the categories were neither discrete nor fixed. Some individual interview transcripts contained elements of all these readings, emphasising the fluid and situated character of prejudice practices. Moreover, within these broad groupings, I also found sub-themes, particular patterns of response, which are specific both to the museum context and to the content and nature of the inscribed messages the museums intended to convey.

Although this approach to analysing and interpreting the data from my case studies helped to shed some light on the efficacy of different interpretive strategies deployed by the museum in generating intended audience responses, it became clear that this text–reader model for investigating agency (located within Abercrombie and Longhurst's IRP) was limited in its capacity to explain the role of museums in combating prejudice, providing only a partial picture. In particular, the presence within the data of visitor responses which could not be neatly categorised as confirmatory, oppositional or negotiated, as we shall see, exposed the need for additional, complementary but distinct, ways to conceptualise and understand the museum's social agency.

Confirmatory responses

Confirmatory readings were the most commonly occurring type of visitor response and took many forms. I include here responses from visitors who identified a message and decoded it in the way intended by the museum (and directly and explicitly articulated their support for it) and those responses where the visit simply appeared to prompt individuals to talk about issues of cultural difference in ways which can be considered to suggest concurrence with the values espoused by the museum. Though these responses appear with considerable regularity in visitors' discourses, it nevertheless remains problematic to celebrate the powers of the text simply on the basis of these declarations of support for equality and tolerance and condemnations of discrimination. For example, it might be argued that visitors may already be predisposed to discuss difference in this way (without exposure to the museum) or visitors might simply be responding in ways they feel the interviewer wants to hear or which they feel are appropriate or acceptable to their co-visiting peers. It is, nevertheless, possible to see within the data a repertoire of visitor responses, recurring phrases and arguments which represent relatively distinct ways of seeing, thinking, talking about and negotiating difference.

Three particular interpretations, each drawing on and giving emphasis to a different concept – *equality*, *universality* and *tolerance* – emerged especially strongly from the data. Though these interpretations contain different emphases they cannot be understood as neat or discrete forms of response. Rather they often co-exist and overlap – an individual visitor may potentially employ one or all of the interpretations in a single conversation. The considerable frequency with which they appear in visitors' accounts, I would argue, suggests the presence within exhibitions of constraints, parameters or cues which can contribute to the framing of individual interpretations. The interpretations often appear to draw on (either directly or indirectly) or be shaped by the resources of the exhibition, lending support to the notion of textual agency.

Though overlapping, the emphasis within each of these categories of response is relatively distinct. The recurring terms and metaphors in *interpretations of equality* draw on the discourse of rights (sometimes explicitly but more often through inference) to evoke a sense of equity, legitimacy and equivalence in status between social groups. *Interpretations of universality* privilege humanistic responses and emphasise the common ground and mutuality of experience that exists between culturally different groups. Lastly, *interpretations of tolerance*, perhaps most interestingly, contain the highest degree of contradiction. They are often deployed by visitors to argue for the need for mutual understanding between different constituencies but can sometimes reflect a somewhat grudging acceptance of an otherwise unwelcome minority.

Interpretations of equality

Interpretations of equality are examples of visitor responses that perhaps most powerfully reflect the outcomes intended by the museums. Here, visitors not only acknowledge sameness between culturally different groups but discuss those groups in ways which suggest equitable (rather than hierarchical) social relations. Roy, a retired foundry worker who lived outside Glasgow, said:

> What I get out of it is that there's a diversity of religions and cultures and they're all alright. I don't find anything particularly disagreeable about it, I just think it's all very interesting. Now, I believe that who are we to say that because we're Christian that we're right? It could be Mohammed or anything as long as you believe in a higher person then I think that's fine.

Eric, a dentist visiting from the United States, commented:

> There's a very strong statement, especially in the evangelical church in the US ... that there is one way to God, that the Christian faith is the one way. In fact, for me, I think, there *is* one way but that's just one way in the whole scheme of things and I think the slant of the museum is that the one way for me is a tiny portion of the whole mosaic where there are so many other ways where people reach enlightenment and I think the message I get is that my way is no more valid than anyone else's for them.

'I didn't imagine this museum would be as interesting as it is really. I thought a museum of religion was a kind of a turn-off really,' explained Sally, a retired teacher from Birmingham, England, visiting with her husband. 'I thought it was going to be boring but ... I think it's brilliant the way they've done it so inclusively. It's terrific to see the Pope next to an image from Ghana and all seen with the same importance.'

Sometimes, visitors draw more explicitly on a human rights discourse to articulate their understanding of the museum. For example, one visitor wrote the following in the comments book at the Anne Frank House:

> This museum is truly a testimony against discrimination, against persecution based on race, gender, religion, creed, sexual orientation or any other constructed difference. It stands for human rights and dignity.

Within the audience data it is also possible to identify comments that constitute what might be understood as minority perspectives on the exhibitions and the museums' overall messages of equal rights. For example, one visitor to the Anne Frank House wrote in the comments book, 'I can't tell you how much I appreciate the House's spotlight on the gay issue! How about the Iraq war and Bush's madness next?' Clodagh, an administrator from Glasgow in her early thirties who described herself as a Pagan, similarly welcomed inclusion in St Mungo's temporary exhibition of diverse faith practices within Glasgow. When asked why this was important to her she responded:

> Well, our religion has always been represented as something really scary and associated with strange practices so the opportunity to be represented in a room with other mainstream faiths on an equal footing is significant. We're represented as a proper faith not as a cult.

A nurse who had recently moved from India to live in Glasgow was especially pleased to find diverse religions validated through their inclusion in the museum:

> I saw my home country's religions, all various types of religions – Hindu, Sikhism, Buddhism, Islam – all that. I see that my country is appreciated here. My country's values, the lifestyles is appreciated here and I was proud of that – I feel good. Even my own state language is in here.

These examples recall responses found in other studies. Corinne Kratz, for example, describes the reaction of one Kenyan visitor to her exhibition of

Okiek. 'It was a matter of pleasure and pride to find scenes and people from an area he knew presented respectfully in the Nairobi Museum, a national institution' (2002: 138). This response begins to hint at the power and authority which museums hold to provide legitimacy and to confer respect and equality to those groups who seek and secure representation within them. I shall revisit this theme in the next chapter and discuss, at some length, the implications it holds for understanding the social agency of museums.

Interpretations of universality

Interpretations of universality appeared most commonly in the conversations and comments cards of visitors to St Mungo's. Here, many spontaneously highlighted commonalities and shared experiences between the different cultures and religious groups depicted. Eunice, who works in catering in Bradford, expressed her support for the museum's position:

> If the schools came to these kinds of places it might help. Just show people that we're basically the same, that there's so much intermingled. We believe the same things, the Jews believe a lot of what the Christians believe and a lot of the Muslim stuff is the same. People just don't realise it's so close together.

Valerie, a retired nurse from Hertfordshire visiting with her daughter Carol, a self-employed bookkeeper, commented:

> I think it's a good cover of all aspects, spiritualism and all sorts of things. Some of the religions that are outside the mainstream so that was quite good, that it encompassed all that and the pagan rites as well. God – it doesn't matter what you call him – we all come under the same umbrella.

In assimilating cultural difference to their own experience, it sometimes seemed to me as if visitors found reassurance in articulating and reconfirming this sameness. For example, quite commonly visitors were prompted by their visit to reflect on issues of conflict related to cultural difference beyond the museum, either in their personal lives (for example, in relation to their neighbours, personal memories and anecdotes from friends and families, 'race riots' experienced in their home town and so on) or on a global scale (the current war in Iraq and the events of September 11, 2001 were most often invoked). These reflections on conflict were sometimes accompanied by the interpretations of universality I have described – where visitors drew upon the museum's messages to restore in their minds a more optimistic image of intercultural relations at the global and local scales.

Messages of universality were not, for the most part, drawn from single elements of the exhibition but rather appeared to be embodied in multiple, interconnecting aspects of displays. At St Mungo's, the juxtaposition of objects representing different faiths within unifying, thematic narratives appeared to be most influential in informing or framing these interpretations. Jeff, a civil servant from Glasgow, commented, 'there seems to be a bit of everything in the way that the Christianity is mingled with the Islam and the Buddhism'. Sometimes, however, visitors drew very directly on the exhibition format and content to make these assimilating connections. When Anna, a student on vacation from Finland, was asked 'What do you think is the overall purpose of this museum?' her reply reflected both the layout of the *Gallery of Religious Life* and the text it contained:

> All I can say is that I think it was basically a good idea to mix together many different religions because there are basically the same elements in there … all the big things – birth, death and that – they concern all people and in every religion there is some kind of explanation or stuff like that for these events.

Deploying these interpretations of universality sometimes required visitors to position themselves directly in relation to the subjects of display. As Corinne Kratz states:

> People produce senses of identity in relation to objects and subjects on display, in relation to experience they bring to the exhibition, as well as in relation to particular politics of representation. Recognizing similarities and contrasts with other people and situations is an essential and ongoing aspect of such subject formation. Situating ourselves entails imagining other lives and places even as it brings particular aspects of our own lives and identities into focus.
>
> (2002: 94)

So for example, Maria, a school secretary in her early forties visiting St Mungo's with her husband Jim, stated:

> Well, you've got your own views before you come. The way you look at other faiths you tend to compare it with your own and think 'is that right or is it wrong?' I mean we believe in the Bible as the word of God and that's the thing we work to so it affects the way we look at other religions. Yeah, but it's funny how certain things in books like the Qu'ran and that sound very, very similar to verses in the Bible and stuff. Yeah, and I mean we've got relatives in South Africa and we once went into this particular house and it was just so *similar*. It was depicted in different ways and different pictures

and it all happened in Africa but it was very, very similar and that was what they believed.

Analysing visitors' conversations at both sites (though this was especially marked at St Mungo's) highlighted a variety of ways in which visitors positioned themselves in relation to those perceived to be culturally different. This variety was similar to the responses which Kratz found in her analysis of audience responses to her exhibition of Okiek portraits:

> At times exhibition visitors emphasize commonalities, assimilating what is depicted to their own experience; at others, they accentuate differences, exoticising the people or places featured. Most commonly, visitors relate to an exhibition in ways that combine both assimilating and exoticizing interpretations, as circumstances and identities they bring to an exhibition engage with the material shown.
>
> (2002: 94)

So, Lynne, a school teacher, found common ground between her own experiences and those of followers of different faiths portrayed in St Mungo's:

> I love angels and I find it interesting here to be reminded that, although my own religion is Christianity, a lot of other religions recognise the history of angels as well, that it's not just a thing you're aware of because you're a Christian.

Maria's later comments revealed an interesting interplay between assimilating and exoticising elements, acknowledging certain shared experiences with people from religious backgrounds different from her own but drawing on the museum's reference to female genital mutilation simultaneously to maintain a degree of distance.

> I think the basics on some religions are very similar. You know, bowing down to one god … but I think it's the, you know, the physical rituals and stuff of some that I don't like. The mutilation and stuff like that. I don't think God'd like us to do that to ourselves or he would have made us like that in the first place.

The frequency with which interpretations of universality were deployed by visitors (in particular at St Mungo's) might suggest that the use of universalising, thematic narratives is one interpretive strategy which museums might purposively pursue in order to explore cross-cultural differences in ways which enable and support non-prejudiced text and talk. Indeed, such approaches have become increasingly common in museum exhibitions

(Kratz 2002). The challenge for exhibition-makers, however, lies in enabling these assimilating responses while simultaneously avoiding romantic, reductionist notions of cultural commonality which can serve to disguise important cultural differences and to elide inequalities in power between different dominant and marginalised groups. As Kratz points out:

> The humanism that enables and underlies ... connections [between viewer and subject] can lead towards serious engagement with the social, cultural and political economic differences that also charac-terize all human life. But it can also suggest a false or sentimental universalism that effaces significant differences in meaning, history and life circumstances.
>
> (2002: 10–13)

Displays which attempt to offer a utopian vision of intercultural relations – which emphasise (at an abstract level) the importance and value of respect for diverse religious or cultural groups – can also be criticised for over-looking (or purposefully side-stepping consideration of) those situations in which religious or other beliefs should *not* be respected or tolerated because they infringe on the basic human rights of others (for example, by permit-ting the abuse of women or the subjugation of sexual minorities). Museums are generally very wary of tackling contested topics such as these, a point I shall return to in the concluding chapter.

Interestingly, some visitors also notice and comment on the emphasis on sameness (as opposed to difference) within displays at St Mungo's, echoing one of the standard critiques of multiculturalism. One visitor to the museum wrote in the comments book on 17 February 2003:

> Interesting but not as informative as I had hoped. Can't help feeling there is a tendency to make all religions alike. Only by looking at differences can we appreciate other religions and our own (for those few of us who actually have one).

The inclusion within displays at St Mungo's of examples of discord, hostility and violence arising from religious differences is one strategy purposefully deployed by the museum to render visible the realities of inter-community conflict and to prick nostalgic or romantic notions of universal harmony and equity. Interestingly, however, many visitors appear to prefer the sanguine optimism of the evocations of a shared humanity. Many complaints about the content of displays at St Mungo's are linked to the inclusion of specific issues (for example, the Northern Ireland conflict, sectarianism in Scotland and so on) which appear to disrupt this more palatable, preferable reading.

It is also worth remembering that some marginalised communities themselves (or specific constituencies within them) may wish to resist incorporation within universalizing interpretative strategies. Some may value being included within culturally pluralist displays, believing them to infer equal status and rights for the minority group to which they belong. (Clodagh's appreciation of Paganism being presented on an equal footing with majority or mainstream religions might be seen as an example of such a viewpoint.) In different instances, however, others may argue that such 'gains' are offset by the potentially totalising and essentialising effects of displays which emphasise sameness between groups and which may, in doing so, deny difference and demand an unacceptable level of assimilation into the mainstream.

Interpretations of tolerance

The third category of interpretation that visitors deployed in a mostly confirmatory manner (expressing support for the museums' perceived intentions) positions difference as something that is deemed reasonable and permitted, but within a framework of cultural relativism which appears to retain some hint of disapproval. These interpretations of tolerance emphasise the importance (at an abstract level) of accepting or 'putting up with' difference but, in practice, this may fall short of supporting culturally different practices as equally valid or as legitimate as one's own. In the following interview extract, Jennifer, a social worker visiting Scotland from Australia, is prompted by her visit to St Mungo's to ponder differences between her beliefs and practices and those of her friends:

> The museum reinforces some of the things that you don't think about every day because you're not living them. It reinforces that all of that diversity is still happening in the world, that people believe their own things but still co-exist. Even though everyone now, with multiculturalism, is drifting towards this common plane where we all mix and go out and do all sorts of things together, there are strong forces that pull you all back into your respective religious backgrounds and, you know, we've been staying with a group of good friends who are of Indian origin and you can see how strong that influence is, even though you might think that they would never necessarily have an arranged marriage. I mean you just wouldn't think that they would do that but it's a very strong pull family-wise and obviously religiously, and they may fall back into that category and might have an arranged marriage which I find ... I mean I fully support it. I think it's great that we live in a world where people can continue to do that, although I don't necessarily like it myself, but I think it's great people can do that.

Similarly, James from Glasgow, a bus driver in his late thirties and visiting St Mungo's with his father, commented:

> I've been in here quite a few times. The interesting thing about it is, it's good to look at other religions. Obviously, I don't hold to what they say and what they believe but it's good to get a bit of information about other religions because you meet people of different religions and you can talk to them roughly about what they believe ... It's a good way to get a 'level par'.

Rita, a retired secretary who lived outside Glasgow, reflected on the message of St Mungo's deploying a similar interpretation of tolerance:

> I think it's trying to say that we should tolerate all different religions, even if we don't agree with them, and let people believe in what they like and freedom to worship, that sort of thing. It wants to make all the foreign people that come to live in Glasgow feel welcome and comfortable here.

Negotiated readings

In line with other studies of audience reception in wide-ranging media contexts, it was also possible to identify within visitors' responses readings which can be considered 'negotiated'. Negotiated readings are those where the audience, in broad terms, accepts the message as it was intended but may find reason to question its universal applicability. As Stuart Hall states:

> Decoding within the *negotiated version* contains a mixture of adaptive and oppositional elements: it acknowledges the legitimacy of the hegemonic definitions to make the grand significations (abstract), while, at a more restricted, situational (situated) level, it makes its own ground rules – it operates with exceptions to the rule. It accords the privileged position to the dominant definitions of events while reserving the right to make a more negotiated application to 'local conditions' ...
>
> (1990b: 516)

Perhaps not surprisingly, these negotiated readings occur with relative frequency in museums that seek to construct and communicate particular (non-prejudiced) ways of seeing. Since the process of reception can be understood as the outcome of a dialogic interplay between what museums and visitors bring to the exhibition encounter (framed by the social and political context within which the encounter takes place), the capacity for complexity, variability and contradiction in the production of meanings is considerable. Interestingly, whilst Hall and other media theorists have often viewed the practice of 'negotiation' in a predominantly positive light – as evidence of the capacity for audiences to resist or challenge attempts at (coercive, manipulative, oppressive) media influence – the negotiated readings I discuss here can be seen to take a rather negative turn. Within the context of museums that aim to tackle prejudice, these negotiated readings might more appropriately be considered unwelcome since they contain prejudiced and illiberal arguments which run counter to the purposes and intentions of the museums.

Though contradictory elements were found in many visitor responses, the construction of negotiated readings is most clearly illustrated in the following examples from St Mungo's. Here, the visitors identify and declare support for the museum's message (of mutual respect and understanding) at an abstract level but refuse to apply this universally. In both examples here, the visitors seek to exclude Islam in particular, from their acceptance of the validity of the world's main religions as represented in the museum (Fig. 4.1). One comments card pinned to the exhibition wall just two months after the events of September 11, 2001 stated:

> Very good. However, I think that in light of recent events the section
> on Islam should be removed. Never to be returned.

A couple in their late seventies concurred that the museum's message was one of ecumenism and discussed their (joint) support of it with considerable enthusiasm before a disagreement arose. It is useful in this instance to quote from the interview at some length to give a flavour of how the discussion evolved. Partway through the interview I asked Eleanor, a retired anthropologist, and her husband Cameron, a retired vet, 'What parts of the museum did you like most or find most interesting?'

> ELEANOR: Well I think that, for me, the representation of all the different religions was very valuable and, I thought, well portrayed. We both agreed as we walked down the stairs it was a marvellous museum, fabulous.
> QUESTION: *Were there any parts of the museum you didn't like, or found least interesting?*
> CAMERON: I just felt we could stay here for days. There's so much to appreciate and learn – particularly at this time with world events, you know, and the Muslims and so on. And upstairs is just preaching moderation and preaching ecumenism.
> QUESTION: *Do you feel the museum is trying to communicate any particular message?*

Figure 4.1: 'The Attributes of Divine Perfection' inspired by a Prophetic Hadith, by Dr Ahmed Moustafa, 1987, St Mungo Museum of Religious Life and Art

Source: By kind permission of the artist

CAMERON: I've said it already – ecumenism. Yes absolutely, the appreciation of all the different faiths by each other, you know. We were talking about the Rangers and Celtic football teams and the great division there between the Protestants and Catholics which has persisted for centuries and it's a good job we don't all have teams that follow one particular religion or the other. I didn't realise until about a year ago that in England, Liverpool and Everton are the same way. I had no idea that ...

ELEANOR (*interjecting*): Yes I would agree with you. It seemed to be portraying the fact that, you know, every religion has its own worth.

QUESTION: *Were there any aspects of this message that you especially agreed or disagreed with?*

CAMERON: The message of ecumenism you mean?

ELEANOR: That more people should come and be influenced by it!

CAMERON: Well, particularly the Muslims. Yeah, they're a really dreadful crowd.

ELEANOR: You're being taped aren't you?

CAMERON: I'm very happy to go on about that and keep saying they're dreadful because they, you know, they have a religion of hatred ...

ELEANOR (*interjecting*): But it isn't ...

CAMERON (*interjecting*): No ... I am saying what *I* think not what *you* think. I mean it is a religion of hatred because they have these guys preaching 'kill these ... kill the Americans ... kill the Jews' you know ... and we get none of these religious leaders standing up and denouncing their fellow men who are making those remarks about killing Americans and so on ... and we have this terrible fear of them all the time. I really think all Muslims should be made to swear on their Qu'ran that they will not get involved in British terrorist acts or else they should be sent out of the country.

ELEANOR: But they're British too!

CAMERON: Many of them have said that they are British but they won't fight for Britain and ...

ELEANOR (*interjecting*): That's one point we don't agree together.

QUESTION: *Do you feel museums like this one are important?*

CAMERON: I would certainly say so and increasingly important in the light of what we've just been talking about.

It might be argued that these comments reflect the rise of anti-Muslim prejudice which has been widely discussed in the news media following the events of September 11, 2001. Anti-Muslim prejudice (or Islamophobia as it has also been termed) involves the deployment of reductive and essentialised notions of what it means to be Muslim. These stereotypical representations of Muslims are drawn from the beliefs and behaviours of a minority (generally understood to be extremists) to produce a totalising picture of all Muslims, concealing internal diversity and emphasising Islam as necessarily violent, threatening and supportive of terrorism (Runnymede Trust 1997). Although the nature and extent of Islamophobia in Britain has been fiercely debated[5] it has nonetheless been argued that media reporting of events and the representation of Muslims in the media have often been imbalanced and unfair.[6] The Runnymede Trust's report *Islamophobia: A Challenge for*

Us All, contends that an imbalance in the presentation of Muslims in the media has contributed to the exacerbation of anti-Muslim prejudice. Their report states that whilst 'freedom of expression is an essential component of democracy ... There need however to be certain rules of engagement such that media coverage overall is less distorted and negative'.

These negotiated readings begin to suggest the wide range of influences on visitors' processes of reception and interpretation. Although it is problematic directly to attribute Cameron's comments to news media influence it is nevertheless worth noting that the interview took place at a time when mainstream media contained especially negative representations of Muslims. This draws attention to the possibility for messages from different sources within the mediascape to collide and interact with each other in the interpretive processes of individual actors. This understanding of media messages as potentially competing and/or complementary will be discussed in more detail in the next chapter.

Oppositional and resistive readings

Many studies of audience reception of media have highlighted the possibility for oppositional readings, sometimes highlighting and celebrating the active character of much media consumption as evidence of reader resistance or heroic obstinacy in the face of a manipulative media, intent on pernicious, self-serving outcomes. However, as with the negotiated readings described above, these oppositional responses might be seen in a rather different light when considered in the context of museums that seek to confront prejudice. Inevitably, it seems rather more problematic to celebrate responses that challenge the museum's preferred reading when those responses might be racist, misogynist, homophobic or otherwise discriminatory and oppressive.

The active audience presents a challenge (as well as interesting opportunities) to those museums aiming to disseminate particular social messages, to make non-prejudiced ways of seeing and thinking more permissible. Wide-ranging research has highlighted the potential for 'misunderstandings' (Hall 1990b) or for occurrence of the 'boomerang effect' (Brooker and Jermyn 2003) where intended meanings are not simply resisted but are turned around by audiences in ways which result in the construction of entirely oppositional meanings. As Sharon Macdonald found in her research at the Science Museum, London: 'Of interest here was not only that visitors made connections between exhibits that were neither spatially nor conceptually linked according to the Team's own plans, but that they specifically interpreted the exhibition contrary to a "message" that the Team had hoped to convey' (2002: 227).

Oppositional readings in my study ranged from the subtle and covert to the unambivalent and direct. Some responses that might be considered oppositional suggest 'misunderstandings' whereby visitors are not directly and openly challenging the museum's message (as they perceive it) but rather do not *decode* the message in the way that it was intended. This form of 'misunderstanding' is well illustrated in the following comments card from St Mungo's, written and displayed within the museum on 1 February 2003:

> I came to St Mungo's especially to show my husband Salvador Dali's painting 'Christ of St John on the Cross' – truly magnificent – which I saw for the first time 5 years ago. I was dismayed then as now that it is displayed in a room surrounded by objects from other religions. To me it deserves to be in a room of its own in order that one can meditate on it and have quiet undisturbed reflection on it and the meaning behind it without any other visual distractions. Also I feel that the exhibition about 'Religious Life' is very confusing especially for children, as all the artefacts from the different religions are in a 'jumble' together and it's difficult to follow what the teachings are, especially the Christian religion which I believe is still officially taught in Scottish schools albeit these days along with other religions in some way.

For Stuart Hall, these 'distortions' or 'misunderstandings' arise out of a 'lack of equivalence between the two sides of the communicative exchange' (1990: 510). In his discussion of television, he argues that:

> more often broadcasters are concerned that the audience has failed to take the meaning as they – the broadcasters – intended. What they really mean to say is that viewers are not operating within the 'dominant' or 'preferred' code. Their ideal is 'perfectly transparent communication'. Instead what they have to confront is 'systematically distorted communication'.
>
> (ibid.: 514)

Interestingly, it is possible to detect the appropriation of interpretations of tolerance (discussed earlier in the context of confirmatory readings) to construct what can be understood as illiberal or prejudiced (oppositional) arguments. In these next examples, visitors to St Mungo's express their support for tolerance but criticise other religions for their perceived inability or unwillingness to reciprocate. Maria – a secretary from Leeds, England, whose comments have previously been cited to illustrate confirmatory responses – also stated:

> And I think what you find today is, Christian things are the last things to be taken note of. I mean everybody else is more important. There's a lot of Christian people out there but in this country we've

got to be so tolerant of everybody else and we're supposed to push ours in the background.

Winifred, an elderly woman who had lived in Glasgow all her life, enjoyed visiting the museum with her friend Irene but her comments, nevertheless, exhibit some discontent. When asked what she would take away from her visit, she replied:

> I think it makes you realise that you've got to think about all the different religions, all the various beliefs and how you can make it all work, particularly in a city like this. And I think that, if I may be honest, we feel some of them tend to put their religion first whereas if we were going to India we could not put ours first, we would have to go by their way. I know it's a bit mixed up but I'm sure you know what I'm trying to get at. There's a lack of tolerance in some of them.

These responses hint at a degree of dissatisfaction, among some respondents, with the demands of accommodating what are perceived as 'new' faiths into mainstream (Christian) society.

Many of the most fervently expressed rejective comments appeared in written form – in the comments books at the Anne Frank House and on the comments cards exhibited at St Mungo's. Although it is difficult to draw definitive conclusions from this, it is possible that visitors felt more comfortable making these comments anonymously (in written form) than making them within the interview context. In the following examples, visitors not only decode the message *as intended* but directly challenge it, producing interpretations which clearly exhibit prejudice and intolerance. One visitor took exception to the *Out of Line* exhibition's support for lesbian and gay rights to equality, leaving the following message in the comments book on 29 April 2003:

> What a shame that you would manipulate the tragedy that was this girl's life into a defense [sic] of deviant sexual behaviour.

Similarly, the following set of comments directly challenge the St Mungo Museum's message concerning the equal validity and importance of different religions:

> I think the museum is preaching rubbish. I don't believe that all religions save. I only believe in God and Jesus Christ.
>
> (24 August 2001)

I strongly object to the deconstructionist and post modernist interpretation on the world's religions. This museum contributes to
the dismantling of Judeo-Christian civilisation. I recommend the
museum's closure. In addition the Dali is poorly hung and in any
case does not fit in with this exhibition.

(27 August 2001)

In these instances, it can be argued that, although visitors identify the
preferred meaning encoded within the museum's message, since it is so
antithetical to their existing worldview (in the examples above, on homosexuality and religious pluralism – issues about which the visitors clearly
hold strong opinions), they wholeheartedly reject it and take the opportunity to offer their own, opposing perspectives and to address these to both
the museum and to other visitors.

Situated boundaries of tolerance and prejudice

Many of these negotiated and oppositional readings illustrate the relational
and situated character of prejudice, discussed in chapter 2. Many visitors
expressed generalised support for concepts of tolerance, mutual respect
and understanding and were critical of practices which contravened human
rights or which were perceived as discriminatory. In this way, they aligned
themselves with the museum's perceived messages and position. However,
these responses often contained contradictions and inconsistencies which
brought into focus the fluid boundaries of prejudice and tolerance which
can shift in response to different geographical and temporal contexts. At St
Mungo's, for example, the museum's message of mutual understanding and
tolerance was most commonly disputed in relation to Islam. Whilst visitors
were often content to see a range of religions legitimised and portrayed as
equally significant, some questioned the museum's decision to include Islam
amongst them. At the Anne Frank House the museum's perceived support
for universal equal human rights was most frequently challenged in relation to lesbians and gay men. Sometimes these challenges were explicit and
forthright, as in the examples cited earlier. At other times, the challenge was
still present but couched in rather less direct or explicit terms.

The uneven nature of visitors' discourse on cultural difference raises
interesting questions about the role of museums in combating prejudice. To
what extent might museums be capable of remapping prejudice practices,
of extending, blurring, even redefining the boundaries that delimit socially
unacceptable from socially sanctioned forms of prejudice? Might museums
expand visitors' capacity for making non-prejudiced interpretations to
include forms of difference with which they have generally been uncomfortable? How might museums reconcile the tensions between universalist
claims embedded in human rights discourse with more localised, restricted

and popular conceptions of equality? I return to these vexing questions in the concluding chapter.

Rethinking media–audience agency

The broad categories of audience response – confirmatory, oppositional, and negotiated – which I have borrowed from a number of earlier audience studies (that build on Stuart Hall's classic model of the communicative exchange process) have helpfully highlighted the extent to which audience readings can both subscribe to, and deviate from, the intended or preferred meaning of the museum. Moreover, they have enabled me to identify frequently occurring interpretations which appear to draw directly on exhibitions, enabling visitors to negotiate and relate to difference in ways which reflect the museums' goals of tackling prejudice. However, the use of this 'text–reader' approach to investigate media agency has also highlighted significant limitations in its ability adequately to explain the processes actuated by the visitor–exhibition encounter.

This approach suggests, rather simplistically, that a museum's 'success' is measured by the extent to which visitor responses can be understood to reflect acceptance of the museum's (anti/non-prejudiced) values encoded within the preferred messages of the exhibitions. In these simplified terms, the potential for rejective (prejudiced and illiberal) meanings, evidenced in visitor responses to St Mungo's and the Anne Frank House, highlights the considerable capacity for 'failure' (understood as an inability to coerce visitors or to 'convert' them to the museum's position). Three main weaknesses or tensions are evident in this approach.

Firstly, although the data suggests the presence within exhibitions of textual cues which appear to equip visitors with non-prejudiced ways of negotiating difference, within and across visitors' accounts there is, nevertheless, tremendous variability and unpredictability in response. Secondly, the encoding and decoding model and much of the research within audience studies over the past two decades has taken place within what Abercrombie and Longhurst call the IRP – the Incorporation/Resistance paradigm – that is built on hegemonic theories of power which are increasingly being challenged. Although the IRP's central focus on power clearly has relevance to an investigation of prejudice, the notion that the relationship between media and audience is understood (in broadly binary terms) as a *struggle* for primacy remains problematic. Moreover, there is growing theoretical and empirical support for an understanding of power as fragmented and diffused. According to Abercrombie and Longhurst, this shifting nature of power reveals tensions within audience studies. They argue that 'If power is indeed diffused, and is not exercised in a unitary way on behalf of a dominant power bloc, then it makes *less* sense to see the culture of a society as driven by the twin forces of domination and resistance. Encounters with the media then become just that – relatively more isolated events not conducted within a unitary framework of domination' (1998: 36).

Dynamic and dialogic interpretations of difference

The presence within audience responses which, during analysis, I had identified as especially significant and interesting, but which could not be neatly categorised as either confirmatory, oppositional or negotiated, exposed the third and arguably most significant tension in this theoretical approach. The act of categorising responses in this way has the effect of both fixing them in time and suggesting a degree of internal consistency and stability which conceals the complexity and dynamism which many visitor accounts contained. For example, one visitor, Harold, a retired teacher from Newfoundland, was prompted by the *Out of Line* exhibition to reflect on homosexuality in a way which demonstrates engagement with the museum's message and – most importantly – suggests a shift in position and perspective:

> Well, if you just think about the homosexual situation. Some people say it's a disease or it's something you learn OK? Well, I don't believe that, so consequently I don't have any problem about seeing a couple of fellas or a couple of girls walking towards me on the street, hand in hand. But anything can become blatant right? So that sometimes, homosexuals might behave in a blatant way, but then again, I say 'hold on, I just saw a heterosexual couple kissing on the street as well and that didn't bother me right?' It's just, because of the way, you know, in a heterosexual society we're growing up, it's hard to be accepting obviously when you think it through, but then if the homosexual group have a real bunch of renegades who are really causing a lot of trouble then, of course, it's damaging your own cause right?

Harold appears to draw directly on ideas presented in the exhibition (the likening of homosexuality to a disease is a reference to the comments of a religious leader, included in the audio-visual presentation, whose opinions have angered gay and lesbian groups in the Netherlands) to position himself as, at least in relative terms, liberal and accepting. He then debates the relative acceptability of heterosexual and homosexual behaviours and appears to acknowledge and *adjust* his own position in a way which suggests a degree of acceptance of the museum's implied message. His response is neither entirely accepting of, nor resistant to, the message of equal rights for gays and lesbians. Whilst it might be argued that this could be seen as a 'negotiated' reading (he broadly accepts the overarching message of equal rights regardless of sexual orientation but at a situated, personal level is uncomfortable with witnessing behaviours which he feels are too provocative and inappropriate), this classification would fail to capture the change (albeit subtle) in position on homosexuality and the dynamic interactions between the exhibition's message and the visitor's values and prior experiences.

Another example of this *interplay* between the perceived message of the museum and visitors' prior experiences can be seen in these comments from Winifred (the elderly resident of Glasgow whose responses earlier illustrated the deployment of interpretations of tolerance), interviewed after visiting St Mungo's. Partway through the interview I asked Winifred, 'Do you feel the museum is trying to communicate any particular message?'

> Yes, I think it's trying to say that we should all be tolerant of each other but, in this climate, it must be very difficult, you know what's going on abroad … and what the Arabs say about 'kill this and kill that'. I mean, what's that got to do with their religion? That's based on a very peaceful religion.

Winifred's response suggests to me, a process of negotiation between the ideas and arguments she encountered in St Mungo's and those, drawn from many different sources, with which she came to the museum. Islam and Muslims, as John Richardson observes, are 'made known' to us through their representation in a number of different settings (2004: 33). In recent years, as I stated earlier, a number of countries in the West have witnessed a rapid rise in anti-Muslim prejudice which has been attributed, at least in part, to negative and distorted news coverage (ibid.; Runnymede Trust 1997). Anti-Muslim prejudice constructs Muslims as a homogeneous and monolithic group, as static and intransigent, as both separate from and inferior to the West. It further draws on and reinforces negative stereotypes which operate to emphasise and naturalise associations between Islam and violence, aggression and terrorism. For Winifred, 'what the Arabs say about "kill this and kill that"' – comments which reflect Islamophobic conceptions of Muslims – appears to be at odds with the representation of Islam and the portrayal of Muslims which she finds in the museum's displays. Winifred's engagement with the museum, I suggest, has called into question the negative associations and totalising stereotypes which she has encountered in other aspects of her everyday life, for example in the news or in everyday conversations with friends and family.

Other visitors were conscious of the way in which exhibitions had served to challenge, perhaps prompted them to change, their pre-existing ideas and attitudes. Adrian, a student in his early twenties visiting the Anne Frank House from England, commented:

> I found that screen in there really interesting. It made you think about what your views on freedom of speech are and I found myself in some situations going towards 'freedom of speech' and [in others] going towards 'protection of anti-discrimination'. I think it really changes the way you think and it's good.

And his friend Andrew, also a student, added:

> You see one side of the argument and you're thinking, 'good argument, good argument', then you get the other side and think 'hold on – that's a good argument too'. And it really forces you to actually think about where you actually place yourself.

Similarly alluding to a transformative experience, one visitor to St Mungo's wrote the following on a comments card dated 15 August 2001:

> So often we miss the things which stand before us. This museum, for example, I did not even know existed. Furthermore, as someone who is anti-religion I never suspected to find myself here. However, after today visiting the museum, I feel compelled to re-evaluate my ideas and philosophies. Your displays have opened my mind.

Asked if he felt the Anne Frank House was trying to communicate any particular message, Michael, a community organiser visiting from the United States, commented:

> OK, you know you're looking at a historical situation and the story of a young woman's capacity to be able to record what happened and live through it but, at the same time, I think it's connecting with what's going on around us today. I think that's the value, it's not just a tourist attraction you can go round and just enjoy it because it's not that kind of situation. So I think it's quite provocative in terms of what it's trying to do and I think that's where it steps beyond the period in which the Anne Frank story is set. Initially when I came here I was thinking, this is a set piece set in a particular context, but I came out looking differently at the world around me a bit.

These comments, I would argue, help to highlight and evidence the dynamic and dialogic character of the interpretive process that can occur in the museum setting, revealing the interplay between 'what visitors bring to the exhibition' and 'what exhibitions bring to visitors' (Kratz 2002: 94). The possibility of change that they point to was at least partially concealed by the tripartite model of confirmatory, oppositional and negotiated readings commonly deployed in studies of audience reception. The presence of dynamic and dialogic interpretations of difference suggests that the agency of museums cannot be understood simply in terms of the extent to which visitors concur with or resist the museums' messages. Rather, they suggest that the interpretive processes actuated by the visitor–exhibition encounter contain transformative possibilities. Agency is exclusively attributed to neither exhibition nor visitor but rather distributed between them with the potential to generate and disseminate ways of seeing, thinking and talking about difference that are both informed by the ethical constraints established by the museum and simultaneously filtered through individual and social frames.

Exhibitions as resources

This recasting of audiences, not as recipients of (or resistors to) fixed and non-negotiable messages but rather as participants in the co-production of meaning, can be seen to dissolve many of the tensions and inconsistencies that have been referenced in the earlier discussions. Museum exhibitions, purposefully designed to combat prejudice, are no longer simply *texts* (to be accepted, rejected or negotiated) but rather *resources* (alongside those of other wide-ranging media) available for appropriation and use by active audiences. The museum's intention is no longer conceived of in terms of 'influence' or 'coercion' but rather as the engagement of audiences in critically rethinking issues of equality and human rights and in co-producing ways of understanding and talking about difference. Those museums that seek to address prejudice might then be considered as offering resources to enable visitors to make, articulate and disseminate non-prejudiced accounts of society. Visitors might therefore employ the museum's resources to counter competing media resources that promulgate and legitimate prejudice (such as those identified in the discursive analyses reviewed in chapter 2). Alternatively, they can be seen to co-exist alongside complementary, anti-prejudice resources made available through other media. Importantly, this approach does not replace or invalidate but rather builds on textual analyses, offering new opportunities for exploring contemporary media–audience relations.

Moreover, this understanding of media as resource is broadly consistent with discursive approaches to understanding prejudice (although, as we saw in chapter 2, discursive analyses focus primarily on those resources that support, permit and legitimate, rather than combat, prejudice). Reviewing a number of different research projects investigating racist discourses in Britain, New Zealand, Australia and the Netherlands, LeCouteur and Augoustinos suggest that the common interpretative repertoires and rhetorical devices which have been found in text and talk in these different contexts should be 'seen as resources that can be drawn upon, combined and elaborated in complex and flexible ways in the articulation of accounts that suit the varying needs of particular local situations' (2001: 228).

101

Support for this repositioning of media as providers of resources that are utilised by audiences in varied ways can also be found from within audience studies. Abercrombie and Longhurst argue that both theoretical and empirical difficulties within the Incorporation/Resistance Paradigm as well as actual (real) changes in the constitution of audiences (influenced by changes in media production and modes of consumption) present increasing challenges to the ways in which audiences are conceptualised. They argue that a new paradigm for conceiving of media–audience relations is emerging – the Spectacle/Performance Paradigm (SPP). The SPP, in which the roles of producer and consumer, audience and performer are increasingly blurred, is produced in part by the emergence of what they term the 'diffused audience'. The diffused audience refers to the ways in which being a member of an audience is no longer an exceptional event since wide-ranging forms of media have become an increasingly integral part of everyday life, and on an unprecedented scale. For Abercrombie and Longhurst, 'Beside being regulative or constitutive of everyday life, the media also provide images, models of performance, or frameworks of action and thought which become routine resources of everyday life. People, in other words, *use* what the media provide in everyday life' (ibid.: 104).

Conclusion

Before moving on, it is helpful at this point to review the arguments developed thus far. The relationship between the preferred or implied messages of museums designed to counter prejudice and the interpretations of difference manifested within audience responses led us to consider questions of what Ruddock (2001) terms media 'influencability' and effect. However, as evidence within audience studies increasingly lends support for a theory of the active audience, claims of media effect and textual influence emerge as increasingly problematic. This, combined with audience responses that could not neatly be categorised as either confirmatory, oppositional or negotiated, led us to recast the museum not simply as 'text' (designed to persuade or convert the prejudiced individual) but rather as a 'resource' that can be appropriated in ways that facilitate and support the articulation of (non-prejudiced) accounts and interpretative repertoires.

The media – in their many forms – are ever-present and pervasive of everyday life. In this 'media-drenched society' (Abercrombie and Longhurst 1998: 69) where individuals are faced with a multiplicity of resources on which to draw, it might be argued that it is impossible to isolate the 'influence' of any individual medium. However, as we shall see in the following chapter, the particular, even unique, role and influence of the museum as a knowledge provider is reflected in visitors' own accounts of their perceived truthfulness and reliability. Furthermore, the emergence of the diffused audience suggests that it is less relevant to seek to isolate the 'effect' of individual media resources. Rather these must be understood as part of the mediascape of everyday life. For Abercrombie and Longhurst, the media can be viewed as resources for the imagination:

> Within the intense mediascape that modern societies provide, there is much that is unregarded or discarded by audiences; it is not that every magazine article, piece of music or television programme is instantly taken in as fuel for the imagination. ... What audiences are doing, therefore, is drawing from the endless media stream that passes them by a set of diverse elements out of which they can construct imaginative worlds that suit them. We have very little empirical evidence about the constitution of these worlds. It must be a fair guess, however, that they are socially constructed. In other words, the use of particular media resources for the imagination is not a random process. People will build particular imagined worlds around their previous experience and existing lives in the worlds of work, family and household and general social relationships.
>
> (ibid.: 107)

The media then can be understood as providers of resources that can be purposively mobilised towards politicised ends – to fashion individual and collective understandings of difference that might be prejudiced, egalitarian or contradictory. Moreover, museums are increasingly deploying devices which invite audiences to participate in processes of cultural production, to 'perform' in ways which enable them not only to construct their own meanings but to present these viewpoints within the setting of the museum. In this way, exhibitions provide not only 'resources' for visitors to draw upon but also stages or platforms from which individual meanings can be articulated, shared and disseminated.

The resources provided by museums can take diverse forms and support many different interpretations and ways of seeing. Those exhibitions that aim to confront and counter prejudice embody resources which do not purport to be neutral in tone, content or purpose. Rather they are constructed in ways designed to establish clearly defined ethical parameters and moral constraints within which visitors' conversations and their understandings of difference can be developed. The decision-making process through which these parameters and constraints are determined is a complex one, inevitably fraught with difficulties, and whilst a social consensus is unlikely to be forthcoming, the precepts of human rights nevertheless provide a starting point and a degree of guidance upon which exhibition-makers might draw.

This rethinking of media agency raises a further set of questions. How might the particular resources of the museum (in comparison with those offered by other media forms, such as television, newspapers and so on) be perceived, approached and appropriated by audiences? Are there characteristics of the experience of exhibition visiting that hold particular salience for understanding the agency of museums in confronting prejudice? In what ways, and with what kinds of social effect, are audiences *using* museums to negotiate understandings of difference? It is to these difficult questions that I shall turn in the next chapter by exploring the role that museums play, alongside other knowledge providers in the mediascape.

5

MUSEUMS IN THE MEDIASCAPE

In Abercrombie and Longhurst's (1998) vision of the mediascape, audiences have opportunities to draw upon an almost limitless, potentially overwhelming, array of resources from wide-ranging media forms. These may be ignored or (more actively) rejected, cast aside or taken up and utilised in myriad ways. In this analysis, museum exhibitions that seek to tackle prejudice can be conceived as resources (among many others in the mediascape) which audiences can potentially dismiss or draw upon in their negotiations with, and interpretations of, cultural difference. However, whilst audiences are undoubtedly discriminating in their consumption, selecting those elements which suit their needs, there are also other factors, linked to the character of specific media which, I wish to argue, can also help to account for the fate of the resources they provide – how audiences perceive, approach and appropriate them, whether they are taken up or passed over, how they might be utilised in ways which compete with or complement other resources.

The opportunities that audiences have to access increasingly diverse sources of information might suggest that museums occupy a relatively marginal place in the broader mediascape. While exposure to media such as television or radio is commonly counted in hours per day or week, museum visiting (if this was countable) would, for most people, most likely be measured in hours per year. Furthermore, the relatively limited 'reach' of museums (in terms of audience size and composition) might similarly support the view that there are more pervasive and efficacious media, with the means to engage and more profoundly to influence larger and more diverse audiences. Ultimately, why might museums be viewed as especially significant sites for interventions aimed at tackling prejudice?

To consider these arguments, I begin by briefly considering the nature of the museum experience in the context of newly emerging forms of the audience before drawing, once again, on data generated from visitor responses to the Anne Frank House and St Mungo Museum of Religious Art. I present evidence to argue that an understanding of the significance of museums in the combating of prejudice must take account of two interrelated factors.

The first concerns the act of museum visiting itself which, I suggest, stimulates and enables especially *active* (and thus potentially labile) audience experiences. The second concerns the extent to which audiences perceive museums to be relatively more trustworthy, objective and reliable sources of information about cultural differences than many other media forms. My intention is not to make claims that museums are relatively more influential and effective than many mass media and other agencies in tackling prejudice. Nevertheless, I do wish to suggest that the characteristics I identify (that relate to both the *experience* of museum visiting and perceptions of the museum as a *resource*) suggest that they are uniquely placed to engage audiences in debating questions of cultural difference and, in doing so, to contribute to broader social change. This potential contribution is, in most museums, largely unacknowledged, unexplored and untapped.

A typology of audience experiences

Abercrombie and Longhurst (1998) distinguish between three audience forms – simple, mass and diffused – an analysis which provides a useful starting point for understanding both the qualities of the museum experience and the attributes of the museum resource. The *simple* audience experience is typified by attendance of a music concert, a play or sporting event. Here communication takes place between distinct categories of 'performer' and 'audience' and a distance (both geographical and social) is maintained between them. Events generally take place in public spaces and are marked by a high degree of ceremony and ritual. The simple audience experience is immediate and unmediated and takes place outside of the everyday. Since these experiences are more exceptional than routine or mundane they can demand a relatively high degree of attention and involvement from audiences.

The advent of mass systems of communication – for example, radio, television, recorded music and newspapers – led to the development of *mass* audiences. Relative to those performances for simple audiences:

> mass audience events do not involve spatial localization, the communication is not so direct, the experience is more of an everyday one and is not invested in quite the same way with ceremony, less attention is paid to performance, which is typically received in private rather than public, and there is even greater social and physical distance between performers and audiences.
>
> (ibid.: 58)

Mass media consumption can be such an integrated part of everyday life that audiences may be relatively distracted and often simultaneously engaged in other forms of activity – one might do the ironing whilst watching television

Table 5.1 Modes of audience experience

	Simple	*Mass*	*Diffused*
Communication	Direct	Mediated	Fused
Local/global	Local	Global	Universal
Ceremony	High	Medium	Low
Public/private	Public	Private	Public and private
Distance	High	Very high	Low
Attention	High	Variable	Civil inattention

Source: Abercrombie and Longhurst (1998: 44)

or read a book whilst listening to the radio. This is not to say that all mass media consumption is low attention but commonly mass media audiences 'move in and out of attention' (ibid.: 68).

The third form of audience experience produces what Abercrombie and Longhurst call the *diffused* audience. 'The essential feature of this audience-experience is that, in contemporary society, everyone becomes an audience all the time. Being a member of an audience is no longer an exceptional event, nor even an everyday event. Rather it is constitutive of everyday life' (ibid.: 68–69). Diffused audiences then, are fundamentally different from mass or simple audiences. They arise out of the pervasiveness, ubiquity and constitutive capacity of media. The boundaries between performer and audience that, for simple and mass media experiences, are relatively distinct, are increasingly blurred and overlapping. 'Since people are simultaneously performers and audience members, cultural consumers become cultural producers and vice versa' (ibid.: 75). The characteristics of simple, mass and diffused audiences are summarised in Table 5.1. These forms of audience co-exist simultaneously.

Museum audiences

How might museum audiences be understood in the light of this model of media experience? Whilst museums increasingly create opportunities to engage mass audiences, for example through the provision of experiences via the internet, the more conventional forms of museum visiting that I have so far focused upon can be understood, relatively straightforwardly, to conform to the simple audience experience. The encounter between audience and 'performers' (objects and other elements of the exhibitionary mix) is relatively direct and takes place in specific public spaces, set apart from daily life. The experience is imbued with ceremonial and ritualistic qualities (Duncan 1991, Fraser 2005) that contribute to the prescription of what are perceived by audiences to be 'appropriate' behaviours. However, as we shall see, museums also provide settings for *diffused* audience experiences which arise partly from changes in the nature of audiences (at a macro-social level) and, in a more localised fashion within museums, through the trend towards more interactive and participatory forms of exhibition experience. The blurring of the boundaries between producer and consumer engendered by the purposeful introduction of interpretive devices that enable visitors to enact 'linguistic performances' (LeCouteur and Augoustinos 2001) of their own, holds significance, I intend to argue, for an understanding of the museum's agency in combating prejudice.

Audience activity and performativity

Within sociological, cultural and media studies, 'activity' is, as I discussed in the previous chapter, generally viewed in terms of the capacity for audiences to operate autonomously to generate polysemic interpretations that potentially oppose or resist the producer's intended meanings. Visitors to museums display this form of activity in their verbal and written responses to the messages they decode. However, activity can be understood more broadly to encompass not only the capacity for agency in the determination of meaning but also to encompass a range of behaviours and modes of response. As media theorist Denis McQuail states, 'Individual acts of media choice, attention, and response can also be more or less active, in terms of degree of motivation, attention, involvement, pleasure, critical or creative response, connection with the rest of life and so forth' (1997: 22). Although, in this chapter, I wish to explore activity in this broader sense, I also aim to challenge the assumption that all forms of activity are necessarily evident of audience empowerment and autonomy. Sharon Macdonald (2002) helpfully alerts us to the possibility that devices, introduced to exhibitions with the aim of enhancing visitor choices and encouraging participation and interactivity of experience, are equally capable of constraining and disempowering audiences.

Many simple audience events are characterised by efforts on the part of the medium/performers to delimit and constrain outwardly 'active' audience behaviours. Indeed, Abercrombie and Longhurst (1998) point out that the distance between performers and audiences found in many of these events has contributed to the perception of audience passivity that framed much of the early research into media influence. So, expectations are placed on concert attenders, for example, to refrain from activities other than listening during the performance. Attempts by audience members to conduct conversations with others or to make a telephone call are likely to be frowned upon! However, they also point out that passivity (in outward behaviour) cannot be assumed to imply that audiences are not attentive to, and highly involved in, the performance. They cite Bennett's work on theatre audiences to illustrate the dangers of conflating audiences' *physical behaviours* with their *interpretive processes*:

Spectators are thus trained to be passive in their demonstrated behaviour during a theatrical performance, but to be active in their decoding of the sign systems made available. Performers rely on the active decoding, but passive behaviour of the audience so that they can unfold the planned on-stage activity.

(Bennett 1997: 206)

In general then, media which address simple audiences, 'allow, encourage, demand a *condensed*, intense experience' (Abercrombie and Longhurst 1998: 55) that is less readily provided by mass or diffused audience experiences. Museums, as the data generated by this study suggests, can stimulate audience activity in a number of different ways which together provide the conditions for this condensed experience. This lends weight to the notion that, whilst there are factors which potentially delimit the influence of museums in the mediascape (not least the relatively modest size of audience in comparison with many mass media), it might also be argued that their 'influencability' (Ruddock 2001) is enhanced by the relative intensity of the experiences they offer in comparison with more ubiquitous and pervasive, but also more everyday, forms of mass media. Evidence from the interviews with visitors lends considerable support to this hypothesis. The data suggests that heightened levels of audience activity mean that audiences are indeed likely to 'notice', attend to and engage with the museum.

In many areas of media research, audience activity is equated with diminished textual powers – the more active the audience, the greater the capacity for polysemic interpretations and the weaker the powers of the media or text to establish preferred meanings. However, in the revised understanding of museum agency I proposed at the end of the previous chapter (which suggests that the role of museums is not to *coerce* visitors into alignment with preferred readings but rather to *engage* them as co-participants in the process of making meaning and in negotiating interpretations of difference) audience activity takes on rather different implications. Here, I wish to argue that the highly active engagement exhibited by visitors expands, rather than constrains, the museum's capacity to combat prejudice by providing the conditions for the production and dissemination of (often non-prejudiced) discursive interpretations.

Indicators of three main forms of audience activity emerged from my analysis of visitors' responses. The first relates to the *purposive* character of museum visiting and the perception (amongst visitors) that exhibition viewing offers enhanced levels of choice and control to visitors. The second concerns the readiness with which visitors made *connections* between concepts and narratives embodied within exhibitions and aspects of their own lives, memories and experiences. The third manifestation of activity concerns the opportunities provided by museums for audiences to make and enact their own *performances*, to share and disseminate their views with others.

During the interview, visitors were asked whether they felt people respond differently to museums in comparison with other media (such as television or newspapers) that deal with similar topics to those they identified as present in the exhibitions. Many visitors seemed to find the question more challenging than previous ones but eventually offered very clear, articulate and rich responses. Many appeared to be acutely aware of the different attributes of different media forms, confidently contrasting museums (often favourably) with television and newspapers. Their responses appear to suggest that museum visiting is perceived to offer enhanced levels of choice and control, demands higher levels of attention than other media and offers many opportunities for connection with personal lives and contemporary events at global and local levels.

Although many sought to distinguish museum visiting favourably from other forms of media consumption, it is important to recognise that these perceived characteristics are likely to be influenced by widely held, normative perceptions of different media. Indeed McQuail suggests that 'evaluative attitudes expressed toward media are somewhat superficial and learned as socially desirable rather than deeply internalized' (1997: 106). It might therefore be suggested that visitors in my study were simply recycling clichéd, normative views of media quality and popular distinctions between high culture (museums) and low culture (mass media). Although it is useful to recognise that audience perceptions may be influenced in this way, I wish to argue that they nevertheless remain significant in affecting the ways in which audiences approach and engage with museums.

Purposive and 'free-choice' viewing

Several visitors emphasised 'free-choice' in their decision to visit museums, talking about 'coming of their own volition' and contrasted this most notably with television viewing, a pursuit which was recognised as more mundane, routine, even inevitable. Aneesa, an art student from London visiting St Mungo's with her boyfriend, commented:

> Well, TV you're just flicking through the channels. You might just watch it 'cos it's on TV. The museum, you have to get out of the house, have to come for a reason, you come to explore, to know about culture.

In a similar vein, Julie, a call centre worker from Manchester interviewed at the Anne Frank House, suggested, 'It's more effort to go to a museum and it costs more so that people in a museum *want* to be there, but on television you just end up on that channel really.'

The purposiveness of museum visiting, and the associated efforts required to plan and execute a visit, appeared to influence the way in which audiences approached the medium itself. Visitors believed themselves to be in greater *control* of their consumption and it seemed as if the perceived absence of manipulation – the lack of an agenda on the part of the museum (an important point to which I shall return later in this chapter) – combined with the special-ness, the extra-ordinariness of the museum visit, to result in more attentive and focused viewing. Jeff, a civil servant from Glasgow, stated:

> It's more personal when you come to the museum as well, you're picking and choosing, like when you go to an art gallery there's some bits I don't particularly like. Taking Glasgow as an example, I'm not fond of the Burrell, it's a nice building but I'm not fond of the Burrell because that was one man's collection and things like tapestries and plates, they don't interest me. I would gravitate more towards paintings. It's much more personal because you as an individual are taking what you want out of it.

Beki, a student visiting St Mungo's, argued that:

> Museums have cultural significance. Going to a museum is not like switching on your TV. You're in a different frame of mind when you come to a museum than when you're just watching the telly, watching a documentary or reading the paper or whatever. You're more inclined to dismiss it if you're watching the TV, you could be vegetating. If you're reading the paper, you could just be lazing about on a Sunday morning or whatever. If you come to a museum, you come here for a specific purpose and your mind's going to be more active and open so I think from that point of view you're in an environment which is conducive to this kind of thing.

Carol Duncan, drawing links between museums and religious institutions as sites of ritual, has also argued that this specialness inclines visitors to attend to museums in a certain way. 'Museums do not simply resemble temples architecturally', she suggests:

> they *work* like temples, shrines, and other such monuments. Museumgoers today, like visitors to these other sites, bring with them the willingness and ability to shift into a certain state of receptivity. And like traditional ritual sites, museum space is care-fully marked off and culturally designated as special, reserved for a particular kind of contemplation and learning experience and demanding a special quality of attention.
>
> (1991: 91)

Although individual choice and control is perceived to be heightened, there is also the sense that the museum visit can expose you to things that are unexpected, that you might otherwise 'filter out' in your consumption of other media. Martin, an unemployed man in his twenties from Fife, Scotland, said:

> It's really difficult to say, but I don't know if I'd have the same opinion if I watched it on TV because perhaps you don't concentrate as much. Being here you're in tune with what you've just seen and you're more willing to concentrate on what's being presented to you, the messages that are there. Perhaps if you're at home, or just reading the paper, you might only see what you want to see.

Whilst the presence of choice can have the effect of *suggesting* control and empowerment to audiences it is interesting to consider the potential for museums to frame and delimit choices in ways which might prompt people towards preferred meanings. The *Out of Line* exhibition at the Anne Frank House invites visitors to choose between two responses to a range of different scenarios concerned with equality and discrimination. Whilst visitors' responses are, as we have seen, immensely variable, the possibilities for expressing these within the exhibition itself are, as I earlier described, contained by the museum through the voting format which permits and legitimates only two possible reactions – the selection of 'the right to freedom of expression' or 'the right to protection against discrimination'. Significantly, both 'choices', framed by the museum and the exhibition-makers, are underpinned by (and predicated upon) notions of equal human rights for all, regardless of gender, race, religion, disability or sexual orientation. Though some visitors may choose to make discriminatory comments to others within their group or to write them for viewing by a wider audience in the visitors' book, significantly there is no opportunity within the voting format of the exhibition itself to express support for a prejudiced (for example, homophobic, sexist or racist) position. Visitors are encouraged to dwell on these issues and to formulate their own opinions but the museum's stance on equal human rights remains non-negotiable. (The implications associated with museums adopting an authoritative and potentially challenging, even unpopular, position are significant and will be discussed more fully in due course.) However, regardless of this potential framing and constraining of visitor choice, it can nevertheless be argued that the more *purposive* and choice-laden the act of consumption, the greater the degree of perceived control by audiences and the more attentive the act of viewing.

Connection, identification and use

The second dimension of 'activity' that emerged strongly from the audience data concerns the extent to which visitors forged connections between what they encountered within exhibitions and issues and events that were external to the museum. These connections were made at both a personal level (for example, prompting reminiscence or reflection on events and experiences in visitors' daily lives or those of their family and friends) and at a more abstract or global level (for example, broad reflections on social or demographic change or references to specific world events). Visitors *used* the material they encountered in exhibitions in various ways. For example, some visitors to the Anne Frank House reflected on issues of conflict and discrimination in their personal lives and the prior experiences of family members. Towards the end of the interview, Amanda, a health visitor from Middlesex, England, was asked if there were any aspects of her identity that made the museum particularly meaningful to her:

> There's only one little thing, and I don't know if it's significant to what you're saying, but really the 'No Jews Allowed' notice, I could link to my own mother's experience being Irish, remembering when she was over here and wanted to apply to be a civil servant but there were signs saying 'no Irish'. That was in England, not Amsterdam … and she was deeply upset by that. It's only a little thing, it's not comparable, but I just made that little link when I saw it.

Robin, a geography student visiting the Anne Frank House from Canada, said:

> My mum is from the US and when she was younger she had to go to … they had segregated schools. My mum's not old, she's forty something, so just imagine not too long ago they still had a certain thing happening, still going on in the States. She went to high school outside New York City and she said it was weird that everyone was in one school. It's just weird that some of this stuff is still going on.

Connections were also made with events reported in the news, both internationally (most frequently the war in Iraq and the events of September 11) and locally (for example, news reports on conflict between rival football clubs in Glasgow, or issues relating to local immigration and the presence of asylum seekers). For example, Eunice a woman in her early fifties who worked in catering and lived in Bradford, believed the message at St Mungo's to be that 'everybody's the same'. When asked if she supported that view she responded:

Well I have to, coming from Bradford, I mean they're going to have to do something there, trying to keep it all together, 'cos it's falling apart. We've had the riots 'cos of the Muslims, Christians, and everything, it just wants to get sorted out. We could do with something like this down there to sort it out.

Responses such as these might suggest a role for museums as settings for audiences to reflect on contemporary social issues. Interestingly, Abercrombie and Longhurst argue that the simple audience experience offered by theatre is especially suited to societal reflexivity. Theatre is generally performed in separate spaces, at special times, outside of routine, everyday life. Drawing on Turner (1982) they argue on the one hand that, like ritual, theatre performances are liminal, creating environments which lend themselves to reflection on society and the means for addressing social conflict. On the other hand, however, they also suggest that 'modern mass media may be more effective providers of raw material for the imagination than simple audience forms' such as theatre (ibid.: 106). This, they suggest, is not only because mass media are relatively more pervasive and ubiquitous but also because of the disconnectedness from everyday life that characterises many simple audience experiences. Drawing on Horton and Wohl (1956) they appear to suggest that, whilst theatre experiences are potentially highly intensive and involving, the fact that they are spatially and temporally discrete from everyday life constrains their capacity to function as providers of resources for the imagination. 'Television, cinema and radio, on the other hand, produce a continuous interplay between the two worlds of mundane reality and performance' (ibid.: 106), creating an intimacy between medium and audience. This analysis might suggest that the ubiquity and infusion into everyday life that characterises mass media serves to relegate museums to a relatively less significant role in the broader mediascape. However, I wish to argue that the ease with which audiences connected museum narratives with their own biographies potentially challenges this view.

Humanistic connections were also made through identification with the subjects on display. The use of highly personalised narratives in both museums offered visitors avenues to identify links and common ground between their own views and experiences and those of people from different cultural backgrounds. Not surprisingly, at the Anne Frank House, the delivery of the narrative through extracts from the diary as well as personal testimonies of those who knew the Frank family was an especially powerful device (Fig. 5.1). Wendy, visiting from Chicago, commented:

I think the people in the video ... they were the *real* people. That was good, and of course the excerpts from the diary. When you see the excerpts from the diary and you hear the voice, even though you know it's not Anne's voice, it gets you emotionally so I did have to wipe away a tear more than once.

Similarly, at St Mungo's, several visitors commented on the presence of multiple voices (linked to specific, named individuals) within the exhibition – text labels featuring comments made by people representing different faith communities and headsets through which visitors could listen to different individuals talking about the objects on display. The contemporaneity of these personal testimonies further reinforces the possibilities for visitors to make connections with their own lives and experiences. Ethnographic exhibitions often amplify the distance between subject and viewer (Riegel 1996, Karp and Kratz 2000), suppressing connective responses by emphasising temporal (as well as geographical) distance between the museum visitors and the people whose cultures are displayed.[1] In contrast, the exhibitions in St Mungo's, by depicting diverse cultures as coevally resident within the city of Glasgow, serve to narrow the distance between viewer and subject. Similarly the use of contemporary scenarios in the *Out of Line* exhibition at the Anne Frank House disrupts visitors' sense of historical distance by demanding engagement with present-day issues relating to discrimination and prejudice. Although these devices are effective in forging connections between the subject matter of an exhibition and visitors' lives, this emotional engagement is not always welcomed. The preference amongst some museum visitors to maintain an emotional and cognitive distance from the material and stories they encounter in order to avoid unpleasant memories or discomfort has also been found by Bagnall (2003) and Riegel (1996). In Gaynor Bagnall's study, some visitors found exhibitions at a history museum to be 'too emotionally resonant and did not want this emotional closeness as part of their visit' (2003: 92). Henrietta Riegel's earlier study of an exhibition in Stuttgart, which sought to immerse visitors in re-creations of war and post-war scenarios, similarly found that some visitors complained about feeling too close to the subject in ways which evoked difficult memories for them.

Museums have become increasingly aware of the power of interpretive devices that personalise and humanise stories to facilitate connections between visitors and the subject matter of exhibitions. The Museum of Tolerance in Los Angeles and the United States Holocaust Memorial Museum in Washington DC, for example, both issue visitors with identification cards which tell the story of one individual's experiences of the Holocaust. Timothy Luke describes the visitor experience at the Holocaust Museum:

On each floor during the tour, one must turn a page in this document. Journeying through time by going through space, visitors turn over the pages of this *Pass* to advance with their Holocaust

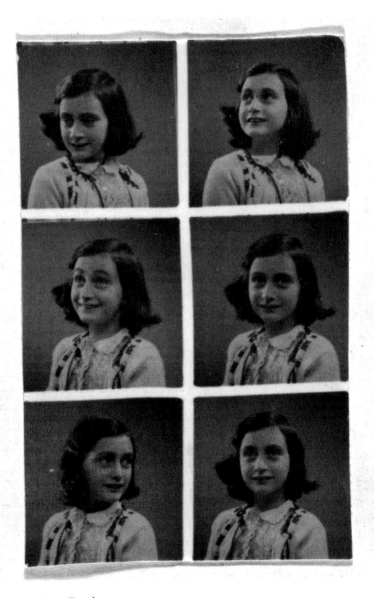

Figure 5.1: Anne Frank

Source: By kind permission of Getty Images

persona, experiencing how they conjointly fare in their passage through the museum's displays and the Holocaust years.

(2002: 42)

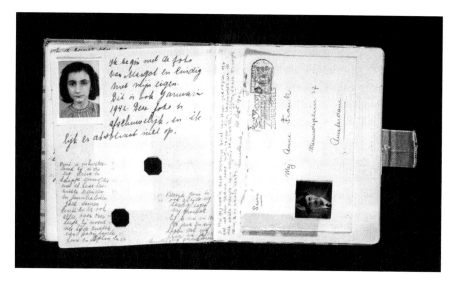

Figure 5.2: A handwritten page of Anne Frank's diary

Source: By kind permission of Getty Images

The potential for the use of personalised testimonies to facilitate empathetic connections between viewer and subject was also noted in Corinne Kratz's evaluation of her exhibition of portraits of the Okiek people of Kenya. In the exhibition she used reflections and comments by Okiek people on the subjects and events portrayed in her photographs. This interpretive device, though still relatively uncommon in many ethnographic exhibitions, is increasingly used in other kinds of museum. Kratz used the technique purposefully, 'to enrich the representation of Okiek and help nudge visitors toward making connections with Okiek despite their differences' (2002:157). Indeed, her evaluation suggested that the captions – alongside other devices which emphasised the individual and personal nature of the stories she was telling – proved effective in forging links between viewer and subject. 'Visitors', she explains, 'most often mentioned the conversational captions but noted other features that contributed to this sense as well: the emphasis on portraits and faces, close-ups, color, the human scale of enlargements, informal tone in descriptive captions, inclusion of names, and hanging photographs at eye level' (ibid.: 207).

Visitors' responses in my study also suggested that the encounter with objects – with 'the real thing' – enhanced museums' capacities to offer especially engaging, emotionally intense experiences (Fig. 5.2). Ronnie, a school teacher from Holland, contrasted his experience of visiting the Anne Frank House in person with television viewing:

When you're watching something on the television you don't experience it as much as you do if you get it firsthand, when you can actually see the diary, look through the same window as she looked through. It's a stronger impression than just getting something as pictures so it makes the experience all the more authentic and realistic.

Sarah, a student from Bedford, England, highlights the multi-sensory experience of museum visiting which she suggests is relatively more engaging than some other media experiences:

Yes, if it's in a newspaper you can always put it down can't you? And people tend to, with the news and things. But here, it's something you choose to do so you're generally going to be interested anyway and having the variety of ways of having messages put across, having the videos and letters and pictures and things like that. It appealed to all your senses and it's much easier to take things in and stay interested.

I shall return to the significance of objects in relation to the museum's claims to authority, objectivity and authenticity and consider their role in greater detail later in this chapter.

The potential for connection and identification between audiences and other (non-museum) media has been noted in a number of studies. For example, in her study of viewers of the television series *Dallas*, Ien Ang (1985) develops the concept of 'emotional realism' to describe the ways in which audience members identified with the fictional characters. Similarly Katz and Liebes' investigation of viewers' responses to the same programme found 'referential critiques', which involved individuals 'referring their reading of the text to their own lives' (Silverstone 1994: 149).

A contemporary example – and one which relates directly to our interest in prejudice – of the ways in which audiences make connections between narratives they encounter in their media consumption and experiences in their own lives, can be found in fan (enthusiast) responses to the US television drama series *Six Feet Under*. In this controversial show, Fisher and Sons – a family-run funeral home in present-day Los Angeles – provides the backdrop against which the central characters' lives unfold. The TV show's unflinching treatment of the central theme of death and dying not only generated controversy but also secured popular success and critical acclaim from 2001, when it first aired on American television, to 2005, when the final series concluded. Fans visiting the official *Six Feet Under* website were invited to share their reactions to the series via a number of themed bulletin boards which encouraged viewers to discuss their favourite characters, make plotline predictions and so on. A key narrative within the drama, concerning the 'coming out' of one of the main characters, David Fisher, and the reactions of his mother and siblings on learning of his sexuality, generated considerable discussion on the bulletin boards and many viewers discussed this storyline in relation to experiences in their own lives. Interestingly, some fans explicitly attributed their ability to come to terms with their own sexuality to their viewing of the show. One viewer wrote:

> I cannot begin to express what a profound effect *Six Feet Under* has had on me ... As the characters have become more and more a part of my life, I have recognized my need to examine my own self-imposed limitations. I have become much more open about all aspects of myself, including my sexuality.

Another viewer used the bulletin board to apologise for his prior homophobic behaviour, thanking the creators of the programme who, he claims, helped him to change:

> This show has really helped me in a way. I'm a straight heterosexual, and I'm not ashamed of it. But a couple of years ago I was a huge homophobe ... The teenage years are confusing and I was trying to show everybody that I was a real straight MAN! By doing this I might have hurt other people who were gay ... I don't have any bad feelings against homosexuals today, mainly because of personal growth, but also 'Six Feet Under'. I am very sorry about my former behaviour. And I would like to thank the creators of the show who have helped my tolerance.

One further referential response, from a mother in her fifties who described the conflicts arising from the different attitudes members of her family held to her son's homosexuality, similarly invested the TV programme with a power to influence. 'Keep up the good work Six Feet Under' she wrote on 19 February 2002, 'you have helped to open up conversations and give strength where needed' (HBO 2002).

These bulletin boards, through providing viewers with opportunities to incorporate the programme into their everyday lives, are examples of what Will Brooker (2001) has termed 'overflow'. Overflow refers to the growing tendency 'for media producers to construct a lifestyle experience around a core text, using the Internet to extend audience engagement and encourage a two-way interaction' (Brooker and Jermyn 2003: 323). Whilst it would be naïve to read these referential accounts necessarily as evidence of the agency of the media in providing resources that counter prejudice, they might nevertheless begin to suggest a role for museums, alongside other forms of media, in providing a range of resources that are used in people's everyday lives to negotiate and make sense of cultural differences.

119

The use of museums

The *use* of the concepts and material embodied in displays at the St Mungo Museum and Anne Frank House could also be discerned in the audience data generated in this study though, in many instances, the form of usage was hard to pinpoint and define. For example, some visitors to St Mungo's who lived within Glasgow, were prompted by the visit to reflect on the changing nature of the city's demography as a result of immigration and the more recent arrival of asylum seekers, an issue that was especially prominent in local news media at the time of the interviews. It seemed to me as if some local residents were using the museum resource as a way to better understand the social change they encountered in their daily lives. Whilst this usage was often implied, in a few instances, it was made very explicit. Jane, a woman who worked for the social security benefits agency in Glasgow, had visited before but this time brought her ten-year-old daughter.

> JANE: I've been before but I thought it would be interesting for her because they're doing some religious study at school.
> QUESTION: *What parts of the museum did you like most or find most interesting?*
> JANE: I liked mostly the top floor, showing her all different religions. That was interesting, that was more aimed at her level.
> QUESTION: *Were there any particular parts of the museum that prompted you to pause for discussion or to share your thoughts with each other?*
> JANE (*addressing her daughter*): There were quite a few, weren't there? The Salvador Dali picture, we talked about that, didn't we? Islam and stuff like that. She's from a multicultural school – in the area there are asylum seekers, refugees and everything so I thought that would be interesting for her to have an insight into the other kids in the school. I think schools should visit places like this, especially the way things are changing, different religions all coming into the country and everything, and war and all that kind of thing. They all play together Monday to Friday, I think if they knew a bit more about each other's culture it would definitely help, I think this is a great place.

Towards the end of the same interview, Jane also highlighted her perceived value of the museum as a source of information that had practical use in her own everyday life:

> QUESTION: *Are there any aspects of your identity that make this museum particularly meaningful to you?*
> JANE: It's the Benefits Agency I work in so, I mean, like having a wee understanding when I have to deal with multicultural people, and me

having a wee background and I can think, 'oh that's what that is. That's why they wear that on their head' – that kind of thing.

The two characteristics of museum visiting considered so far are closely linked and, taken together, suggest that museums may hold a relatively privileged position as providers of resources for the imagination which equip audiences with the potential to engage with issues of difference and social change. Although, as we have seen, visitor experiences are immensely variable, the act of museum visiting is for many characterised by both attentiveness and a capacity for powerful emotional engagement and personal connection. As Abercrombie and Longhurst state:

When members of an audience people *attend* to a performance, they concentrate their energies, emotions and thoughts on the performance and try to distil from that performance a meaning of one kind or another. Commonsensically, it seems likely that attention is related to involvement and involvement is related to effect. That is to say, the more intense the audience attention, the more involved it will be in the performance and the greater will be the intellectual and emotional impact.

(1998: 43)

Social interaction and performative behaviour

The third form of audience activity I wish to highlight as especially relevant for this study concerns the social character of museum visiting (which frequently involves interaction both within visiting groups and between visitors who are unknown to each other) and the ways in which museums potentially stimulate and enable certain kinds of performative behaviour amongst audiences. Limited research has been undertaken into the social interactions that take place between visitors and on the influence of these processes on audience experiences. However, research by Dirk vom Lehn et al. (2001) (using video-recordings of visitor inter-actions within science and art exhibitions) suggests that the presence of both companions and strangers will exercise significant influence over the ways in which other individuals approach and experience particular exhibits. Museums, I shall argue, are key sites for the enact-ment and viewing of performances by visitors; performances which regularly feature negotiations of cultural difference. The fact that these performances take place in a space that is both public and authoritative also has implications for their dissemination and for the ways in which these are subsequently 'received' or viewed beyond the physical confines of the museum.

The redefinition of the roles of audience and performer, consumer and producer, offers a useful way to understand visitor behaviour and action within museums that attempt to offer alternative, non-prejudiced ways of seeing. Exhibitionary strategies that demand audience interaction and response can be seen as means through which visitors are enabled to enact their own 'performances' – through opportunities to debate issues, express personal opinions, share them with other audience members and contribute directly to exhibition content. The democratising strategies, through which audience members are invited, enabled, provoked to perform – to participate in the process of cultural production and dissemination – are increasingly commonplace in museums of all kinds (as well as in other media forms, as we have seen with the earlier example of the television show *Six Feet Under*). Museums then can be understood as settings which offer conceptual and material resources in which visitors can perform their own negotiated understandings of cultural difference. The museum's resources are presented through a variety of interpretive means which may include devices or props designed to enable visitors to enact their own performances but can also function to shape their content and, indeed, to frame and constrain them in varied ways.

Both St Mungo's and the Anne Frank House deploy interpretive devices designed to stimulate audience engagement and participation by inviting visitors to express their opinions and to share these with other visitors and with the museum. At the Anne Frank House visitors frequently wait in line for the opportunity to read the comments book and add their own responses before leaving the museum. The *Out of Line* exhibition not only encourages visitors to express their opinion through voting for either 'freedom of expression' or 'protection from discrimination' but also *displays* the collective responses in the form of illuminated bars on the ceiling which show visitors the results of the vote (amongst the current room of visitors) in each of the dilemmas presented (Fig. 5.3). At St Mungo's Museum, many visitors take the opportunity to share their thoughts with others on comments cards which are then displayed, becoming part of the exhibition in the galleries themselves. These latter devices constitute a greater level of participation than that afforded by comments books (which are generally positioned to enable visitors to comment on exhibitions after they have seen them) as they incorporate the visitors into the displays themselves.

The deployment of these devices, I wish to argue, has interesting consequences for our understanding of the role of museums in ameliorating prejudice. The invitation and legitimation of audience responses can be seen to represent not simply a remapping of the boundaries between audience and media, between consumer and producer, but also a narrowing of the social distance between the powerful, expert media and the lay audience member (McQuail 1997). It is in this sense that the museum experience can

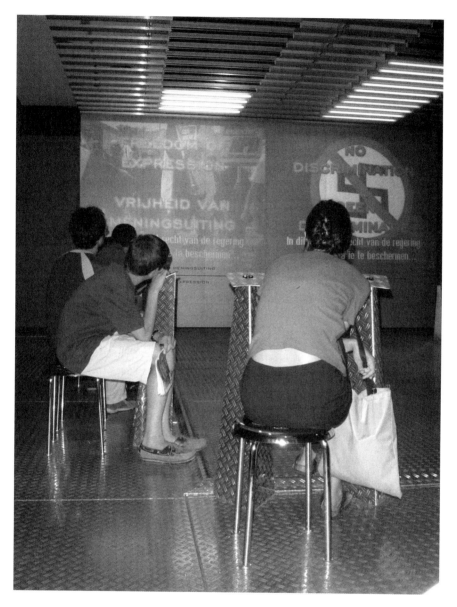

Figure 5.3: *Out of Line* at the Anne Frank House

be understood as not only 'simple' but also 'diffused'. As Abercrombie and Longhurst state:

> the diffused audience arises from the interaction of two processes, both of which are modern. On the one hand, there is

the construction of the world as a spectacle and, on the other, the construction of individuals as narcissistic. People simultaneously feel members of an audience and that they are performers; they are simultaneously watchers and being watched.

(1998: 75)

The exhibition encounter proved highly effective in provoking talk and text amongst and between visitors. Many, as we saw in the confirmatory readings discussed in chapter 4, took the opportunity to perform their own toler-ance (through their conversations and their written responses), condemning prejudice and intolerance in others. In this way, performance can be seen as a means through which audience members both affirm and, through the possibilities for change opened up by the visitor–exhibition encounter, remake their own identities.

Some visitors reflected on interaction stimulated between members of their own visiting party. Vince, a mechanical engineer from New Zealand, had visited the Anne Frank House with his fourteen-year-old daughter:

> The 'choice room', that was a little bit extra, and that's quite good actually because my daughter was getting very angry at me for choosing one option. I was choosing the 'freedom of speech' option all the time and she thought that that meant that you were pro the neo-Nazis and things like that – which told me, as well, that she's still got a way to go with the maturity of her thinking. She's still seeing things incredibly black and white and I thought she'd actually moved into the grey area of thinking a little bit more but she hasn't.

However, interactions are stimulated not only *within* visiting parties but also take place *between* visitors who are unknown to each other. Many interviewees were acutely aware of other visitors and intrigued by how their responses might differ from their own. Robert, an insurance salesman from Derby, visiting Amsterdam with his wife and son, was intrigued by the reac-tions of other visitors to *Out of Line*:

> It made you think about how liberal you are or aren't or whether freedom of speech is important to you personally ... what you find offensive and what you don't, and how other people react to what you think. I'm also wondering whether their reaction was slightly tainted by what they've just seen and whether yesterday they'd have done the same voting.

In other instances, for example visitor comments displayed in the *Gallery of Religious Life* at St Mungo's or written in comments books at both sites, responses took the form of conversations or debates in which individuals either endorsed or challenged the expressed opinions of others. On 3 April 2003, the following two comments appeared on the 'talkback' board at St Mungo's:

> I think this display is an offence to the one true God, Father and son and Holy Spirit.

> The above comments show intolerance, narrow thinking with no intention of understanding others. It is unchristian and is the cause of conflict.

And in another example, from 18 and 20 November 2001, respectively:

> Very good. However, I think that in light of recent events the section on Islam should be removed. Never to be returned. John Davis[2]

> I disagree completely with John Davis. Islam = terrorism. There are fanatics everywhere and in every religion.

'Conversations' between individuals unknown to each other were also found by Sharon Macdonald (2005) in her analysis of visitor comments books at the Documentation Centre of the Former Nazi Party Rally Grounds in Nuremberg.

The capacity to stimulate talk is similarly evident in other forms of media consumption. For example, there has been considerable discussion around the role of television in prompting conversations amongst viewers. Taylor and Mullan observe that:

> Although 'television conversations' may often be about the comings and goings of fictional characters or 'personalities', they provide ways of talking about a great many features of the world: sex, sin, retribution and death. Indeed … in some cases it seems that television drama has only properly occurred, been thoroughly realized, when the plots and the moral messages they contain have been discussed and interpreted and re-dramatized in the company of friends or mere acquaintances.
>
> (1986: 205)

However, the provocation of talk and text within the setting of the museum takes on a particular salience for the countering of prejudice in light of the fact that, in contrast to the responses generated by most television viewing, these discursive performances are enacted within the public sphere. I wish to suggest that audience interactions, mediated by and through the interpretive devices deployed within exhibitions, are lent a certain power and intensity by the uniquely constituted space of the museum in which they take place.

Museums 'contain' visitors' conversations in the sense that they provide a safe environment in which they can occur. Moreover, the museum provides a public forum which serves to disseminate, to give value to (and perhaps, in some instances, to authorise) the verbal and written opinions of visitors. It might also be suggested that the sensitive and contested nature of the topics of prejudice, inequality and discrimination further heightens the emotional intensity of the visit. For example, part of the power of *Out of Line* at the Anne Frank House lies in the shared nature of the exhibition experience. Although it is not generally possible to determine the way in which particular individuals in the room are voting, some visitors are nevertheless conscious of the presence of others and acutely aware of how their own decision relates to the dominant opinion as the results of the vote are displayed visually on the ceiling. Joan, a teacher from Colorado, expressed her anxiety about the sharing of her own views:

> I was at the front and at the very beginning, I was afraid to put my hand up because I was afraid somebody was going to watch me vote.

This sensitivity to others was also observed by vom Lehn et al. (2001) who found that visitors were engaged in a process of mutually monitoring each others' actions and activities within the same space. Whilst this effect is potentially present to a greater or lesser degree in all museums, it seems reasonable to suggest that its impact is potentially heightened in museums that engage visitors in potentially sensitive and contested topics.

Telling the truth: trust, authority and 'facticity'

The act of museum visiting, then, has the potential to be a relatively active (in several senses of the word) mode of media consumption. Visitors can be understood to be active in the purposive and attentive way in which they approach visiting, the readiness with which they connect museum narratives with aspects of their own lives, and in the performative behaviours that are increasingly enabled and encouraged by participatory devices within exhibitions. These modes of audience activity help to position museum visitors as co-participants in the production and dissemination of discursive interpretations. However, there exists a tension between this conception of audiences (as active, as relatively autonomous) and commonly held perceptions that audiences approach museums with a degree of deference, viewing them as sites which possess the cultural authority to depict cultural differences both *accurately* and *fairly*;[3] as places in which they can receive 'a history lesson at a glance, a confirmation of actual life as documented and preserved for [their] value-free absorption' (DaBreo 1990: 104). In what ways then might visitors' responses be shaped by perceptions of institutional authority? How might audience autonomy (and the capacity to generate and disseminate illiberal, prejudiced interpretations) be framed and even constrained, by perceptions of the museum's *accuracy* (a perception that museums are objective, that they can reflect social reality, that they 'tell it like it is') and *fairness* (which acknowledges a degree of subjectivity but implies both impartiality and the capacity to make the 'right' judgement) in representing difference?

The last two decades have produced a growing body of literature, especially from within cultural studies, that has laid bare the role of museums in the construction of narratives with particular purposes and ambitions; narratives which have excluded certain constituencies (as both subject and audience), producing and reproducing inequalities in ways which are shaped by the social norms and political ambitions of the time. Although the specific motivations behind (and political consequences of) different displays have taken many forms, the *'constructedness'* of the exhibitionary medium has nevertheless been taken by most academics (and many practitioners) to be axiomatic. It is interesting, then, given the widespread academic and professional debates which have explored the political uses and consequences of museum exhibitions, that audiences nevertheless appear to have retained considerable faith in the museum as a purveyor of objective, impartial truths.

Of course, the museum's reputation in this respect has not gone entirely unchallenged. Indeed, it is fair to say that growing public and press interest in the museum as a 'battleground' for the Culture-, History- and Science Wars (Macdonald 1998: xii) has contributed to the erosion of confidence and credibility in the museum's probity and capacity for impartiality. Nevertheless, audience responses to St Mungo's and the Anne Frank House suggest that faith in the museum as a reliable source of factual information remains significant. These findings are supported by those from recent research in both the United States and Britain. The results of an American Association of Museums survey found that 87 per cent of respondents considered museums trustworthy compared to 67 per cent who trust books and just 50 per cent who trust television news (Marstine 2005: 4). Similarly, a recent study of public perceptions of memory institutions in Britain confirmed that many believe archives, museums and public libraries are relatively more trustworthy sources of information about current social issues than more everyday mass media. The study found that, although busy lifestyles combined with technological developments facilitated relatively higher use of newspapers, television and the internet, than museums, libraries and archives, respondents distinguished between media forms in terms of trust and value.

> The data show that relatively high percentages of value are placed in museums, libraries and archives in helping respondents to understand social and political concerns ... [The] least trusted sources of information such as tabloid newspapers are regarded as sources of entertainment and speculative gossip rather than real information ... Information provided by traditional repositories of public knowledge are trusted more because of their higher levels of authenticity and neutrality [and] lack of editorial bias or manipulation.
>
> (Usherwood et al. 2005: 4–5)

Karp and Kratz's (2000) analysis, which distinguishes between two closely connected forms of authority – 'ethnographic' and 'cultural' – is especially useful. Ethnographic authority is drawn from the deployment of specific exhibitionary devices and interpretive strategies – the tone and content of text, the selection and arrangement of objects, and a wide array of design features. Cultural authority is rather less tangible; 'It is embedded in educational curricula, part of inchoate attitudes formed through school trips and family holidays, manifested in museum architecture, and claimed in assertions of personhood' (ibid.: 208). As Michael, a community organiser visiting the Anne Frank House from the United States, observed:

> The setting is not a controversial setting, you're coming into a museum ... there's something about it – I don't know if it's the quiet or professionalism or it's a place where people learn, they get a handle on a bit of the past. That ambience, I guess all taken together, seems to maybe open a person up a bit more to learning and being a part of this and maybe being moved by it, whereas if you go into a place where, you know, where the side's already taken, it might be a different situation. You know in a newspaper, they're always either left wing or right wing. Museums, I don't think would tend to have that reputation for being, you know, whatever wing. It's just like 'this is it'.

The ethnographic and cultural forms of authority that Karp and Kratz describe, combined and embodied in all museum exhibitions, may be open to challenge (especially as museums increasingly play with the conventions of exhibition making) but, as I intend to show, they nevertheless retain a powerful influence on visitor responses.[4]

In my study, I was interested to explore the extent to which audience activity (in terms of the interpretations visitors generated through and out of their visit) was constrained and framed not only by the interpretive cues and props embedded in the museum's resources (as I explored in chapter 4) but also by audience perceptions of the institution; the ways visitors approached and viewed the source itself. In their appropriation of media resources, to what extent might audiences be seen to defer to the museum's perceived authority? Faced with a vast array of media resources, how might audiences differentially filter those offered by museums from those provided by other media forms? Although I will necessarily give some consideration to the strategies and devices museums utilise to claim and bolster their authority, my focus here is on audience reception – the ways in which visitors view the museum as a source of information. Are museums viewed as reliable arbiters of cultural difference or as biased and untrustworthy? If museums are endowed with the capacity to 'tell it like it is' what implications does this have for the decisions that are made about who is represented in museums and in what ways?

Telling it like it is

Many visitors invested museums with the power accurately to depict real life, to present certain ideas and narratives as if they are natural or 'real'. Carol, a self-employed bookkeeper from Hertfordshire, stated:

> It's more true in a museum. In the paper or on television, it can be so distorted. Here, it's straight up isn't it? You tend to take the paper and television with a pinch of salt half the time. I think most of the museums are sort of more symbols of establishment, and symbols of permanency and the information that's collected is correct, is a reflection of society at the time, whatever the museum is showing, whatever area.

This equation of *permanency* with *authority* can be explored through a number of spatio-temporal dimensions. Sharon Macdonald (1998) points to the possibility of museum displays – often spatially fixed and in place for many years – holding a greater cultural authority in comparison with other media. Television, for example, may be a more ubiquitous and pervasive medium but its resources are relatively transient. Moreover, it is reasonable to argue that the authority accorded to different kinds of museum is unevenly distributed and likely to be bound up with a number of factors including geographical location, mode of governance, type and quality of collections. Large national museums in receipt of public funding are, in most instances, likely to be more prestigeful than their smaller counterparts (Macdonald 1998, Kratz 2002). Linked to these suggestions, I have elsewhere argued that the representation of difference within relatively more permanent, 'mainstream' museum displays might serve to more powerfully confer equality and convey a sense of inclusion and legitimisation for marginalised communities than (the more commonplace) representation within temporary and often spatially marginalised exhibitions (Sandell 2005).

Comments made by Jeff, a civil servant from Glasgow, highlight the perceived significance of the St Mungo Museum's efforts to reflect the changing demography of the city in which he lived:

> This is all part and parcel of the cosmopolitan nature of Glasgow and that should be recognised and accepted and a museum and a cultural thing like that is, to me, another way of reinforcing that's part of the normality. If we went up there and only saw Christianity, then that obviously would be a very false picture of our current society and that's important.

This notion that museums are somehow 'correct' in their depictions of real life was echoed in comments made by Rita, a retired secretary from outside Glasgow, which suggest that museums can potentially 'fix' or rectify flawed or 'wrong' opinions:

> Although probably some of the people don't agree with the different things they see here but at least it makes them understand more, brings it to their attention or probably they've got wrong ideas and then they come to a museum like this and it explains everything so they can understand.

Interestingly, several visitors commented on the absence of any particular message in the museums. Rather, for these visitors, it seemed as if museums were motiveless, naturally non-partisan, simply providing information – the facts – without any particular agenda or perspective of their own, a perception that is especially ironic in the context of this study. Suzanne, an air steward in her twenties, said of St Mungo's:

> I don't think it's trying to push anything. It's not trying to say 'you should be like this' or 'you should be like that'. I think it was just like an informative way of showing things.

The significance of objects

The presence and use of objects – the 'real thing' – appears to play an important part in constituting what Donald Preziosi and Claire Farago term the museum's 'facticity' – its capacity for 'presenting things in what in a given time and place may be legible as facts' (2004: 13). Peter, a surgeon originally from Australia and now living in Newcastle, believed that people respond differently to information (about cultural difference) that they encounter in a museum compared to other media:

I think it's because it adds a more 3-dimensional feel to it and, well, there's something in front of me that's 500, 1000, whatever, years old. And it generates interest to go away and look at perhaps the historical facts. It generates your own interest in certain areas rather than a lot of the forms of media which are putting the statistics forward in a way that they're trying to tell you something – something that they want you to take away and it's very, well it's very 'constructed' in that way. To an extent, that's the case here [St Mungo's] as well, but I think it's more of an overall presentation of a number of different things which are definitely fact and you've got some physical items as well and you can take away from that what you want, so it's not so constructed.

Megan, a receptionist visiting the Anne Frank House with her family from England, similarly suggests that the museum's capacity for physical encounters with material objects lends it greater impact than other media:

to see her diary, her writing, was great and to see the actual marks on the wall where their heights are and the little map of the Allied invasion, I think that's very good, interesting, and it does mean more when it's actually there in front of you, when you're in the building. It's always better, I think, particularly for children, to actually see things rather than having to read it through a book, I think it's harder. Television's good, isn't it? They've all got their own way of giving information, but I think it sticks in your mind more when you actually see it ... to see the little height chart and Anne's writing and little drawings and the pictures on the wall, I think that means a lot more, I think it stays in your memory more.

Although audience responses suggest that museums, through the display of the 'real', are capable of both stimulating powerful affective responses in visitors and also providing the physical evidence or 'proof' to support their asseverative authenticity claims, they are not the only medium to make such assertions. Roger Silverstone suggests that museums and television share many characteristics as media. He points out that, not only do museums very often combine real with replica objects but that television (particularly in those programmes that concern themselves with real life such as documentaries and news programmes) also makes claims to present reality; claims which audiences generally accept in much the same way as they do for museums (Silverstone 1988: 233). Macdonald and Silverstone (1990) subsequently make the point that museums have faced challenges to their authenticity claims from other media. They argue that the capability of television to place objects within their 'natural' settings (for example, through contexts of production or use) may offer viewers a more faithful and genuine representation than museums, especially those which display objects taxonomically rather than in (simulated) 'natural' contexts. Similarly, they suggest that theme parks offer audiences experiences which engage a range of senses, potentially heightening perceptions of 'realness', whereas museums have traditionally relied primarily on visual experiences. These challenges have led museums to adopt new approaches to display (for example, the development of multisensory, experiential and interactive exhibitions) in attempting to reassert their authenticity claims. Nevertheless, many visitors to both St Mungo's and the Anne Frank House spontaneously cited trustworthiness as a means to contrast museums favourably with television and other media, a point to which I return shortly.

Impartiality and bias

A large number of interviewees at both sites used words such as 'unbiased' and 'balanced' to describe the museum, frequently contrasting it favourably with other media sources perceived to be more partisan. Betty, a retired teacher from Colorado, said, 'And things in a newspaper can be biased, you have to understand that. Here, they try to throw up both sides of the issue', whilst Eunice from Bradford commented that, in St Mungo's, 'You get a bit more of both sides here. Sometimes some of the TV programmes are quite one sided but you can see it from both sides here.'

These comments suggest a hierarchy of trust in which different media are positioned by audiences according to their reliability as knowledge providers – a hierarchy in which museums appear to hold a relatively privileged position. It seems likely that the relative positions within such a hierarchy will determine the degree to which filters are deployed by audience members to counter perceived bias. Indeed, research into mass media supports the view that audiences are aware of, and sensitive to, perceived subjectivity of media. As media theorist Denis McQuail (1997: 106) argues:

> audiences are sensitive to the quality of media on grounds of political bias and fairness, often placing more emphasis on impartiality and reliability than on the media's own rights to freedom of expression ... Audiences can often seem intolerant of the public expression in the mainstream media of extreme or deviant political views. The norms applied by the audience to media information commonly refer to completeness and accuracy, balance and diversity of opinion. News sources are often judged according to their relative credibility.

Though many audience responses suggest that museums are a relatively trusted media source, that is not to suggest that visitors are uncritical in their consumption. The potential for challenging the museum's claims to truthfulness are more than evident in the oppositional readings discussed in earlier chapters. These challenges, or questioning, of the museum's objectivity and impartiality appear to be most readily prompted when the museum's perceived position clashes with strongly held personal beliefs and experiences. For example, a visitor to St Mungo's on 26 September 2001 wrote the following comments:

> As a strong Christian myself, I see your representation of Christianity not 100% truthful. Based more on the Catholic religion and not the love of Jesus Christ. This makes me question whether other religions portrayed are correct. The articles collected are interesting.

Similarly, in the following extract from the comments book at the Anne Frank House on 10 April 2003, one visitor draws on their own personal experiences to mount a challenge to the museum's impartiality:

> This museum is a very powerful and moving testimony to what happened to a young, innocent schoolgirl. Your attempt at dealing with the dilemmas we face where freedom of speech versus the right to protection from discrimination is creative yet you have succumbed to lack of objectivity in your portrayal of the issues. The issue that I find most disturbing is that of Israeli and Palestinian rights. You make a very strong and clear opinion – Israeli policy is inherently wrong and it is unfair to mix Israeli policy and anti-Semitism. As an Israeli who worries daily whether or not she, her family, friends and country mates will make it through the day with terror claiming more victims, I am glad that my country has the tanks this time around and no-one will force me or my family to hide in an attic in the face of any Arab or otherwise enemy. Never again!

Overall, I would argue that these comments suggest that the museum's perceived authority, though open to challenge and by no means wholly determining of audience interpretations, nevertheless provides a powerful framework for the way in which many approach their museum experience. This, I shall further contend, places certain responsibilities on museums – responsibilities for the ways in which they represent and engage with difference which many museums remain reluctant to acknowledge and act upon. However, before developing these arguments, it is useful firstly to consider the growing interest amongst practitioners in playing with, sharing and, in some instances, perhaps subverting this authority.

Playing with exhibitionary conventions

In Corinne Kratz's exhibition of Okiek portraits she sought not only to subvert stereotypes associated with the people who were the subject of the exhibition but also to pose questions for visitors about the authority claims of museums by attempting to render more visible the assumptions that are implicit in the exhibition-making process. These intentions revealed a paradox, as she explains: 'There was a tension between my two goals ... because exhibitionary authority underwrote the exhibition's challenge of stereotypes at the same time that I sought to question it' (2002: 92). These tensions can similarly be detected in the exhibitions presented by St Mungo's and the Anne Frank House and in the practices of museums more broadly. Museums are increasingly experimenting with the conventions of exhibiting in ways which may potentially dilute or undermine the authority associated with traditional modes of display. Two particular strategies evident in both case studies and increasingly utilised by museums more generally are relevant here.

Firstly, the widely discussed move away from a single curatorial narrative to polyvocal exhibitions in which diverse constituencies have a voice is one such strategy. In some instances, different voices provide diverse but complementary perspectives which might together be taken to produce a relatively unified institutional position. The support, in broadly consensual terms, of different faiths for the museum's central mission of generating mutual respect and understanding at St Mungo's is one example of this. In other instances, different voices provide competing, even oppositional, viewpoints on the same topic such as the purposefully biased perspectives arguing for 'freedom of expression' and 'protection from discrimination' in the *Out of Line* exhibition. Here, the overt use of opinion successfully highlights the contestable nature of concepts related to human rights for many visitors but may also result in a weakening of institutional authority. Several visitors distinguished between the *Out of Line* exhibition, which they felt contained a specific, purposeful message, and the remainder of the House which they felt was, in contrast, largely unbiased. For example, Nathalie, a computer technician from Germany, stated:

> [In a museum] it's more neutral because you're not led to a certain opinion except for maybe some of the films here but in the main part of the museum about Anne Frank you're shown facts and then you can make up your mind and I thought it was a good way to do it, not to influence people from the beginning but just to show what it was like.

The second way in which museums are playing with exhibitionary conventions, in ways which are likely to impact upon the authority relations between museum and visitor, concerns the attempts not only to encourage visitors to respond to displays but also to enable them to share their views through the incorporation of responses into the exhibition itself. Here, I am referring to the ways in which visitors' comments cards are displayed within the main exhibition galleries at St Mungo's and visitors' responses to scenarios in *Out of Line* are publicly shared in the form of illuminated bars on the ceiling. This strategy, it might be argued, validates the views and opinions of the visitor, blurring the boundaries between the perceived expertise of the museum and the personal opinions of visitors.

Although the deployment of less didactic modes of interpretation which bend exhibitionary conventions may have implications for audience reception, the cultural authority of the museum has nevertheless proved to be relatively enduring in many contexts. Ken Arnold, for example, describes attempts in an exhibition at the Wellcome Institute in London to disrupt perceived notions of a singular curatorial authority through the presentation of juxtaposing perspectives. Despite this purposeful strategy, 'the exhibition was often not regarded in this way because the institutional context itself suggested a didactic and authoritative stance – "the Wellcome" was assumed to be presenting some kind of definitive, authoritative picture' (1998: 192).

Authority may be undermined not only through the museum's use of unconventional, unfamiliar and discomforting interpretation *strategies* but also through exhibition *content* and *messages* which are perceived to flout the norms of acceptability applied by audiences. This is an important issue to which we shall return in the concluding chapter.

Conclusion

I have so far argued that the resources of the museum are taken up by visitors in various ways and, along with other media resources, prior experiences and beliefs, help to shape their interpretations of cultural difference. Indeed, the qualities visitors attribute to the museum as a medium – trustworthiness, reliability, the capacity to 'tell the truth' – and the potential for museum visiting to be an especially active mode of consumption, together position the museum as a relatively efficacious and highly valued provider of resources within the mediascape. Visitors' interpretations and negotiations of cultural difference can be detected in the performative output of individuals – the comments and conversations in written and verbal form that are stimulated by the exhibition encounter – which are, in turn, viewed by others within the spaces of the museum. Museum audiences are simultaneously performers (for themselves and others) continuously making and remaking their interpretations both through engagement with exhibitions and through social interactions with companions and strangers.

These complex processes, and the discursive outputs they produce, are shaped at a local level by the museum in which they are enacted. However, their effect is not locally confined but rather extends beyond the museum in various ways. Visitors take their experiences away with them and may utilise them in other settings. Here the resources from the museum may interact with other media forms and the resources – both competing and complementary

– which they offer. This suggests that the museum's role in combating prejudice should be understood in the broader context of the mediascape in which people are immersed. In their wide-ranging media consumption, individuals will encounter a diverse array of resources, each of which potentially supports and enables alternative ways of viewing, thinking and talking about difference. However, as I have argued in this chapter, the museum as a provider of resources has certain characteristics which suggest that it plays a significant role in supporting, validating and promulgating interpretations of difference; interpretations that, in many instances, draw on concepts and values that are privileged within exhibitions. These may potentially counter the effects of media resources that might be considered prejudicial or illiberal, that draw on and reinforce negative stereotypical representations of different communities and which enhance inter-community conflict.

The influence of museums also leaks out beyond the micro-interactional processes stimulated by the visitor–exhibition encounter in other ways. Exhibitions and the messages inscribed within them are dispersed not only through attendance by visitors but also through media coverage, promotional materials and other forms of communication. The larger and most prestigeful museums in particular are likely to 'reach' (in various ways) much wider audiences than those indicated by exhibition attendance alone. As Corinne Kratz states:

> Exhibits are not only sites where politics of representation can be debated, but places where they are also developed and disseminated – through visitor interactions, conversations, press reviews, influences on future exhibitions, and other traces that stretch far beyond the exhibition itself. Such development and dissemination can transform the politics of representation and their uneven terrains.
>
> (2002: 96)

Unravelling the influence of museums from other media forms, in both framing individual visitors' interpretations and contributing more broadly to social change through the shaping of norms of acceptability and tolerance, is almost impossible. However, growing interest in museums as sites for cross-cultural dialogue and as settings in which interventions designed to counter prejudices experienced by marginalised communities can be staged, suggests that they are increasingly viewed as loci for the (re)framing of society's conversations about difference.[5]

If, as I have argued, museums hold a significant and privileged position as institutional agents in the combating of prejudice, what obligations and responsibilities does this place on them? What kinds of frameworks – moral, legal, normative – might museums draw upon to navigate the rapidly shifting and inherently problematic terrain of the politics of difference? How can museums respond to conflicts between locally situated norms of acceptability and tolerance and abstracted, universal concepts of equity and social justice? How are the cherished museum ideals of balance and objectivity challenged by a discourse of human rights?

I address these questions with reference to a range of museum examples in the concluding chapter but firstly turn attention to the challenges inherent in attempts by museum practitioners to offer alternative ways of seeing and understanding disability. Drawing on a different body of empirical research – a study that set out to explore the ways in which disabled people are represented in museums – I shall consider, in the following chapter, the particular dilemmas bound up with the staging of interventions that seek to counter prejudices based on physical differences.

6

DISPLAYING DIFFERENCE
Revealing and interpreting the hidden history of disability

> the meanings attributed to extraordinary bodies reside
> not in inherent physical flaws, but in social relation-
> ships in which one group is legitimated by possessing
> valued physical characteristics and maintains its
> ascendancy and its self-identity by systematically
> imposing the role of cultural or corporeal inferiority
> on others. Representation ... simultaneously buttresses
> an embodied version of normative identity and shapes
> a narrative of corporeal difference that excludes those
> whose bodies or behaviours do not conform.
>
> (Garland Thomson 1997: 7)

The chapters thus far have focused predominantly on issues of reception
and consumption exploring the variable, but not wholly unpatterned, ways
in which diverse audiences respond to, engage with and construct meaning
from exhibitions designed to counter prejudice. These dynamic processes
have been explored, for the most part, within the context of museums that
explicitly position themselves – through their missions, goals and practices
– as agents of social change. This chapter extends discussion of the social
agency of museums in rather different directions. Moving away from the
audience, it focuses instead on questions of production – on the museum
processes and practices associated with exhibition-making and representation. Moreover, it draws principally on research that has been undertaken
within a range of museums that, taken together, can be considered rather
more typical of the sector at large than those more specialised museums that
have so far formed the focus of this study. Finally, whilst the discussion thus
far has examined wide-ranging prejudices, purposefully avoiding a narrower
focus, this chapter takes disability (and associated prejudice based on perceptions of physical differences) as a lens through which to explore the particular
dilemmas that exhibition makers might encounter in their attempts to engage
audiences in the task of recasting individual and collective understandings
of difference. It considers the scope for wide-ranging collections – of fine

and decorative art, social history, costume, ethnography and so on – to yield material that might support interventions, or trans-coding strategies (Hall 1997),[1] intended to counter prejudice, by contesting or subverting what Stuart Hall terms the 'dominant regime of representation'; a regime which, I shall argue, undergirds negative and stigmatising understandings of disability in many contemporary Western societies. For Hall, a regime of representation refers to 'the whole repertoire of imagery and visual effects through which "difference" is represented at any one historical moment' (1997: 232). A given regime may be composed of heterogeneous and shifting depictions of difference but, at particular moments, can be understood to take on a dominant character. Hall, for example, describes how a particular regime of representation can be seen across different periods comprising wide-ranging depictions of black people and representational practices which 'have been used to mark racial difference and signify the racialized "Other" in western popular culture' (ibid.: 239).

The arguments I have so far put forward are premised upon (and have attempted to extend and evidence) the idea that museums possess constitutive or generative capacities – the potential to shape, rather than simply reflect, social relations and realities. Museum displays, and the discourses of difference they embody, have social effects and consequences. The poetics and politics of exhibition practice have often combined to shape, reproduce and concretise dominant (negative) understandings of difference, by excluding and marginalising (through elision) or by constructing representations that are reductive and essentialising, discriminatory and oppressive. By casting racial, gender, physical and other 'variations' as inferior or deviant, museums have privileged ways of seeing that have made prejudiced understandings of difference more perceptible and permissible, that close off, rather than open up, possibilities for mutual understanding, respect and social justice.

Building on these concepts of social agency, this chapter explores ways in which museums might also operate as sites for the staging of interventions designed to confront, undercut or reshape dominant regimes of representation that underpin and inform contemporary attitudes towards disability. These interventions, or counter-strategies, are based on the assumption that meaning is never fixed but rather in flux and always open to change, however pervasive and persistent dominant representational strategies might be. Counter-strategies can be deployed to destabilise existing meanings and to surface new ones enabling 'different things to be shown and said' (ibid.: 270). Through displays which contain protean and nuanced interpretations of difference, which mitigate, complicate or subvert prevalent stereotypes, which elicit (and frame) visitor responses and which enable (and inform) society's conversations, museums can offer alternative, non-prejudiced ways of seeing.

This chapter addresses a number of questions. How might such purposive displays be created and what dilemmas and challenges are curators, educators, designers and other actors in the exhibition-making process, likely to encounter along the way? In particular, what approaches might be deployed to interrogate and mine existing collections to investigate the histories of disability and disabled people to identify material evidence that might be marshalled to play a part in countering prejudice? How might museums, including those that have not traditionally viewed themselves as agents of change, draw on their collections (generally amassed and arranged according to very different agendas and criteria) to develop displays that attempt to reframe the ways in which society perceives disability?

I begin by considering the particular inflections inherent in prejudice directed towards disabled people to begin to suggest the most appropriate forms that interventions and counter-strategies within museums might take. The ways in which museums have most often understood and engaged with disability and their relationships with disabled people are then outlined to provide further context. The main body of the chapter discusses the findings from a recent project undertaken by the Research Centre for Museums and Galleries (RCMG) at the University of Leicester[2] which set out to explore wide-ranging collections in institutions in the UK to uncover the 'hidden history' of disability and to identify material evidence that might be (re)interpreted to offer new liberatory narrative forms. The chapter concludes by discussing some of the interpretive dilemmas which exhibition-makers might face in seeking to develop representational counter-strategies intended to offer audiences alternative ways of understanding, thinking and talking about disability.

Specificities of prejudice

Different forms of prejudice, as I described in chapter 2, share in common a number of features. Expressions of prejudice are directed at those who are perceived to be not only *different* but also (though in distinctive ways) *inferior* or *deviant*. Whether blatant or covert, prejudiced discourses of all kinds (regardless of the particular targets at which they are directed) are both *functional* and *purposive*. They are designed and meted out to achieve certain ends; to blame or to justify discriminatory actions and behaviour, to exclude or to marginalise, to intimidate or to belittle, and so on. Moreover, specific prejudices very often mobilise distinctive stereotypes to achieve their purposes. Representations of difference in diverse media forms have often been characterised as prejudiced by virtue of their reliance on (and perpetuation of) a limited and limiting repertoire of demeaning stereotypes that offer reductive and essentialising conceptions of marginalised and oppressed groups.

Whilst diverse forms of prejudice have these features in common, specific manifestations, directed at particular groups, are nevertheless distinctively inflected. For example, in their recent study of attitudes towards a range of minorities in England, Gill Valentine and Ian McDonald found that prejudice directed towards asylum seekers was most often couched in economic terms. Asylum seekers were frequently perceived to be undeserving recipients of preferential treatment for housing and welfare benefits. Attitudes towards transsexuals and transgendered people were most often characterised by 'tolerance born out of pity' and a lack of respect for these groups was very often demonstrated through laughter. Prejudice expressed towards minority ethnic groups was complex and contradictory. British Asian people[3] were sometimes praised for their 'hard working and family values' but were simultaneously perceived as being unwilling and unable to integrate with white people. Black British people were more commonly perceived as 'being good at integrating with white people and as sharing similar social and cultural values' (ibid.: 12). However, these perceptions were also accompanied by negatively stereotypical views, especially of young black men, who were frequently associated by interviewees with drugs and other criminal activity.

These inflections are, to varying degrees, situated and dynamic and are likely to vary significantly across different cultural contexts and through time. Depending on the individuals or groups at which they are targeted, and the social, political and economic contexts within which they are expressed, particular forms of prejudice are therefore fluid, differentially motivated and couched in variable ways. The shifting nature of prejudice has been noted in a number of different contexts but has been most fully explored in the context of evolving forms of racism. The 1970s and 1980s, for example, saw the emergence in the United States of the terms 'symbolic' or 'modern' racism to describe the more subtle, covert and indirectly expressed views, actions and behaviours which, researchers argued, were replacing 'traditional' or old-fashioned racism which was characterised as 'blunt, hostile, segregationist and supremacist' (Walker 2001: 26).[4] Catherine Kudlick's (2003) review of recently published research concerned with disability similarly highlights the contingent and contextual nature of attitudes towards disabled people. Although most of the work she reviews is based on research in Western Europe and North America, the inclusion of a study of images of blindness and blind people in a medieval Islamic society both brings into sharp relief and challenges many of the assumptions about disability that prevail in the West.

Despite this fluidity, and mindful of the situational character of prejudice, it is nevertheless possible to identify some of the features commonly associated with negative conceptions of disability. What characteristics are inherent in prejudiced discourse motivated by perceptions of physical differences? What stereotypes of disabled people are most prevalent and widely deployed in representational practices across different media? In what ways are these used and for what ends? Addressing these questions, I shall draw largely on literature from Western Europe and North America to highlight some of the characteristics of prevalent attitudes to disability although some of those identified will resonate within other contexts.

Disablism

Although there are terms, in relatively widespread usage, which refer to forms of prejudice (or related pernicious, stigmatising conceptions of difference) based on race (racism), gender (sexism and misogyny), sexuality (homophobia and, less commonly, heterosexism), there is no universally accepted label for prejudice on the basis of disability (Kudlick 2003). This omission is perhaps especially surprising given the significance, in raw numbers alone, of disability as a social category. Although definitions are problematic, it is estimated that nearly one in five Americans (Kudlick 2003) and one in seven people in Britain (Disability Rights Commission) are disabled. Catherine Kudlick points out that, in the US, whilst the term 'ablism' is coming into increasing usage it is often 'tinged with the sarcasm people reserve for politically correct expressions such as "physically challenged" and "differently abled"' (ibid.: 771). In Britain, the term disablism, although similarly marginalised in academic and popular discourse has, in recent years, begun to be used more widely. Although its precise definition is contested (as with other terms to describe specific forms of prejudice) a recent report uses disablism to refer to 'discriminatory, oppressive or abusive behaviour arising from the belief that disabled people are inferior to others' (Miller et al. 2004: 9). The absence of a commonly used term to describe prejudice motivated by perceptions of bodily difference reflects the wider marginality of disability as a subject of critical inquiry; a situation which disability studies scholars in recent years have highlighted and begun to redress. It further reflects the unease which continues to surround disability as a topic of everyday conversation. As Snyder et al. suggest: 'Just as sex was the ubiquitous unspoken subject in the Victorian world, disability – the harbinger of mortality – is the ubiquitous unspoken topic in contemporary culture' (2002: 2).

Prejudice directed at disabled people, some have argued, is less commonly expressed with the malevolence and vitriol that other groups may experience. 'Unlike racial, ethnic and sexual minorities', Kudlick argues, 'disabled people experience attacks cloaked in pity accompanied by a widely held perception that no one wishes them ill' (2003: 768). Indeed, many people are perhaps unlikely to view their benevolence towards disabled people as constituting prejudice. In their study, cited above, Valentine and McDonald found that no interviewees openly acknowledged that they held prejudiced attitudes based on disability and many expressed support for an equality agenda (especially in relation to service provision) for disabled people. However, the language respondents used to talk about disabled people was especially revealing. Many focused on notions of help and care reflecting, as the researchers argue, 'the way that disabled people are implicitly regarded as lacking competence, vulnerable, and deserving of pity' (2004: 10). Although interviewees in their study had generally had greater personal contact with disabled people than with other minorities, many participants nevertheless expressed concern about their own language and behaviour. One woman from London, in her mid twenties, stated:

> My brain automatically goes on to the things you shouldn't do, and the things that you've been told are bad to do to people with disabilities. I get paranoid that I am going to do one of those things, or that I'm going to be obviously referring to this checklist of things that I shouldn't do. I can't just act naturally as much as that's what I want to do.
>
> (ibid.: 11)

These comments are illustrative of broader anxieties that reflect unease and discomfort with the idea of disability. As Rosemarie Garland Thomson, describing the encounter between a disabled and non-disabled person, notes: 'The interaction is usually strained because the non-disabled person may feel fear, pity, fascination, repulsion, or merely surprise, none of which is expressible according to social protocol' (1997: 12). Though distinct from other forms of prejudice in several respects, the *effects* of disablism are no less debilitating than those that may be delivered in more hateful and malevolent terms. Disablism, many have powerfully argued, operates to close off opportunities for disabled people in all aspects of everyday life.

The supercripple, the victim and the villain: stereotypical representations of disabled people

> Any casual visitor to museums in Britain would assume that disabled people occupied a specific range of roles in the nation's history. The absence of disabled people as creators of arts, in images and in artefacts, and their presence in selected works reinforcing cultural stereotypes, conspire to present a narrow perspective of the existence of disability in history.
>
> (Delin 2002: 84)

Stereotypes, as I discussed in chapter 2, feature in representational strategies across wide-ranging media and are mobilised in ways which very often support and reinforce prejudiced ways of seeing, thinking and talking about difference. Stereotypes give emphasis to a few distinguishing traits at the expense of complexity, constructing reductive and essentialising understandings of social groups. Wide-ranging studies that have investigated the representation of disabled people in literature, film, television, advertising and other mass media have frequently highlighted the prevalence of recurring stereotypes which are suffused with notions of pity, fear, revulsion and deviance. As Katherine Ott has observed, 'Most interpretations of disability rely in some way upon a handful of stereotypes that include the tragic victim, super cripple or maniacal villain (driven to evil by the misfortune of an unbearable disability)' (2005a: 13).

Early discussion of representation concerned the appearance of disabled people in literature. In 1987, Kriegel proposed stereotypes including the 'demonic cripple' and the 'charity cripple', while Holden (1991) examined the roles taken by disabled people in the Bible. In 1992, Colin Barnes and David Hevey both published influential works looking at the relationship between media representation and the creation and perpetuation of stereotypes. Barnes examined wide-ranging media (citing literature, film, television, radio and news media) and found twelve recurrent stereotypes which included disabled person as curio, as 'supercripple' and as pitiable or pathetic. Hevey (1992) focused on photography used in charity advertising to show how these purposefully constructed images carried messages designed to generate a preordained response in the generally non-disabled audience (understood to be the charity donor). Thus, Hevey studied the use of focus, colour, grain and props to create images of disabled people which suggested infantilism, dependence, passivity and need.[5] More recently, Rosemarie Garland Thomson, in her powerful analysis of literary texts, highlights the ways in which representational strategies have consistently served to construct the disabled figure not simply as exceptional or extraordinary but rather as deficient, inferior or deviant. 'From folktales and classical myths to modern and postmodern "grotesques,"' she argues, 'the disabled body is almost always a freakish spectacle presented by the mediating narrative voice. Most disabled characters are enveloped by the otherness that their disability signals in the text' (1997: 10). Not all of the persistent stereotypes of disabled people that have been highlighted are necessarily overtly demeaning. There are many examples of the representation of disabled people as heroes who, through their heroism and emphasis on their outstanding achievements, transcend the experience of disability and, in some cases, effectively 'pass' as 'honorary non-disabled' persons.

Empirical studies of representation and stereotyping have focused, for the most part, on processes of production (on the ways in which ideas about disability have been inscribed and encoded within diverse media forms) rather than those associated with reception and consumption (the ways in which diverse audiences – disabled and non-disabled – have decoded and otherwise responded to and constructed meaning from the stereotypical representations they encounter). Although there may be relatively limited empirical evidence concerning the social effects of distorted depictions of disabled people in the media, the symbolic power of representational strategies (in particular, their agency in shaping public perceptions and expectations of disabled people) has generated considerable discussion within the disciplines of disability and cultural studies. Moreover, there has been a strongly expressed view among disabled people that media representation has played, and continues to play, a significant (and negative) role in shaping their lives and the opportunities that are open to them. Colin Barnes (1992: 2), for example, has spoken of 'a growing awareness among disabled people that the problems they encounter are due to institutional discrimination and that media distortions of the experience of disability contribute significantly to the discriminatory process'. Referring to the effects of literary representations, Rosemarie Garland Thompson similarly argues that 'Because disability is so strongly stigmatized and is countered by so few mitigating narratives, the literary traffic in metaphors often misrepresents or flattens the experience real people have of their own or others' disabilities' (1997: 10).

This brief consideration of disability prejudice begins to suggest some of the possible approaches that might be taken by museums in developing interpretive interventions designed to construct new cultural narratives that undermine dominant negative understandings of disabled people. Before exploring these more fully, however, it is useful briefly to review the ways in which museums have most often viewed and engaged with the notion of disability. How have museums typically responded to imperatives presented by the disability civil rights movement and associated political agendas? To what extent have museums engaged with issues related to the representation of disabled people in their collections, displays and exhibitions?

Museums and disability

Museums have become increasingly sensitised to the topic of disability over the last two decades, although in very selective ways. Disabled people have been conceived almost entirely as (under-represented, potential) audiences, who must be accommodated through the implementation of strategies designed to increase access to museum buildings and exhibitions. Whilst legislative drivers for change have ensured that questions of physical (and to a lesser extent, sensory) access for disabled visitors have remained firmly on the agenda for many museums, rather less attention has been paid to other questions posed by disability.[6]

Janice Majewski and Lonnie Bunch (1998) describe three distinct tiers of disability access that museums should address in developing exhibitions that meet the needs of their audiences. The first tier, which they term 'access to the exhibition's physical elements', is concerned with enabling visitors

145

to gain entry to the museum building itself and to navigate successfully through and around exhibitions. This level of access encompasses those elements which most readily spring to mind for museum professionals when questions of disability are raised – the visible 'hardware' of access, such as the provision of lifts, ramps, handrails and accessible toilets. The second tier they consider is 'access to the exhibition's content' which requires an acknowledgment that visitors experience displays in different ways. 'In exhibitions', they argue:

> museums must give consideration to issues that range from label legibility to label text comprehension; from video captions and audio description to multiple levels of understanding and enjoy-ment of the exhibition's themes and content. Accessibility to content means accessibility to the written word, the objects, the media presentations, and the interactives.
>
> (ibid.: 156)

Although some museums have made significant progress in this area, others have barely begun. This unevenness in provision is powerfully illustrated in Catherine Kudlick's (2005) personal account of the experiences of visiting a local history museum and neighbouring fine arts museum in a major American city. As a person with a visual impairment visiting museums with a blind companion, Kudlick describes the multiple barriers – physical, sensory, attitudinal – to gaining access at one venue compared with the much more positive experience at the other. Having described the unhelpful, even hostile responses of staff at the local history museum to her enquiries about facilities for visually impaired visitors, Kudlick reflects on the impact of disability legislation and highlights the need for further change:

> Why is it that when America seems eager to open its civic places to the broadest possible audience, certain public institutions appear so ill-informed about people who require alternative ways to fully participate? Here we are, at a time when the [Americans with Disabilities Act] has been in effect for over a decade, people with disabilities have seen the promise of increased social awareness and powerful technology, and a generation of people like the women in the [local history] museum have grown up in large urban centers pouring money into their civic places. And yet in the early twenty-first century, two people still couldn't visit this museum on the spur of the moment or at the very least encounter employees sensitized enough to treat them with anything but contempt. Why is it that some people view visitors like us as problems rather than as opportunities to present exhibitions in new and interesting ways?
>
> (2005: 78)

The third tier of access described by Majewski and Bunch is concerned with the representation of disabled people and the inclusion of disability-related narratives and interpretation within exhibitions. This, they argue, has been almost entirely overlooked.

Representing disability

Museums in many parts of the world have become increasingly preoccupied with the challenges associated with representing (at least some forms of) cultural difference within their collections and displays. This concern has been especially marked amongst museums in post-colonial contexts and those in societies which have undergone dramatic social, political and demographic changes. Countries and contexts vary in terms of the forms of difference that are acknowledged as legitimate (and therefore deserving of museums' attention) but might include group identities defined in terms of gender, ethnicity, sexuality, nationality, disability, religion, age and so on. Museums then have faced increasing pressure to reform, to reinvent themselves as agents of inclusion and to accommodate, through display, multiple forms of difference. Despite widespread rhetorical support for the notion of representing diversity and a growing body of research concerned with the poetics and politics of representing and working with previously excluded or marginalised groups, museum practice nevertheless remains selective and uneven. On the one hand, for example, it has become increasingly unacceptable for public museums in many contexts to present exhibitions which overtly perpetuate negative racist stereotypes or for major city museums to persist in sidelining the contributions of minority ethnic groups that have had an established presence in the community for many decades. On the other hand, it has been argued that change is both too slow and too slight. Jane Morris, for example, in a newspaper article published to coincide with the start of Black History Month in the UK in October 2004, wrote: 'Few British museums tell the story of black or Asian people in anything but the most cursory fashion'. Similarly, Bourne (1996), Liddiard (2004) and Vanegas (2002) highlight the very limited display of material that relates to gay and lesbian lives.

It is only relatively recently that the representation in museum exhibitions of disability and disabled people's lives has begun to receive much attention, and two distinct but interlinked concerns can be identified. The first refers to the absence or invisibility of disabled people within most museums' displays. There is growing support for the view that, by neglecting to depict bodily difference in their exhibition narratives, museums not only reify the idealised human form but, in doing so, present a historically inaccurate view of the past. As Katherine Ott suggests:

147

The ideal which we imagine in history is unquestionably able-bodied ... People present a spectrum of body types, and until recent decades, the most common physical traits included being arthritic, stooped, pock-marked, scarred, toothless, or bent and injured in some way. Difference was everywhere, yet it is missing from the history we present to the public. The healthy, idealized figures in exhibits, films, and re-enactment are as false as the landscaped and manicured grounds of a Civil War battlefield.[7]

(2005a: 21)

The second concern relates to the extent to which museums' depictions of disabled people – where they do exist – rely on (and reinforce) the limited range of negative stereotypes found in other media forms. What part do museums play in buttressing the dominant regime of representation in relation to disability?

Buried in the Footnotes

These linked concerns provided the impetus for a major research project, *Buried in the Footnotes*, undertaken by RCMG between 2003 and 2004. The project set out to address a deficit in knowledge and understanding around the hidden history of disability by investigating museum collections and displays in the UK to identify evidence attesting to the lives of disabled people. It further aimed to identify and examine curatorial practices and other factors which may have contributed to historical and contemporary under- or mis-representation of disabled people. Though based on fieldwork across collections in the UK, the findings of the project, as I shall argue in due course, have relevance and implications for museums internationally.

Research aims and methodology

The rationale for the research grew out of earlier preliminary investigations undertaken by Annie Delin which had suggested that museum collections may hold material that could attest to the lives of disabled people but that this was only relatively rarely displayed and then only in particular, most often stereotypical, ways. Delin (2002) had argued that disability history qualified as a hidden history using a definition proposed by Anne Laurence:

The term Hidden History is used when the history of a hitherto neglected group begins to appear: as, for example, in the case of black history, women's history, lesbian and gay history ... The phrase is not simply used to describe the group's emergence into mainstream history: it also has an explicit message that these groups have lacked a history because society has been unwilling to see them as a separate group with particular rights. Groups hidden from history are hidden for three reasons. They are hidden because of prejudices against the group in the past, because of modern prejudices; and because of the absence of records.

(Laurence 1994: 3)

Building on Delin's hypothesis, the research team developed a project underpinned by the idea that, if museum collections held the hidden history of disabled people, they might potentially be viewed as resources with which to contribute to a reframing of the ways in which contemporary society viewed disability. The project then set out to explore a number of questions. In particular, what evidence exists within museum collections and associated documentation that relates to the lives of disabled people, both historical and contemporary? How, if at all, has this evidence been interpreted, displayed or otherwise made accessible to the public? If so, within what categories have disabled people been represented? What factors, historical and contemporary, have affected the way in which information about the lives of disabled people (linked to material held in museums) has been collected, documented and made publicly available? Finally, what factors influence, or have influenced, curators' attitudes towards this information and its dissemination?

Buried in the Footnotes used a mixture of quantitative and qualitative methods to address these questions. Befitting the exploratory nature of the investigations, our approach was open and flexible. Project funding from the Innovation Awards scheme administered by the UK's Arts and Humanities Research Board was especially significant in this respect, as it enabled us to approach the field with the possibility of failure (for example, finding few objects linked to disability) and to allow for unexpected outcomes which could then be explored and tested in the process of research. Importantly, the project team was composed of both disabled and non-disabled researchers with different experiences, specialist knowledge and insight – of disability, of museums and of research methods. Researchers with disabilities played a central role both in shaping the research agenda and in gathering, analysing and interpreting the data.

The primary research consisted of two main stages. First, a self-completion questionnaire (see appendix 2) was sent to a sample of curators to achieve variety in terms of geographical distribution, mode of governance, size of organisation and collection type (including fine and decorative art, social history, archaeology, local, industrial, maritime, medical and military history). The questionnaire had two main objectives: first, to identify levels of awareness amongst curators of the existence of relevant material within collections and to gauge their attitudes towards its collection, documentation and interpretation and, second, to identify a shortlist of appropriate case studies for the next (qualitative) phase of the research.

Two hundred and twenty-four questionnaires were distributed and seventy-three were returned, a response rate which was higher than expected. (Some curators who did not submit completed questionnaires nevertheless contacted us to give their reasons for non-participation which included shortage of staff time and resources, existing commitments to recataloguing or redisplay and temporary museum closure.) Of those who did respond, twenty-nine stated that they would be willing to be involved in further research as a case study museum. From these, ten case studies were subsequently selected[8] to include a variety of organisation types. In addition to size, geography, mode of governance and collection types, we wanted to include known examples of good practice, museums with a potentially 'obvious' connection to disability (such as medical or military connections), and also an example of a museum that had stated in its questionnaire return that it held nothing relevant to the project within its collections. Each case study was visited by members of the research team, interviews were conducted with curators and other staff, displays were reviewed and collections databases were searched for relevant objects. The database searches used a wide range of search terms (many of which might be perceived as offensive in a contemporary context but were nevertheless widely used in the past), to see if this would elicit new information about possible relevant objects in the collection. The key search terms used were: disabled, disability, blind, deaf, lame, surgical, cripple, dwarf, giant, lunatic and invalid. Additional search words were used where relevant to the collection type, including adapted, altered, crutch and peg-leg.

A key element of the research process was a colloquium, following completion of fieldwork and data analysis, bringing together knowledgeable commentators from a number of fields to assist us in interpreting the significance of our findings, to generate new insights into the material we had identified and to test our preliminary conclusions. Participants from different constituencies were selected to participate – disabled people with an interest in cultural practice or issues of representation, the museums profession (at curatorial and directorial level), research communities, and strategic bodies (for example, MLA: the Council for Museums, Libraries and Archives and the East Midlands Museums, Libraries and Archives Council). Our research generated a wealth of material and findings that addressed each of the research questions. For the purposes of this chapter, I intend to focus on those findings which relate primarily to the material we found within collections and their potential use in representational counter-strategies.

Identifying relevant objects

Buried in the Footnotes started with the premise that museum and gallery collections were likely to contain material attesting to the lives of disabled people or otherwise linked to disability. Although we had no idea of the nature, quantity, or condition of that material (or of the information attached to it that related to disability), our assumption was that there would be a certain amount of evidence to be found. We subsequently discovered that wide-ranging collections of all kinds did, indeed, contain a wealth of relevant material, in fact, on a much larger scale than we had originally anticipated. Our questionnaire asked curators: 'Are you aware of any material in your collections which relates to disability and/or the lives of disabled people?' To assist respondents, we provided some indication of the kinds of material that might be considered relevant including, for example, objects, clothing or personal items used or owned by disabled people; works of art or objects which portray disability as a feature or central topic; and art works or objects created by artists/makers who had a disability.

Of the seventy-three questionnaire respondents, whilst a high proportion (fifty-eight) identified some objects within their collections, the majority of these felt that they had only one or two items that would be deemed relevant for our research. Subsequent in-depth research with case study museums revealed many more objects than those initially identified by curators in their questionnaire responses. A number of factors were suggested which could account for the significantly higher number of objects identified during our visits compared with those identified via the questionnaires. Curators had time during the preparation for the visit to consider the issues raised and had usually identified some additional items before the researchers arrived. There was also time during the case study for curators to think about their collection in the light of this research. Moreover, the researchers brought subjectivities and specialist perspectives to bear on the investigation of collections and were able to identify items where the connection with disability was perhaps not so immediately apparent to a non-disabled curator. Finally, the wide-ranging search terms used to interrogate the databases (with which some museum staff were initially uncomfortable) revealed many of the additional items.

False teeth, spectacles and walking sticks

During the course of the research, a number of questions were raised by curators and subsequently discussed by the research team which linked to definitions of disability and the criteria which might be used to determine whether or not an object was deemed to be relevant to disability history. For example, what conditions or experiences were included within our definition of 'disability'? Whilst some impairments or bodily variations appeared to fall relatively straightforwardly into widely accepted understandings of disability, experiences of mental ill health, sickness and disease, war injury, and learning differences (such as dyslexia), for example, were deemed relatively more problematic, mirroring broader (and highly politicised) debates surrounding definitions within the disability world. Objects of contested relevance included walking sticks (which may have been used to aid mobility or simply as a fashion accessory) and false teeth and spectacles which, though commonplace today and not regarded as signifiers of disability, may have been differently perceived in the past.

Some curators also asked what relationship between an object and disability qualified it for inclusion within our study? For example, should objects collected and donated to the museum by a person known to be disabled but which otherwise bore no readily apparent relationship to disability be construed as relevant? Would we want to include a medal given to an (apparently non-disabled) lifeboat man for saving a crippled man's life?[9] Some of these concerns resonated with dilemmas posed by attempts to mine museum collections for material linked to the histories of other marginalised groups (such as those defined by ethnicity or sexuality) whilst others were especially pertinent to disability. In particular, the relative permeability and fluidity of the boundaries which distinguish disabled from non-disabled people (compared to those which may be used to define other marginal identities based on, for example, gender or ethnicity) emerged as especially salient. The dynamic and fuzzy character of the threshold between disabled and non-disabled identities has been similarly noted by Rosemarie Garland Thomson who contrasts the neatly defined disabled figure that often appears in literature with the more ambivalent experience of disability in real life:

> Even though the prototypical disabled person posited in cultural representations never leaves a wheelchair, is totally blind, or profoundly deaf, most of the approximately forty million Americans with disabilities have a much more ambiguous relationship to the label. The physical impairments that render someone 'disabled' are almost never absolute or static; they are dynamic, contingent conditions affected by many external factors and usually fluctuating over time ... The fact that we will all become disabled if we live long enough is a reality many people who consider themselves able-bodied are reluctant to admit.
>
> (1997: 13–14)

We were mindful of the potential sensitivities surrounding definitions of disability – for example, the emergence in recent years of an increasingly politicised social movement of the deaf who have preferred to view themselves, not as disabled but as 'a linguistic minority with distinct cultural and historical traditions' (Richardson 2002: 77) – but also of the potentially negative consequences that might arise from the application of tightly defined parameters. Following discussions within the research team and during the colloquium we eventually decided to resist the establishment of rigidly

Figure 6.1: Stumper Dryden by Frank Meadow Sutcliffe (1853–1941)

Source: By kind permission of Whitby Museum

defined definitional boundaries to determine what 'counted' as disability history and what should be deemed to fall outside the remit of our study, and instead to maintain an openness to the possibilities presented by the collections. Members of the research team were comfortable with the use of the terms disabled and non-disabled to denote the different perspectives we each brought to the project but the application of this binary division was felt to be less appropriate when assessing the material within collections.

Objects by collection type

Whilst we expected to find significant numbers of items within specialist collections that related to medical, military or industrial history – because of the (perceived) 'natural' links with disability history – a rich variety of disability-related objects were, in fact, discovered across collections of all types. Table 6.1 shows the main types of collection within which material was found.

The discovery of large numbers of objects across such wide-ranging types of collection has significant implications for the generalisability of findings from this research project, suggesting that many museums in different countries

Table 6.1 Disability-related material identified by collection type

Collection type	Material identified
Social history	Social history collections held a vast range of material types including objects and images associated with home life, childhood, education, personal relationships and working life (Fig. 6.1). A large number of aids and items of equipment such as crutches, callipers, prosthetic limbs, braces, spinal carriages and wheelchairs are also included in this category (Fig. 6.2). Some of these objects were accompanied by information which linked them to named individuals, but many were not.
Fine art	Numerous paintings, drawing, photographs or sculptures were either suggested by curators in their questionnaire returns or subsequently identified during case study research. These included works by disabled artists, both historical and contemporary, and works portraying disabled people as a subject (Fig. 6.3). Some artists used unorthodox methods of working because of their disability (for example, using their shoulders, feet or mouth to paint), some explored disability-related themes in their work and some are known to have been disabled through documentary material linked to the artworks. A large number of drawings and sketches for stained glass panels depicting healing scenes with lame, blind and crippled figures were identified. In paintings, blind people figured as a popular subject (for example, blind fiddlers, pipers and beggars), some of real named individuals and others of possibly fictional characters.
Archives	Archives proved to be an especially rich source of disability-related material. They included material from Cripples Guilds – photographs, logs and registers, annual reports and fundraising records. Medical archives, not surprisingly, were found to hold large quantities of information including personal medical records, records of treatment, and admission registers for hospitals and asylums. There were numerous letters, journals, ships' logs and collections of ephemera in archives specialising in military and naval history, fairground history and personal collections relating to disabled individuals.
Oral history	Where oral history records existed, they were found to provide one of the richest sources of anecdote about disabled 'characters' in recent history. They also included the personal testimony of disabled people who featured as interviewees.
Decorative arts	Collections contained a wide range of decorative items, particularly ceramics, featuring beggars, war veterans or other disabled characters. Depictions of healing scenes featured on a number of items. There were also decorative or craft items (embroidery, quilts and so on) made by individuals who were described as 'invalids' or 'cripples'.

Table 6.1 continued

Collection type	Material identified
Archaeological	Archaeological collections included both human remains showing evidence of impairments and a limited number of artefacts depicting disability in decorative or symbolic form. Examples included mummies with amputated limbs and Roman pottery fragments showing dwarf and hunchbacked figures.
Costume	Costume collections revealed a few pairs of shoes and a small number of textile items made for, or worn by, people with disabilities. Several curators noted difficulties associated with identifying disability in the wearer. Many costume items were associated with 'freaks' or characters, for example Charles Stratton's (Tom Thumb) suit and Arthur Caley's (the Manx Giant) boots. Other items included back braces, built-up shoes and adapted items of clothing.
Military	Items noted in armaments collections included guns and other weapons adapted for use by people with one eye or one arm/hand.
Ethnographic	Ethnographic collections included figurative pieces, vessels and other objects depicting blindness, limblessness and other impairments. It was recognised that further, subject-specialist research was needed to understand more fully the meanings of these objects within their originating contexts.
Contemporary	Items within this category included contemporary material resulting from museum outreach projects with groups of disabled people, items relating to the Paralympics, disability action/politics and government initiatives (such as the European/International Year(s) of Disabled People) as well as contemporary art and craftworks.

and contexts are likely to contain material with relevance to disability history or with the potential to support disability-related narratives.

Meanings and narratives

In what ways were disabled people most commonly represented in collections and displays? What did the wealth of material found within museums have to say about disability, past and present? The representation of disability across a variety of media, as I have earlier stated, has generally been characterised as limited (in scale and scope), often reductive and negatively stereotypical. Disabled people as victims, as passive, sexless and low achieving are dominant in both historical and contemporary cultural narratives. Disabled people who are perceived to defy these negative stereotypes (for example, by virtue of their heroism or super-achievements) may be presented as 'overcoming' or transcending their disability (Delin 2002).

Figure 6.2: Wheelchair

Source: Photo courtesy of Royal London Hospital Archives

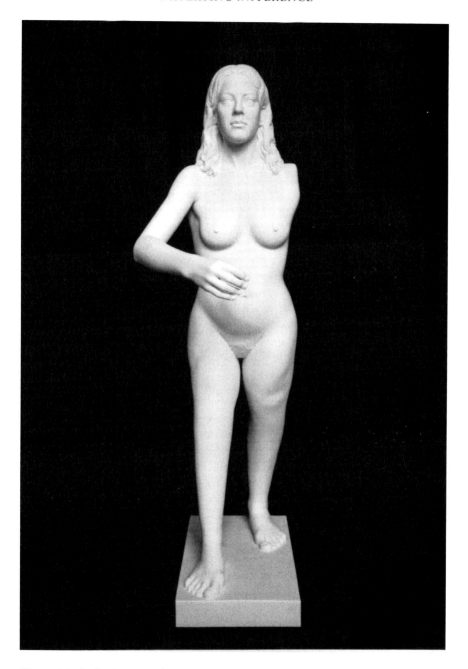

Figure 6.3: Catherine Long by Marc Quinn, 2000. Copyright: the artist

Source: Courtesy of Jay Jopling/White Cube (London). Collection of the Art Gallery and Museum, The Royal Pump Rooms, Leamington Spa

Beggars, heroes and freaks

Many of the items identified by museums in their questionnaire responses resonated with these dominant stereotypical representations and three distinct categories emerged from our analysis. The first category referred to objects which tended to cast disabled people in passive roles – as recipients of care, support, charity or biblical miracle cure; typically nameless beggars, vagrants, asylum residents and hospital patients. The second category featured items linked to narratives in which known individuals overcome the constraints presented by their impairments and transcend their disability, perhaps through creativity or heroism – for example, military heroes and successful artists and sportspeople. The third category most commonly suggested by the material offered to us in our questionnaire presented disabled people as freaks or local characters defined by their physical oddity and viewed as objects of amusement or pity – the extreme 'others' generally perceived to be outside the range of ordinary human appearance. (The term 'freak' is used here to denote people who, at any stage in their lives, were exhibited or exhibited themselves to be stared at for money. Material linked to a number of well-known individuals such as Charles Stratton (Tom Thumb) and Joseph Merrick (the Elephant Man) appeared in collections.)

In contrast, the many objects revealed during the second stage of data gathering, through in-depth case studies, unearthed objects which suggested the occupation of a much wider range of roles by disabled people. Here the research techniques deployed were designed to draw out and reveal unexpected evidence. The researchers offered both an alternative perspective and the time and opportunity to search for material in different ways. Material evidence of disability revealed during this phase of the research suggested the permeation of disability through a much wider range of roles in society, at different class levels and to differing extents of integration and marginalisation. Alongside the asylum residents, freakshow performers, beggars, dependent invalids and recipients of charity funding, we also found evidence of disabled people fulfilling roles including those of teacher, naval commander, parent, lover, collector, benefactor, painter, cooper, miner, musician, linguist, quilter, embroiderer, sculptor, fundraiser, radiographer, nursing educator, politician, merchant and so on.

The study revealed only a small number of displays in which these more varied roles were interpreted to the public or in which prevalent stereotypes were resisted. Examples included exhibitions at the National Maritime Museum in London which emphasised the humanity of Lord Nelson (Fig. 6.4), several displays at Hollytrees Museum in Colchester which represented disabled people in nuanced and wide-ranging ways, and rich narratives exploring the lives of disabled staff as well as patients at the Royal London Hospital Museum and Archives. For the most part, however,

Figure 6.4: The collections of the National Maritime Museum, London, included numerous items depicting or otherwise related to 'disabled hero' Lord Nelson

Source: Research Centre for Museums and Galleries

we found that disabled people were absent from museum displays. Where objects were exhibited, their link to disability was seldom made explicit in labels or they were interpreted in mono-dimensional ways which echoed stereotypical and reductive representations of disabled people which have been found to be prevalent in other media. Disabled people were often represented as poor, passive, sexless and dependent, frequently seen as an economic drain, needing to be cared for, and unable to be productive in terms of employment or creativity or depicted in ways which emphasised their physical difference at the expense of other qualities or attributes.

Interviews with curators suggested that this situation stems from a lack of consensus about the significance and importance of these issues (whether or not museums have a responsibility or a role to play in engaging with issues around disability and countering negative stereotypes), coupled with considerable anxiety about how to display and interpret the material held within collections. Together these concerns accounted for the cultural invisibility and distorted representation of disabled people in museums.

Display dilemmas

The representation of disability is a largely uncharted area of museum practice and one which many of the practitioners encountered during the study perceived to be especially fraught with pitfalls and challenges. Whilst a few organisations had experimented with the inclusion and interpretation of material connected with disability and disabled people's lives most were inhibited from exploring this issue by a range of concerns and anxieties. Many staff cited a fear of making mistakes and of offending disabled people, for example, by inappropriately drawing attention to or stigmatising differ-ence or by using language which may be judged by some to be outdated, distasteful or disrespectful. Others made various conjectures regarding the anticipated and unwelcome behaviours (staring, ridiculing) and responses (shock, distress, discomfort) that might be stimulated amongst museum visitors by exhibitions depicting visible bodily difference. Although many interviewees were interested in exploring ways of incorporating disability-related narratives within their displays, there was a perceived need for guidance that could enable them to move forward in this area.

The concerns felt by staff were very often articulated in the form of interpretive dilemmas or challenges which, it seemed, prevented them from tackling an issue which they were otherwise open to exploring. The dilemmas I shall now consider were those which were most frequently raised by museum staff in our study. These are, for the most part, specific to the context of disability but some nevertheless resonate with concerns raised in relation to the representation of other minorities that have, in recent decades, sought increased visibility through representation within museums and other arts and media forms.

Staring (and the shadow of the freakshow)

The one thing that everyone knows about staring, Rosemarie Garland Thomson has observed, is that you were told by your mother not to do it (2005). Whilst the practice of staring may be discouraged or frowned upon in many social encounters and public settings, museums, in contrast, are sites in which the prolonged, attentive and intense gaze is both actively encour-aged and sanctioned. Staring that is directed at displayed objects or images is generally valued as an appropriate and desirable response in museum visitors, indicative of stimulated interest, surprise, wonder, awe and height-ened curiosity. However, when viewed as a response to the display of objects linked to disabled people or to the depiction of the disabled body, staring might be understood to take on very different meanings and connotations. Being stared at is part of the lived experience of many disabled people. As Garland Thompson observes:

Disabled people have variously been objects of awe, scorn, terror, delight, inspiration, pity, laughter or fascination – but they have always been stared at. Staring at disability choreographs a visual relation between a spectator and a spectacle. A more intense form of looking than glancing, glimpsing, scanning, surveying, gazing and other forms of casual or uninterested looking, staring registers the perception of difference and gives meaning to impairment by marking it as aberrant. … Because staring at disability is considered illicit looking, the disabled body is at once the to-be-looked-at and not-to-be-looked-at, further dramatizing the staring encounter by making viewers furtive and the viewed defensive.

(2002: 56–57)

The freakshows that flourished in the late nineteenth century, in which individuals perceived to possess unusual or inexplicable bodies performed for and were stared at by the paying public, may have largely disappeared by the middle of the twentieth century but, it seems, they nevertheless continue to cast a powerful shadow over contemporary museum practice. Several curators interviewed for this research invoked the freakshow – and a desire to avoid freakshow-style approaches – as reasons for not displaying some material in their collections. Anxiety and uncertainty were especially pronounced when curators were discussing the challenges linked to the contemporary display of material linked to individuals who were, in their own time, known freakshow performers although this concern very often extended to other objects or images that depicted or referenced physical differences.

Although the practice of staring at displayed objects or images within exhibition settings differs from that which occurs in a face-to-face encounter between the disabled person and the non-disabled viewer, many curators nevertheless expressed anxiety about the implications of displaying material in ways which might invite and authorise disrespectful and otherwise inappropriate forms of looking. One curator in our study commented:

If we show pictures of people, we are sending them out on their own and you might get reactions like kids laughing at them. You can't write a label saying 'you mustn't laugh at these people'.

How then might disabled people be made visible within museum displays but in ways which do not simply encourage visitors to gawk at bodies perceived to be anomalous and deviant and which resist the authorisation of staring as a negative and reductive response to oddity? What strategies might museums deploy to frame the encounter between the viewer and the viewed in ways which result in respectful and reflective forms of attentiveness in the museum visitor? In Spring 2005 a new exhibition, *Whatever Happened to*

Polio?, opened at the Smithsonian's National Museum of American History. The fiftieth anniversary of the development of a vaccine to prevent polio provided the impetus for the exhibition but, for the project's director and lead curator Katherine Ott (2005), this was only part of the story.

> Most publicly available histories of polio have tended to focus on medical advancement and the development of the vaccines. People who had polio only make cameo appearances for dramatic effect, usually as children and cautionary reminders. After many conversations with friends and colleagues in the field of disability studies it became clear that the experiences of people who had polio could be the counter-weight to the story of the medical breakthrough. We wanted to include the people who are central to the story but we also wanted to influence the way in which museum visitors would look at them.

Although preliminary research for the exhibition revealed large numbers of images of people with polio, the majority of these depicted individuals in an explicitly medicalised context. Most photographs emphasised dependency, passivity and illness, showing people as patients, completely or partially naked, often being examined or attended to by a physician or a nurse who was touching a part of their body or supporting them. For Ott, 'These images effectively annihilated the humanity of the person shown. In the end, we included only one of them within the exhibition and accompanied it with a quotation from a polio patient that referenced the lack of autonomy that many individuals experienced' (ibid.).

To counter the medicalisation of the story of polio, the exhibition includes numerous photographs displayed as if part of a family album. These highly personal images show people with polio in everyday situations, going to parties and picnics, getting married and playing with their children (Figs. 6.5 and 6.6). Laid out along the entire length of two walls of the gallery, they effectively frame (physically and conceptually) the entire exhibition. For Beth Ziebarth (2005), head of the Smithsonian's Accessibility Program, 'the family album device encourages visitors to stare but at the same time challenges their preconceptions of disabled people by embedding people with polio in everyday social settings rather than solely medical situations'.

Dilemmas linked to the encouragement of inappropriate forms of looking are perhaps inevitable in any attempts to enhance the visibility of disabled people in museum exhibitions. 'The feeling of being on display', David Gerber suggests, 'is something with which almost all disabled people have had to deal; it is, in fact, a singular form of oppression – the oppression of unwanted attention – that disabled people share with few others' (1996: 44). However, there are perhaps, as the example cited suggests, ways of redressing the cultural invisibility of disabled people by framing the visitor's gaze in particular ways.

Figure 6.5: Wedding of Dan and Carol Wilson

Source: Courtesy of the National Museum of American History, Smithsonian Institution, Medical Science Collections

Passing, outing, naming

A further set of dilemmas emerged from our study concerning the circumstances in which a disabled person's identity might or might not be revealed to the public, the implications of 'outing' a person as disabled (who might not themselves want, or have wanted, their disability to be made known) and the contextual factors which influenced decisions regarding whether or not to interpret an object or artwork through a disability-related narrative.

Figure 6.6: A family outing

Source: Courtesy of the Archives of Post-Polio Health International, St Louis, Missouri, USA

Passing

Discussing disability identity, several writers have used the concept of 'passing' to refer to the ways in which an individual might, for varied reasons and motivations, deny or conceal their physical difference and attempt to 'pass' (in certain contexts) as a non-disabled person. Catherine Kudlick has argued

164

that, 'like the pioneers in gay and lesbian history, many disabled scholars try to "pass" worrying that "coming out" will lead to stigma and isolation as long as our culture consciously or subconsciously equates *dis*-ability with *in*-ability' (2003: 769). Related issues emerged through our research in the museum context, for example regarding whether or not artworks by disabled artists should be interpreted in ways which referenced their disability, a topic which provoked strong feelings and sometimes divided opinion (between and amongst) museum practitioners and disabled people. On the one hand, it was felt that labelling an artist as disabled (especially where this was not perceived to be reflected in or relevant to understanding their artwork or life) was unhelpful, inappropriate and might be viewed by audiences as clumsy and tokenistic. Some curators felt that including information within an exhibition regarding an artist's disability might be a reductive rather than an enlarging process, effectively constraining the ways in which audiences perceived or related to the work on display. In contrast, others argued that there were benefits to be gained from stating an artist was disabled, particularly in terms of destigmatising disability and challenging persistent negative stereotypes. As many museums have attempted to broaden the appeal of exhibitions by including within their interpretation not only art historical but also, increasingly, biographical information, some felt that it might be increasingly appropriate to include reference to their disability, alongside information regarding their personal relationships and working life. Most agreed, however, that there could never be a straightforward universal solution and that curators should weigh up a range of contextual factors in determining whether or not (and also the extent to which) disability should feature in exhibition content. Whilst the wishes of individuals (and those of their descendants) were deemed to be very important, it was also recognised that these needed to be considered in the light of contemporary (changed) social attitudes to disability and be weighed against the potential benefits to be gained from the sensitive and thoughtful inclusion of disability-related interpretation.

Outing

Curators, not surprisingly, expressed anxieties concerning the practice of 'outing', a term more commonly used to refer to the public disclosure of a person's sexuality rather than their impairment. They were wary of identifying as disabled a person who concealed their disability in the public sphere, of retrospectively imposing on an individual a disabled identity that they may have resisted or, in the case of a living person, may be unready or unwilling to adopt. This is a controversial and contested area, and for many good reasons.

The 'outing' of a prominent historical figure whose disability has tended to be denied or (more passively) overlooked might usefully be understood as a form of 'representational counter-strategy' (Hall 1997: 272) through which negative and stigmatised perceptions of difference are reversed or subverted.

The controversy surrounding the addition to the Roosevelt (FDR) memorial in Washington DC of a bronze statue depicting the President seated in a wheelchair provides an especially high profile example of this type of strategy. FDR, who contracted polio in 1921, spent his entire presidency from 1933 until his death in 1945 in a wheelchair although, until the new addition was unveiled in 1997, the memorial had included no acknowledgement of his disability. Opponents to the new statue argued that FDR's preference for concealing his disability should be respected and insisted that public memorials should not be appropriated to make social statements in this way. Disability culture advocates, on the other hand, argued that FDR's wish to hide his impairment was shaped by the mores of the time in which he lived and that, in the present-day context, an honest portrayal of the President provided a powerful means of challenging negative attitudes towards disability.[10]

How then should museums approach these difficult issues? In what circumstances might it be appropriate for a museum to address a disability that historically has been denied or hidden? Can museums successfully reconcile the wishes of a person (or those of their family) who may wish to remain silent about their disability with the views of disability culture advocates who seek recognition from society of the presence and the contributions of disabled people? Majewski and Bunch (1998) highlighted these challenges facing curators and concluded that the decision whether or not to refer to a person's disability had to be carefully considered. They cite a number of specific dilemmas including an exhibition at the California Afro-American Museum in 1988 entitled *Black Angelenos: The African American in Los Angeles, 1850–1950*, which aimed to explore the history of some of the city's pioneering black families to understand when and how leadership and influence evolved over time. Researching the life of Robert Owens, an influential political and cultural figure until his death during the Great Depression, the curator found medical records which showed that Owens had struggled with clinical depression which ultimately led to his suicide in 1932.

> When the curator interviewed Owens' ninety-year-old daughter, she was adamant that 'the shame' of Owens' illness and death should remain a family secret. While the curator felt that this information was an important historical note that would help to explain the decline of the family's influence, he was concerned about the living family's real fear of embarrassment.
>
> (ibid.: 153)

Subsequently, the museum decided not to explicitly explore this aspect of the story within the exhibition narrative but chose instead to include the material in an accompanying book to make the history available to scholars (ibid.).

Naming

Many curators we interviewed suggested that images of disabled individuals within exhibitions should, as a general rule, be accompanied by a label which included the subject's real name. Similarly it was felt that, in most circumstances, the interpretation of artefacts linked to the life of a disabled person should also reveal to visitors the personal identity of the user or maker. Anonymity, some felt, might be construed as dehumanising and, especially when viewed alongside material linked to named non-disabled people, to suggest an inappropriately hierarchical relationship. Failing to provide the names of disabled people, some suggested, might inhibit visitors' capacities to make personal connections, and encourage them to focus on a person's impairment rather than to see the multifaceted individual.

In practice, however, we found many instances of displays in which material featuring or linked to disabled people did not carry their names. This issue appeared to be especially problematic in museums with collections linked to medical history. Examples included photographs and paintings depicting groups of hospital patients; residents of asylums for the insane (in some of these the names of staff were offered but not the names of the disabled people); crutches, braces, and prostheses (which were sometimes accompanied by the name of the object donor but not the disabled user themselves). A range of reasons were posited for the omission of a name including missing information regarding the identity of the individual; not having permission from the person depicted or their family; fear of causing offence to visitors with personal connections to the individual featured; and adherence to legal and medical protocols regarding anonymity of patients and sensitivity surrounding the feelings of living family members. (This last reason was most notably offered in relation to the depiction of residents of asylums for the insane.)

Alison Plumridge, then Senior Curatorial Officer at the Royal Pump Rooms in Leamington Spa – a museum and gallery housed in one of the last National Health Service-funded spa therapy centres in the UK which continued to treat people until late in the twentieth century – explained the particular challenges she faced in relation to the issue of naming.

> A lot of the pictures we have were taken between the 1920s and the 1980s to publicise the baths and consequently it is rare to have any information about the people in them. In certain cases we have identified patients and members of staff and there is a real possibility that if information is not recorded now it will be

lost forever. But how can you reconcile patient confidentiality with the need to present patients not as curiosities of medical science, but as real people whose stories should be told? It's not easily resolved.

(Nightingale 2004: 29)

Finally, a third display dilemma emerged from our research in relation to what might be termed 'difficult' material – disability-related objects which were linked to stories of pain and loss, of disempowerment and discrimination.

Telling difficult stories

Interventions designed to enhance the visibility of previously marginalised groups in wide-ranging media forms are, to a large extent, underpinned by a desire to celebrate and destigmatise difference, to offer new ways of seeing and understanding which replace, challenge or subvert dominant negative modes of representation. Thus Stuart Hall (1997) describes a series of trans-coding strategies deployed since the 1960s which have attempted to contest, in varied ways, racialised regimes of representation in film, photography and advertising, for example by attempting to reverse negative racial stereotypes or by seeking to substitute 'positive' images of black people and culture for the 'negative' representations that have tended to dominate across different media forms.

A similar desire to re-present disability in *positive* ways can be seen to underpin many of the arguments proposed in this chapter thus far. Museums, it has been suggested, might usefully explore ways of redressing the absence of disabled people in displays and developing new cultural narratives which counter persistent and prevalent negative stereotypes that define individuals solely in terms of their impairments, typically equating physical difference with passivity, vulnerability, dependency, non-achievement and so on. Our study suggested that many museum collections hold considerable poten-tial to represent disability differently, in more positive ways – to construct empowering, respectful and rounded ways of seeing physical differences not as deficient, inferior or deviant but as both natural and extraordinary.

The tension between, on the one hand, celebrating and affirming difference through positive forms of representation and, on the other, acknowledging and exploring the sometimes challenging, painful and difficult stories associated with disability surfaced in our study. Along-side the objects which might be deployed to present disabled figures which confront or displace negative images we also found many objects which were linked to aspects of disability history which lent themselves to rather less celebratory interpretations. These more challenging mate-rials, present in diverse collections, were linked to a range of histories and

168

events including war injury and mutilation (and associated experiences of vagrancy, mental illness and poverty); freakshows; the experiences of the disabled victims of the Holocaust; histories of asylums, hospitals and workhouses; medical treatments and cures which were experimental, brutal or unsuccessful; and industrial illness and injury created by, for example, mining and fishing.

These difficult stories again prompted considerable debate amongst the disabled people and museum practitioners consulted during our study although ultimately there was considerable consensus surrounding the view that museums should not shrink from these sometimes discomforting subjects but rather should explore ways of enabling audiences to engage with both their historical and contemporary significance. Interventions motivated by attempts to destigmatise difference, the research team concluded, play an important role in extending the range of representations of disabled people and complicating reductionist and totalising understandings of disability that are manifest within prevalent stereotypes. However, it was also acknowledged that the deployment of such strategies was accompanied by a danger that the difficult questions posed by the realities of life for disabled people in the past, the ways in which society has dealt with their presence, and current prejudices towards disability could potentially be overlooked or obscured.[11]

Museums relating to medical history, not surprisingly, held a lot of material that was seen as potentially difficult for visitors to deal with and for curators to interpret. The Royal London Hospital Museum's treatment of the story of the X-ray martyrs was, however, viewed by colloquium participants as particularly thoughtful. The museum's displays explore the history of the hospital and developments in medical practice and include many references to disabled people who were not only patients but also pioneering staff and influential benefactors. These interpretations, the research team concluded, offered humanising, empowering and often surprising representations of disabled people. Alongside these 'celebratory' stories were others which dealt with more painful and challenging themes. One panel which tells the story of the X-ray martyrs features a number of images of Ernest Harnack and his assistants, the pioneer radiographers who continued to experiment on themselves despite losing their health through radiation injuries when the dangers of X-ray work were not fully known. One of these images, showing the hands of one of the X-ray martyrs (Fig. 6.7), although deemed potentially distressing to some visitors, was sensitively displayed and contextualised alongside other images and material.

Conclusion

In their attempts to engage with the imperatives posed by the politics of difference that has emerged over the last fifty years, museums have often

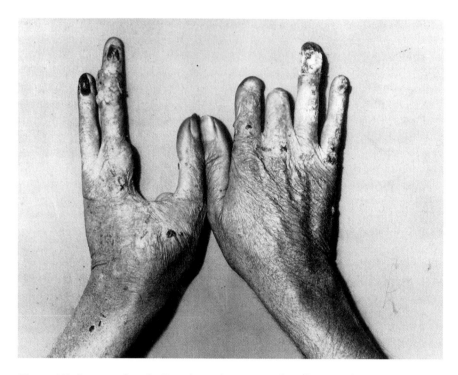

Figure 6.7: One panel at the Royal London Hospital Archives and Museum tells the story of Ernest Harnack and his assistants, the pioneer radiographers who continued to experiment on themselves despite losing their health through radiation injuries when the dangers of X-ray work were not fully known

Source: Photo by courtesy of Royal London Hospital Archives and Museum

struggled with the legacy of historic collections which have supported (or been *perceived* to support) the telling of only partial or biased histories – histories that reflect the experiences and values of a dominant or majority social group. In recent years, there has been a trend towards mining and reinterpreting existing collections to identify material through which new cultural narratives that redress the prior exclusion or marginalisation of, for example, women and minority ethnic communities can be constructed. Alongside these initiatives, proactive contemporary collecting projects have attempted to enrich collections to enable museums to engage audiences whose experiences and stories have been hitherto neglected. Despite these trends the representation of disability within museum displays and exhibitions has remained largely a *terra incognita*.

The study on which this chapter primarily draws suggests that many museums' collections hold material that might be interpreted in ways intended to offer new, liberatory disability narratives and which begin to fray, destabilise and subvert dominant (negative) representational practices.

Despite the richness of material held by museums, the representation of disability remains a neglected area of practice. Many reasons account for this inaction but the presence of dilemmas which are perceived to be bound up with attempts to enhance the visibility of disabled people has played an important role in inhibiting practice. Considerable uncertainty surrounds the most appropriate ways of tackling the subject of disability and many are fearful of making mistakes and causing offence.

Although the dilemmas highlighted by curators arise from genuinely vexing questions (to which no concrete right answers exist) they might also be seen to function for some as excuses; as convenient reasons for not tackling the under- and misrepresentation of disabled people in their museum's displays. There are, after all, processes and mechanisms, tried and tested in other areas of museum practice, which can be used to explore ways to move forward. Anxieties and uncertainties surrounding the most appropriate ways to represent disabled people arise from a model of practice in which the curator is expert and the authority for determining the ways in which material is displayed and interpreted lies within the museum. Where this model holds sway, practitioners are much less accustomed to consulting with communities and other stakeholders about issues of representation than they are in contexts where collaborative and partnership-based approaches to exhibition development have been more widely adopted. In North American and Australian Museums, for example – where the presence and activity of local Indigenous populations have transformed museum practices – advisory groups, consultative panels, joint management practices and so on are now widely viewed as essential for the development of exhibitions of Native materials (Peers 2000).[12] These processes of consultation and collaboration offer one means through which museums might equip themselves with the expertise and the perspectives to inform the ways in which they tackle the representation of disability.

Concerns regarding the encouragement of staring, the practice of outing, the telling of painful stories and so on constitute legitimate dilemmas but they are not wholly intractable and do not, in themselves, entirely account for the lack of activity in the field of disability representation. Underpinning all of these concerns is the continuing debate around the social roles and responsibilities of museums. To what extent should museums concern themselves with addressing issues of contemporary social inequality and discrimination? What opportunities (and, indeed, obligations) might museums have to represent disabled people more fairly and accurately in ways which counter negative stereotypes and prejudice?

Some practitioners in our study were open to, and enthusiastic about, the idea of museums developing displays which attempt to offer alternative, respectful and non-prejudiced ways of thinking and talking about disability. They believed that museums of all kinds were places for exploring and valuing cultural differences and that collections should be viewed and interpreted not solely through the lens of 'disciplinary specialism', but also through that of 'contemporary social concerns'. Others, however, called into question the appropriateness of museums engaging in purposive attempts to shape audience attitudes and perceptions. One curator's discontent with contemporary museum trends and discourse was expressed as follows:

> We steer clear of these issues. I would feel uncomfortable about trying to change someone's perceptions unless there is something which has been a common belief and has been proven wrong. At the moment it's all about education and social inclusion and we just stand back from that because in two or three years it will be something else. We don't take on fads.

Between these extremes of opinion were those whose comments demonstrated openness to exploring these issues further but who remained uncertain about the capacity for museums to counter prejudice.

I have not attempted in this chapter to offer definitive solutions to the dilemmas which emerged from the research. Given the complex and contested issues surrounding the subject of disability, clear-cut answers are unlikely to be forthcoming. Instead I have sought to highlight, and explore through examples, some of the challenges inherent in attempts to reconfigure the museum's representational practices as they relate to disability and to point to possible ways forward that have been pursued and developed in other contexts. My intention has been to draw attention to directions which might fruitfully be explored and through which an enhanced understanding of the museum's potential to reframe conceptions of difference, and disability in particular, might emerge. Such exploration, it is hoped, will take the form not only of further research and debate but also further experimentation in exhibitionary practice.

In the final chapter I pull together the themes that have threaded throughout this investigation of the social agency of museums and discuss, with reference to a number of different examples, the larger and especially vexing questions that have been posed.

7

(RE)FRAMING CONVERSATIONS

A decade ago Stephen Weil articulated a question with which, he suggested, museum practitioners, policy makers and funding bodies had become increasingly preoccupied. 'What kinds of positive changes can museums really effect in the world beyond their doors?' (1996: 95). In responding to the question he argued that, while they could not single-handedly 'stop a war, end injustice or cure inequality', museums were nonetheless influential organisations with the capacity to make a significant contribution to 'the task of building a just, stable, abundant, harmonious, and humane society' (ibid.). In highlighting their potential influence, however, Weil also drew attention to the lack of understanding and knowledge concerning the ways in which museums might make such a contribution.

My purpose in this book has been to respond to this deficit in understanding through a theoretically-informed, empirical investigation of the ways in which audiences respond to exhibitions developed with particular social intentions and exploration of the challenges posed by attempts to reconfigure representational practices in museums. I have sought to offer a set of concepts which together constitute a way of understanding and articulating – and a framework for interrogating – the agency of museums. I have argued that museums can counter prejudice by reframing, informing and enabling society's conversations about difference. I have identified both interpretive strategies and specific display devices, cues and props which appear to be especially effective in stimulating audiences to engage with exhibitions (in ways which fulfil the museum's mandate) and have explored the characteristics attributed to museums as knowledge-providers that illuminate their potentially unique contribution to the task of tackling prejudice. Finally, I highlighted the difficulties exhibition makers encounter in developing representational interventions intended to offer alternative ways of understanding difference.

The idea that museums are places with the capacity to stimulate conversations and sites in which individual and collective social understandings are fashioned is not a new one (Cameron 1972, McLean 1999, Luke 2002, Leinhardt and Knutson 2004). I have attempted, however, to investigate beyond the sometimes abstract concept of the museum as a site for social dialogue to explore, in some detail, the nature of the interpretive processes that emerge out of the audience–exhibition encounter and the character of the meanings that are generated by visitors. Furthermore, I have explored the idea that museums can function as forums for discussion within the explicitly political context of contemporary issues of prejudice that, in many societies, have become increasingly fractious, pressing and contested. This explicit politicisation of the museum as a site for conversations about difference has surfaced a number of especially challenging tensions and dilemmas which are explored in this concluding chapter.

It is, perhaps, unsurprising that I conclude by arguing that museums have a significant (though largely nascent) contribution to make to the development of a less prejudiced society. From the outset, the study was driven by a conviction (albeit inchoate and unsubstantiated) that museums were potentially powerful institutions in configuring relations between social groups. Nevertheless, the findings from my investigations have led me towards explanations of the processes through which this agency is achieved which differ starkly from the ways in which I initially imagined them. Discursive understandings of prejudice, which remain on the margins of prejudice research, challenged the 'conveyor belt' model of visitor transformation with which I began – a model in which the attitudes of inherently prejudiced individuals are, in some way, modified (corrected?) by the predominantly cognitivist intervention afforded by the experience of visiting an exhibition. Most museum visitors, I have attempted to show, are most appropriately conceived of not as 'prejudiced' or 'unprejudiced' but rather as struggling to manage anxieties about difference. Moreover, engagement with contemporary theories of the audience, and of media–audience relations, was critical in repositioning an understanding of the museum not simply as 'text' (with which audiences might acquiesce or wage battle in determining meaning) but as a resource, amongst many, on which audiences might draw in shaping their individual and collective social understandings. Museums, I have argued, emerge from this analysis as agents in the broader mediascape, their exhibitions potentially competing with (or indeed complementing) discursive resources generated by other media which are undoubtedly more ubiquitous and pervasive. I have further argued, however, that the attributes – veracity, authenticity, credibility – with which audiences endow museums, secure them a relatively privileged, authoritative and potentially influential position in the media hierarchy.

(Re)framing, informing and enabling conversations about difference

Museums have always been sites in which differences of various kinds have been invented, constituted, made visible and made to appear natural (Macdonald 1998, Karp and Kratz 2000, Hooper-Greenhill 2000, Bennett

2006). Museum displays, as Eilean Hooper-Greenhill suggests, 'are cultur-ally generative; they construct frameworks for social understanding' (ibid.: 20). Exhibitions embody and materialise discourses of difference, often characterised as oppressive and excluding, that have come under increasing scrutiny in recent decades and, as a consequence, museums have faced increasing pressure to revise their practices.

Although more inclusive approaches to display can be discerned, it would be inaccurate to suggest that these have wholly replaced past museum practices which have been understood to have divisive and excluding conse-quences. Indeed, Tony Bennett usefully cautions against accounts 'in which museum objects are said to be disconnected from one configuration to be inscribed in another governed by entirely different epistemological princi-ples' and instead highlights the 'flux and fluidity of museum practices' (2005: 13). The understandings of difference that are embodied within museum displays are therefore complex and potentially contradictory. Moreover, individual exhibitions, both historical and contemporary, cannot be neatly categorised and contrasted as either wholly oppressive, excluding, discrimi-natory (and thereby attributed with the capacity to reinforce and reproduce prejudice) or liberatory, inclusive, egalitarian (capable of ameliorating preju-dice and fostering respect and mutual understanding). Such analyses are not only unhelpfully reductive but also, as the variability of audience responses evidenced in my study suggests, both inaccurate and misleading.

The social effects of the representational practices embodied in museum displays can only be fully understood through consideration of the ways in which diverse audiences engage with, draw upon and utilise exhibitions to generate and disseminate their own understandings of difference. I wish to argue, however, that a celebration of audience agency should not be misap-propriated to deny the influence (and the concomitant responsibilities) of exhibition makers who determine what is displayed, how and with what intentions. Museum exhibitions present audiences with authoritative, cred-ible and permissible ways of thinking and talking about difference. These ways of thinking and talking have more than symbolic significance – they shape normative truths, social relations and material conditions; they can inhibit, or potentially nurture, possibilities for equity, mutual understanding and respect.

Museums frame (and can potentially reframe) society's conversations about difference in a number of ways. They establish the boundaries and shape the substance of debates about equality and rights through the decisions they make to include or exclude different groups and to address or overlook different manifestations of prejudice within their programmes. They offer resources which influence, in varied ways, the content, character and tone of conversa-tions through the ways in which they depict racial, gender, sexual and other variations. They enable conversations by providing a public forum within which understandings of difference can not only be refashioned but also shared and disseminated. These understandings have influence that extends beyond the confines of individual exhibition spaces, leaking out through a variety of ways including media reporting, promotional communications and the ongoing social interactions of visitors (Kratz 2002). This understanding of agency presents exciting opportunities, as well as challenges, for museums that view themselves as agents of social change and might also be understood to place certain responsibilities on the museum community in general.

Of course the particular explanations that I offer are inevitably shaped by many factors, including my own worldview and experience and the choices I made in building both a theoretical framework and a research design. This then is one amongst a range of possible ways of viewing the social role and agency of museums. The limitations of my research point to the need for further empirical investigation in a number of different areas. It would be valuable, for example, to apply the same method of investigation that I have developed in this study to a wider range of museums with different kinds of goals. It would also be useful to undertake studies which explore potentially interesting issues that my research design neglects to address. This study, for example, has only captured responses at a particular moment in time, immediately after the exhibition visit. Whilst longitudinal studies present a number of methodological challenges, it would nevertheless be valuable to explore the ways in which visitors continue to utilise the resources they encounter during the museum visit over time and in different settings. More-over, studies which explore the influence of visitors' characteristics (gender, ethnicity, religion, etc.) on the ways in which they respond to exhibitions would also provide additional insights.

Although the arguments I have posited concerning processes of audience reception offer a particular understanding – based on empirical investiga-tions in two sites which are in some ways atypical of museums in general – the study was nevertheless driven from the outset by a desire to generate insights which would contribute to broader academic debates and be of value to museums and practice in settings beyond those in which the research was undertaken. With this overarching goal in mind, I have welcomed the many opportunities afforded to me during the research process to discuss emergent findings with practitioners in different kinds of museum operating in widely differing social and political contexts. Though these discussions have been invaluable to me, they have also made me acutely aware of the fact that the findings I have presented, and my interpretation of them, are likely to elicit mixed responses from amongst the museum community, not least because questions concerning the purposes, roles and responsibilities of museums continue to provoke fierce debates.

My intention in the remainder of this conclusion is to focus on the implica-tions of my findings for museum practice and the rather broader questions, dilemmas and tensions which emerge from my analysis. I do not attempt to offer definitive guidelines for practitioners but rather seek to identify the issues which might usefully be explored in developing the potential of museums to tackle prejudice. To assist me in this task, I use a number of examples to contextualise the findings from the St Mungo Museum of Religious Life and Art and the Anne Frank House, which begin to explore their applicability both to other museums concerned with combating prejudice and to museums in general. I begin by discussing a set of interlinked issues that are primarily concerned with the detail of exhibition content, design and interpretive strategy. These are explored in an attempt to identify and enrich understanding of the strategies and devices that appear to be most successful in stimulating and eliciting certain (non-prejudiced) responses from audiences. This discussion highlights dilemmas and tensions which practitioners at St Mungo's and the Anne Frank House – as well as other museums that are actively engaged in seeking to combat prejudice – are already thinking about and experimenting with. I then move on to consider a set of broader issues and implications raised by my research which speak to larger and contested questions surrounding the purpose, role and responsibility of cultural organisations.

Taking sides

In developing exhibitions, many curators are anxious to avoid adopting positions which lay them open to accusations of bias or of inappropriately taking up the role of advocate for a specific cause, choosing instead to aim for (and to claim) impartiality and balance. The untenability of this position and the inevitably political role of museums in privileging certain forms of knowledge have, of course, been widely discussed (Karp and Lavine 1995, Macdonald 1998, Hooper-Greenhill 2000, Luke 2002). As Timothy Luke states, 'while their public pose most frequently is one of cool detached objectivity, museums are unavoidably enterprises organized around engaged partisan principles' (2002: 228). All museums embody sets of values which communicate a particular vision of society but this tendentiousness is very often denied by exhibition makers, both explicitly and implicitly, and rarely openly acknowledged to visitors. Practitioners who fervently maintain that museums are inappropriate settings for initiatives purposefully designed to promote and engender support for egalitarian social values are very often content to promote other sets of values which they themselves take as axiomatic. Most science and natural history museums, for example, implicitly or explicitly promote environmentalism and are generally comfortable with the idea that museums can be used actively to shape visitors' attitudes towards the natural world.

On which topics, and in what circumstances, are museums willing to put aside their claims to impartiality in favour of explicitly articulating a particular moral standpoint, one that offers an unequivocal admonishment of prejudice? This question speaks to the tensions that exist around the extent to which museums might strive unambiguously and explicitly to steer their visitors towards what they believe to be the 'correct' conclusions and also the degree to which they assist audiences in making connections between what is encountered in the museum and manifestations, causes and consequences of prejudice in everyday life. Many practitioners are uncomfortable with, and critical of, approaches which are felt to be overly tendentious, didactic or moralizing or which offer relatively 'closed' interpretations that leave little room for visitors to formulate their own responses. As Irene Hirano, Director of the Japanese American National Museum, states, 'What we've found is that people are really looking for safe places, forums that don't advocate a position but really enable dialogue to happen' (2002: 78). On the other hand, there is a concern that exhibitions, more open in their framing of the topics and issues at hand, might leave too much room for the formulation of meanings which are potentially undesirable or might be less effective in encouraging visitors to reflect on contemporary prejudice and their own values and behaviours.

At the United States Holocaust Memorial Museum in Washington DC, for example, these questions have taken on particular significance as the organisation has sought to expand and enhance its purpose. During the museum's first decade of operation, its function as a memorial to the millions of people who were murdered in the Holocaust was at the forefront of its thinking. More recently, following a major strategic review, enhanced emphasis has been given to its educational role in assisting audiences to understand and engage with the significance of the Holocaust for contemporary society.[1] Reflecting on this enhancement and expansion of purpose, Sarah Ogilvie (2006), Director of the National Institute for Holocaust Education at the Museum, comments:

> We now have a better understanding of what happens between our audience and our content that allows us to be more purposeful in stimulating discussion around contemporary issues. Changes in the world around us and in the perception of the Holocaust as it recedes in time are also influencing factors.

The Museum's permanent exhibition, which opened in 1993, was designed, as far as practically possible, to offer an objective presentation of the history of the Holocaust. In a presentation to the 1994 American Association of Museums conference, Jeshajahu Weinberg, the museum's founding director, acknowledged the specious nature of claims to objectivity but nevertheless stated:

> to teach does not mean to preach. The Museum meticulously tries to refrain from any attempt at indoctrination, from any manipulation of impressions or emotions, from any visual or textual

over-statement and over-dramatization. It restricts itself to dissemination of knowledge, to dispassionately presenting the facts as
established by historical research. Whilst the factual story of the
Holocaust is imbued with a multitude of moral lessons of enormous
human importance, the Museum leaves it to each visitor to draw
his own conclusions, each according to his individual background,
upbringing and personality.

(Weinberg 1994)

This approach reflects adherence to a constructivist view of museum learning,
widely and increasingly supported within museums, which is primarily
concerned with the personal, individual construction of knowledge and
eschews an approach in which visitors' individual meanings are only validated by the extent to which they concord with the conclusions intended
by exhibition-makers or to which they conform to some predetermined and
fixed standard of truth (Hein 1998). But what if these personal meanings are
ones which exhibit prejudice or which fail to establish connections between
historical and contemporary manifestations of oppression? Surely there are
some issues on which there is such an overwhelming consensus that it is
reasonable to unequivocally adopt, and attempt to unambiguously communicate, a particular moral standpoint that leaves little room for opposition?

  Clearly, at the Holocaust Museum in Washington DC, the overarching
ethical message is unambiguous and visitors are extremely unlikely to
construct meanings and draw conclusions from the displays which directly
oppose the institution's condemnation of Nazi ideology. That is not to say,
however, that all visitors will make connections between the Holocaust and
contemporary discrimination or that they will not express their own prejudices in different ways.[2] Although the Museum retains a strong commitment
to the value of providing the conditions in which visitors can determine
their own personally mediated responses, it is nevertheless aware of the
tensions inherent in this approach and is increasingly concerned to explore
and devise exhibition strategies which assist audiences not simply to experience sadness, horror and disgust at what happened in the past but also to
understand the contemporary significance of the Holocaust and to reflect on
their own roles, attitudes and behaviours as citizens (Ogilvie 2005). As Ted
Phillips (2005), Deputy Director of Exhibitions at the museum, explains:

The museum's philosophy is to avoid telling visitors what to think.
We work with our staff to try and maintain a balanced approach
and, in developing exhibitions, we keep running back to the history,
to the facts. We stop short of that final exhibition panel which
would tell people what the lessons of the Holocaust might be for
how we live today. Whether or not we should be more didactic is a
big debate amongst the staff.

Recasting cultural authority

The notion that museums are endowed with an authority which permits them to 'serve as ontologues, telling us what reality is' (Luke 2002: 220) is critical to my argument that museums can shape conversations about difference. But to what extent is this authority being challenged, eroded, remade through experimentation with new, more democratic forms of exhibition practice? Constructivism, for example, advocates the replacement within exhibitions of a single curatorial perspective with the inclusion of diverse voices which 'validate different ways of interpreting objects and refer to different points of view and different truths about the material presented' (Hein 1998: 35–36). This practice has become increasingly widespread in museums and is deployed, though in differing ways, in the case studies explored in this study.

At St Mungo's, consultation with faith communities generated a range of personal testimonies and wide-ranging responses to objects which are included within the displays, whilst *Out of Line* at the Anne Frank House purposefully presents opposing perspectives, drawn from mainstream news media, on contested human rights issues. It might be argued that the inclusion of multiple perspectives serves to strengthen the museum's authority claims especially when the opinions, however diverse, evidence a normative consensus and, in doing so, offer a more powerful endorsement of the museum's overarching messages. As Corinne Kratz argues, 'The consultative trend seeks to respond to questions about how representations and knowledge are produced in exhibitions and the institutional authority that imbues them. It broadens the basis of knowledge and participation in exhibition development, creating new grounds for institutional authority' (2002: 101–102). At St Mungo's, for example, although the voices of individuals from communities represent wide-ranging ways of engaging with and responding to specific objects, they nevertheless avoid contradicting or challenging the museum's espousal of the importance of mutual respect and understanding between people of different faiths.

However, museums are also seeking to elicit, give space to, and validate the wide-ranging opinions of visitors; opinions over which they, inevitably, have far less control. This practice takes many different forms with which museums are increasingly experimenting. At St Mungo's, visitors write their comments on cards which are subsequently displayed for others to read in the exhibition galleries. The National Constitution Center in Philadelphia invites visitors to share their own views on controversial, contemporary topics which are subject to widespread current debate in the news media. These include, for example, the possible introduction of national identity cards and the implications this might hold for national security, individual liberty and privacy as well as the controversy around the amendment of the constitution to allow foreign-born United States citizens to become

President. Visitors are provided with 'post-it notes' on which they can set out their own views and place them onto exhibition panels. In response to some especially provocative topics, these notes build up, layer upon layer, with visitors challenging, endorsing or elaborating upon the views of other visitors and those presented by the museum. At the Lower East Side Tenement Museum, New York, visitors share their responses to the issues raised by their guided tour via a moderated face-to-face discussion in the *Kitchen Conversations* programme facilitated by staff. These diverse techniques afford visitors varying degrees of freedom in expressing their own opinions but each, nonetheless, offers opportunities for expression which can, as we have seen, lead to the articulation of personal interpretations which potentially run counter to the intended message of the museum.

My study suggests that many audiences welcome these opportunities to enter into spirited dialogue with the museum, and with fellow visitors, on the subjects they encounter in exhibitions. But what impact might these interpretive devices have on the museum's ability to fashion authoritative enunciations on issues of prejudice? To what extent might the inclusion (and, perhaps, perceived validation) of diverse, potentially oppositional opinions serve to undermine the agency of museums in privileging and engendering support for non-prejudiced interpretations of difference? The findings from this study provide little in the way of answers to these questions and further investigation in this area would be valuable. However, despite the paradoxes inherent in their use, devices which stimulate conversations and facilitate dialogue (which takes place within the ethical parameters and the framework of values represented and provided by the museum) emerge as valuable, perhaps critical, tools in enabling museums to combat prejudice in the ways which I have described.

Transgressing boundaries of prejudice

To what extent might museums concern themselves with addressing the specificities of particular forms and manifestations of prejudice, targeted at relatively distinct groups, or instead identify opportunities to communicate and engender support for overarching (potentially universalist) principles embodied in human rights frameworks and discourses?

Although their practical application in specific contexts is often fraught with complexity, contradiction and contestation, more abstracted notions of equality and human rights enjoy relatively widespread mainstream support across cultures (Cowan et al. 2001). As Jack Donnelly argues, 'human rights have become a hegemonic political discourse' (2003: 38), one which has contributed, in many societies, to the marginalisation from the political mainstream of proponents of arguments which deny their importance and value. 'Even where citizens do not have a particularly sophisticated sense of what a commitment to human rights means', Donnelly suggests, 'they respond to the general idea that they and their fellow citizens are equally entitled to certain basic goods, services, protections and opportunities' (ibid.: 39). The tensions between the universal and the particular, that are exposed by the situated application of human rights frameworks that hold normative appeal, I would argue, present museums with potentially interesting opportunities for engaging audiences in reflecting on their own prejudices.

These tensions are surfaced, for some visitors, through their encounter with *Confronting Hate in America*, an exhibit at the Museum of Tolerance, Los Angeles, which presents the repugnant consequences of eight different manifestations of hatred in contemporary American life. The abstract notion that hatred is inherently bad, and its consequences socially undesirable, is one that is unlikely to generate dissent, especially among visitors to a Museum of Tolerance. However, some visitors are provoked to question the museum's equalising treatment of wide-ranging hate crimes that are motivated by diverse beliefs, values and forms of prejudice. Alongside panels which present events or actions which have provoked more or less universal public condemnation (for example, racially motivated attacks on individuals who are, or are perceived to be Muslim or Arab-American in the aftermath of the events of September 11, 2001) are others which prompt some visitors to question their inclusion in the exhibit. A member of the museum's visitor services staff explained that the two examples of hate crimes which most commonly elicit this questioning amongst visitors are those which deal with the anti-gay hate crime which led to the murder of twenty-one-year-old Matthew Shepard and another which considers the murder of a doctor by anti-abortionists.[3] 'Some of our visitors find this exhibit especially difficult and challenging,' she told me. 'They are comfortable with condemning many hate crimes but argue that some, perhaps, are more justified than others.'

Inclusive narratives which aim to engender support for universal principles of equality and rights (and are designed to speak to multiple forms of prejudice) can also be found, though relatively rarely, in museums which are principally focused on the history and culture of a specific minority. Despite its unique position as 'the only museum in the United States dedicated to sharing the experience of Americans of Japanese ancestry', and the primary focus in its main permanent exhibition on the specific events surrounding the incarceration of Japanese Americans during the Second World War, the Japanese American National Museum has adopted an ambitious, outward-looking and inclusive mission which seeks to engage visitors in reflecting more generally on issues of prejudice and discrimination.

> We share the story of Japanese Americans because we honor our nation's diversity. We believe in the importance of remembering our history to better guard against the prejudice that threatens liberty and equality in a democratic society. We strive as a world-class

museum to provide a voice for Japanese Americans and a forum that enables all people to explore their own heritage and culture.

(JANM 2005)

Consistent with the goal of viewing contemporary social and political American life (and its implications for a diverse citizenry) through the historic lens of the experiences of Japanese Americans, the museum has recently been instrumental in the establishment of the National Center for the Preservation of Democracy which aims to communicate, through the development of educational tools for young people, three curricular understandings. '1. We, the people, shape democracy. 2. I too can shape democracy. 3. and those who have struggled for freedom and equality have extended democracy's reach for all' (Okihiro 2005: ii).

Whilst the tremendous diversity of museums suggests that they hold resources which might usefully be directed towards focused attempts to address specific forms of prejudice, some of the most powerful social effects generated out of the visitor–exhibition encounter – perhaps most clearly evinced in the dialogic and dynamic visitor interpretations of exhibitions in my study – appear to stem from attempts by museums to transgress individual and social boundaries of prejudice through the normative appeal of human rights discourse. The deployment of these strategies, I would suggest, need not imply adherence to an assimilationist model of difference in which cultural specificity is denied in an attempt to establish equal rights. Rather, I contend that museums can offer understandings of difference that are complex and nuanced, which attempt to establish an expanded view of rights, one which incorporates the right for groups to assert and maintain their cultural specificity (Young 1990). Audience responses to such approaches, it might further be argued, highlight museums' potential to contribute to the remapping, in albeit subtle ways, of the boundaries that delimit and distinguish between socially acceptable and unacceptable forms of prejudice.

Reshaping the normative consensus

Prejudice has come to be widely viewed as a socially undesirable phenomenon. It is frequently conceived in negative terms – to exhibit prejudice is equated with narrow mindedness and suggests unreasonable and unfairly biased attitudes. In his analysis of toleration – the practice which makes possible 'the peaceful coexistence of groups of people with different histories, cultures and identities' – Michael Walzer (1997: 2) explains its normative appeal:

> I begin with the proposition that peaceful coexistence ... is always
> a good thing. Not because people always in fact value it – they

often obviously don't. The sign of its goodness is that they are so strongly inclined to say that they value it: they can't justify themselves, to themselves or to one another, without endorsing the value of peaceful coexistence and of the life and liberty that it serves.

In practice, however, certain forms of prejudice are more widely condemned than others and normative understandings of acceptability and tolerance are highly uneven and differentiated. These situated social norms, as they relate to questions of difference and equality, inevitably play a part in determining which forms of prejudice are perceived to be most problematic, undesirable and therefore deserving of attention.

I have so far argued that museums have a constitutive, generative role to play in configuring relations between social groups. Museums shape, concretise and legitimise normative understandings of difference. But museum practices are also, to varying degrees, reflective of and constrained by the normative consensus. The representation of difference in museums is socially *determined* and, at the same time, socially *constitutive*. Museums are generally more comfortable in tackling subjects around which there exists a relatively 'settled' narrative or overarching consensus rather than those which are, perhaps, rather less resolved and are likely to divide opinion. Consider a museum located in, for example, the United States that adopts a standpoint, within its exhibition narratives, which attempts to privilege anti-racist perspectives; which presents racism as inherently wrong and socially undesirable. Although race-related prejudice and discrimination remain stubbornly persistent features of American society there is nevertheless relatively widespread support, enshrined in public policy, political discourse and legislation, for the notion that racism is not only undesirable but also morally repugnant. As a result, I would suggest, the museum's overall standpoint – at least in abstract terms – is unlikely to provoke mainstream disapproval. That is not to suggest that museums attempting to confront racial prejudice are uncontroversial. On the contrary, museums that have attempted to represent histories in ways which explore the impact of historical and contemporary racist practices have often provoked fierce debates. The opening of the National Museum of Australia in 2001, which was perceived by some to give too much credence to the perspectives of Indigenous Australians who challenged entrenched historical narratives by viewing colonisation as an act of invasion (Bennett 2003), provides an especially high-profile example of such controversies.[4] I wish to argue however that, at least in abstract terms, certain forms of prejudice are less widely condemned and viewed as more socially acceptable than others. These forms of prejudice are likely to present museums with a different set of problems. What potential exists then for museums to adopt the role of moral leader in challenging forms of prejudice and discrimination which are to varying degrees, politically, legally and socially sanctioned? To what extent might museums seek not simply to *reflect* but to challenge, reconfigure, even *define* the normative, popular consensus on difference?

Many working in museums are uncertain about the appropriateness of adopting a purposefully generative or advocative role, especially in relation to contemporary issues which are characterised by ambiguity and contestation. Indeed, most institutions, perhaps with the exception of some contemporary art galleries, tend to avoid 'hot topics and big controversies' (Ames 1992: 7). Michael Ames highlights some of the reasons which might account for this conservatism. Curatorship, he suggests, is based on 'the scholarly model of extensive research, careful accumulation and assessment of evidence over time, a focus on objects rather than issues, and political neutrality' (ibid). In addition, he suggests that the increasing unpredictability of funding regimes, public expectations that museums should entertain and be uplifting, and the mandate to preserve, all contribute to museums' cautiousness in engaging with topical issues. Challenging topics are also avoided because of high-profile examples of museums that have failed to anticipate and manage the controversial reactions their exhibitions have generated.

Electing to engage only with issues around which there is a relatively settled narrative, however, suggests a somewhat diminished (though arguably safer) role for museums. An unwillingness to address contested topics, however challenging, might be understood to relegate museum practitioners to the role of 'disengaged and impotent archivists, carefully cataloguing the barn doors, those that close them, and the names of the horses, after the horses have gone' (Mead 1970: 24). More particularly, confronting only those forms of prejudice which are viewed with relatively widespread condemnation is, perhaps, equally limiting.

I do not underestimate the challenges that arise from attempts directly to engage audiences in debating contested contemporary social issues related to human rights. The staging of exhibitions that attempt to stimulate debate on these topics and, crucially, that seek to establish moral constraints and parameters within which those debates can take place is a process that is fraught with complexities. However, I would suggest that museums have an especially valuable role to play in this regard, through the framing and facilitation of ongoing and *unresolved* conversations about difference. To pursue this line of argument I shall consider the challenges associated with tackling prejudice against sexual minorities, an issue which in many societies holds the potential to provoke diverse opinions.

Moral leadership

Homophobia, one of the most aggressive but tolerated forms of bigotry and hatred in contemporary society, is not on the radar screen of most American museums and their educational divisions.

(Müller 2001: 36)

185

Although it is possible to detect an increasing receptivity, in some contexts, towards representing lesbians and gay men in exhibitions, there is nevertheless considerable wariness and ambivalence surrounding the issue in the museum community at large. In her investigation into British social history museums Angela Vanegas, for example, found that, 'more lesbian and gay material has been displayed in the last six years than the preceding ten, but the vast majority of social history museums have still done little or nothing to include lesbians and gay men in their exhibitions' (2002: 105). The curators she interviewed cited the possibility of losing their jobs or funding, the lack of material in their (existing) collections, fear of audience complaints and the perceived inappropriateness of sexuality as a suitable topic for family audiences, as reasons for excluding reference to sexual minorities in their displays.

In the United States, the events surrounding the 1989 retrospective exhibition of Robert Mapplethorpe's photography sparked a high profile national and international debate around issues of censorship, definitions of art and pornography, and public funding for the arts. This furore undoubtedly played a part in stalling attempts to recognise gay and lesbian culture and history in museums and galleries for many years. More recently there are some, albeit few, signs of an increased openness to these issues amongst parts of the American museum community but change is extremely slow and examples of exhibitions which make reference to sexual minorities remain extremely scarce. 'In their label texts,' Klaus Müller suggests, 'museums often struggle with a language that hides as much as it indicates. Rarely do curators include reference to lesbian and gay history in mainstream exhibitions, though extensive historical studies on the topic have been produced in recent decades' (2001: 36).

Museums' continued reluctance to take a stand against heterosexism or homophobia is not especially surprising. In his analysis of human rights, Jack Donnelly (2003: 230) highlights their applicability to sexual minorities as an especially controversial and contested topic.

> Discrimination against sexual minorities is widespread and deep in almost all societies today. In many countries, the intimate behaviour and loving relationships of sexual minorities are defined as crimes. They are singled out for official, quasi-official, and private violence. In almost all countries, sexual minorities suffer under substantial civil disabilities.

The prevalence and virulence of prejudice directed towards sexual minorities accounts, at least in part, for the hesitancy amongst museum practitioners in tackling the problem. During the summer of 2005, I posed the following question to directors, curators, exhibitions staff and educators in a variety of museums in the United States: 'In your opinion, which forms of prejudice would it be most problematic for your organisation to challenge through your exhibitions or other public programmes?' Despite the wide-ranging geographical locales and the diversity of institutional settings in which this question was posed, almost unilaterally, museum staff suggested prejudice on the grounds of sexual orientation. These responses are not surprising given the political climate within which the question was posed. Public debates about the rights of sexual minorities in the US were particularly prominent at the time and, in the preceding year, gay marriage had become one of the 'hot-button' issues in the Presidential election campaign. News media regularly featured stories in which gay rights activists were pitted against Republicans and Christian conservatives. The identification by museums of prejudice against sexual minorities as an especially difficult issue for them to confront assists in highlighting the challenges associated with tackling issues around which there exists limited consensus. Although the challenge to social norms bound up with attempts to tackle prejudice against sexual minorities is a substantive one, some museums have nevertheless explored ways of addressing the problem.

Whilst acknowledging that most of the victims of the Holocaust were Jewish the United States Holocaust Memorial Museum has, since its inception, committed itself to documenting the experiences of non-Jewish victims – people with physical and mental impairments, political dissidents, non-Jewish Poles, Gypsies, Jehovah's Witnesses and homosexuals. The Museum considers the treatment of homosexuals within its permanent exhibition, in accompanying leaflets for visitors which focus on 'the other victims' (Fig. 7.1) and most extensively in a temporary exhibition – *Nazi Persecution of Homosexuals 1933–1945* – which, following its presentation in Washington DC in 2004, has subsequently toured to various locations in North America (Fig. 7.2). Staff are aware that the museum's attempts to tell the story of the persecution of homosexuals holds particular and unique challenges for the institution. As Ted Phillips (2005), curator of the touring exhibition, explains:

> There was never a serious lack of commitment within the institution to developing this project. An important part of our mission is what we increasingly refer to as 'enhancement of the moral discourse' even where this might prove especially challenging to visitors. Having said that, it is fair to add that this exhibition was approached with particular care. For example, there was far more discussion than would normally have taken place surrounding the most suitable location within the museum to place the exhibition. Some staff were concerned about complaints from family visitors. The compromise position we finally agreed upon was to use moveable screens which were positioned so that people would not simply stumble across the exhibition but rather would have to make a conscious decision to visit it. Similarly, the exhibition panels and other interpretive materials were subject to review by the highest levels of museum management – a practice which had not been deemed necessary for our other temporary exhibitions.

Figure 7.1: A portrait of two companions, Berlin, Germany, 1926. This photograph features on the cover of the United States Holocaust Memorial Museum's 'other victims' brochure which deals with the Nazis' treatment of homosexuals

Source: Courtesy of the Schwules Museum, Berlin

Figure 7.2: 'Solidarity', by Richard Grune (1903–1983), lithograph, 1947. Grune was incarcerated for homosexuality by the Nazi state from 1934 to 1945. From the exhibition, *Nazi Persecution of Homosexuals*, 1933–1945

Source: Courtesy of the Schwules Museum, Berlin

For the museum, the most challenging aspects associated with the recent temporary exhibition have emerged out of its subsequent tour.

> We purposefully sought to secure mainstream tour venues – museums, libraries, colleges etc – rather than gay and lesbian centres, in an attempt to engage a broader cross section of society in thinking about the issues raised in the exhibition. This has worked well on the whole but some host organizations, notably those in particularly conservative parts of the country, have sought extra support from us to prepare themselves for any adverse reactions from funding bodies and partner institutions.
>
> (Phillips 2005)

Though widely promoted and visited, *Nazi Persecution of Homosexuals 1933–1945* appears to have attracted little in the way of criticism. Indeed, the exhibition organisers were both surprised and delighted when the editorially conservative newspaper, *The Oklahoman* (17 September 2005) ran an article which stated:

> Traveling exhibits that opened this week in downtown Oklahoma City are necessary reminders of mankind's inhumanity to itself. One piece of the Oklahoma Holocaust Remembrance Exhibit tells the story of some 100,000 homosexual men who were persecuted by the Nazis – not unlike other lesser-known victims of the Third Reich's virtual purge of Jews from Europe. A second work … conveys the heroic efforts of ordinary people – 'rescuers' – who risked everything to save Jews. Thanks go to the Cimarron Alliance Foundation [a local gay-rights educational organization] and other local sponsors who brought these important and well-done exhibits to town.

It is interesting to note that, some years earlier, the museum's inclusion of material relating to homosexuals in its permanent exhibition had attracted sharp criticism from a small group of rabbis resulting in some debate in the press.[5]

Clearly, some museums will have more scope to innovate and greater confidence to challenge norms of acceptability and tolerance than others. For Ted Phillips, the Museum's widely accepted authority on the Holocaust helps to explain why the exhibition has sparked surprisingly little controversy. Subject matter, funding and governance arrangements, institutional history, public perceptions and staff views on the social role of museums will all play a part in determining the extent to which individual organisations are inclined or able to adopt potentially unpopular standpoints which challenge mainstream normative understandings of difference. Nevertheless, the Holocaust Museum's position as a large, high-profile organisation and perhaps, most significantly, as a museum in receipt of public funding, offers an especially interesting example of the potential for museums to address challenging topics and to contribute towards the framing of debates which continue to be especially sensitive and hotly contested.

Whilst museums approach some human rights issues with especial caution because of their high-profile and controversial nature, others barely register on the radar. Following an invitation to contribute to a panel that would explore the changing nature of museums' relationships 'with gay, lesbian, bisexual and transgender communities', at the American Association of Museums' 2006 conference, I set about gathering examples of museums that had sought to represent these different groups. Identifying examples of exhibitions with narratives that featured gay or lesbian lives was relatively easy (even if the examples themselves were numerically few) but representations of transgendered people were, not surprisingly, much harder to find. In her groundbreaking study, Vivian Namaste revealed the processes through which transgendered people – a term used 'to refer to all individuals who live outside of normative sex/gender relations' (2000: 1) – have been effectively 'erased' or 'made invisible' across a range of cultural and institutional settings. In the few years since Namaste's study, whilst this invisibility persists, there has nevertheless been some increase in the level of debate within mainstream news media, certainly in the UK and North America, concerning the rights of transsexuals in particular. (In 2006, the nomination for an Academy Award of the film *Transamerica* proved especially effective in generating international television and newspaper media coverage around this issue.) Increasing media and public interest in the question of rights for this minority group has not, of course, been reflected in museums but, whilst conducting research for the conference, one especially interesting example came to light from the Lower East Side Tenement Museum in New York. In line with its mission to promote tolerance and help expand visitors' understandings of contemporary immigration the museum brought a production to its theatre in 2005 which explored the subject of political asylum for sexual minority refugees. The museum's decision to programme *Tara's Crossing* – which drew on interviews with asylum seekers to tell the story of a transgendered woman's experiences of persecution in Guyana and the difficulties she faced in coming to the United States – was a conscious attempt to engage audiences in the debate surrounding the legal and human rights of transgendered individuals (Sze 2006) (Fig. 7.3).

The issues discussed so far, primarily concerned with specific issues of exhibition content, framing and design, begin from the assumption that museums have a significant role to play in contributing to the development of a less prejudiced society. Although recent years have seen a trend towards articulating the value of museums in these terms there are, nevertheless, ongoing debates around the extent to which museums should be viewed (or should view themselves) as purposeful agents of social change. With these debates in mind, I wish now to turn attention to the broader implications of the study to consider the nature of the relationships museums might have with the societies of which they are part, and concomitant issues of purpose, role and responsibility.

Museums and social responsibility

In recent decades many museums have dismantled their most overtly racist and otherwise prejudiced and offensive displays, often in response to anger from under- and mis-represented communities. There is widespread and growing support internationally for the telling of more inclusive stories that reflect (at least some forms of) community and societal diversity. These changes are evidence of the ways in which museums of all kinds have responded to heightened global concern for issues of diversity and the imperatives presented in many contexts by an emergent politics of difference. In many ways, however, museums have adopted a reactive role in relation to these social changes. Relatively few have sought purposefully to contribute to the framing of ways in which societies engage with issues of prejudice and equality.

The debate, in recent years, has focused on the *appropriateness* of social change as a goal for museums; a goal which has been understood, by some, to conflict with other museum aims and agendas. Should museums concern themselves with countering contemporary prejudice through exhibitions that seek to offer ways of understanding difference based on concepts of social justice and equality? What responsibilities, if any, might museums have to take account of contemporary identity politics in shaping exhibitions?

Relatively limited empirical research has been undertaken to gauge the attitudes of museum practitioners towards these questions but there is some evidence to suggest considerable ambivalence and uncertainty. In the previous chapter, curatorial attitudes towards the use of collections to change visitors' attitudes towards disability and disabled people were found to be wide ranging. At one end of the spectrum were those who firmly believed that this is what museums were all about and at the other were those who saw these activities as diverting museums away from their 'core business' of collections care and research. Situated between these polarised viewpoints were many practitioners who remained uncertain about the capacity for museums to effect social change and ambivalent about the degree to which they might be required to do so. This uncertainty and ambivalence continues to fuel debates within the museum community.

In Sharon Macdonald's ethnographic study of exhibition-making, *Behind the Scenes at the Science Museum* (2002), it is possible to detect differential attitudes amongst the museum's staff towards both the *agency* of the museum – its capacity to influence visitors – and the *responsibility* that might accompany such influence. Her analysis reveals that museum staff

Figure 7.3: Aundre' Chin in *Tara's Crossing*, Jeffrey Solomon's play about political asylum for sexual minorities, brought to the Tenement Theater by the Lower East Side Tenement Museum, New York

Source: Photo by Loris Guzzetta

appear willing to acknowledge, and indeed to exercise, agency in relation to some issues but are less comfortable to do so in relation to others. For example, the team working on an exhibition about food discussed how, if

193

at all, they might include reference to alcohol. Their discussions suggest a consensus amongst team members that the exhibition might potentially influence visitors' thoughts and behaviours. As a consequence, the museum was perceived to have a responsibility to treat the topic in such a way as to avoid encouraging (or being seen to encourage) the drinking of alcohol. The final exhibition therefore included reference to beer but alongside a note about government recommended levels of alcohol consumption. In contrast, the team appeared far less comfortable to acknowledge agency and responsibility in relation to issues linked to gender and race inequalities:

> Including images of women and ethnic minorities was talked about by the Team as 'redressing the imbalance' of other exhibitions: theirs was an exercise in the 'remembrance' of the existence of these groups which other exhibitions tended to 'forget'. This they saw as a legitimate and even necessary task. But whether they should go further and try to 'do something' about the way in which women or ethnic minorities were perceived more generally was reasonably seen as beyond their remit: they could seek only to 'represent reality' not to change it.
>
> (2002: 183)

Macdonald also describes another exhibition team within the Science Museum, this time concerned with the 'Information Age', that had been asked by the Museum's management to look for ways in which they could show women and girls to be more involved in computing, in response to government and industry initiatives to address gender imbalance in the sector. As Macdonald found, 'Some on the team, however, saw this as contrary to the Science Museum's representational role: "It's asking us to do social engineering and that's not what we should be in the business of doing. That might be the government's job but it's not the Science Museum's"' (ibid.: 183).

These comments are reflective of the broader debates concerning the social roles and responsibilities of cultural organisations to which I have alluded throughout the book. Within these debates, those who oppose the idea that museums might purposefully seek to instigate positive social change draw seemingly arbitrary limits around what they are prepared to accept as appropriate museological purposes and functions. Why, for example, is it acceptable to draw visitors' attention to the dangers associated with excessive alcohol consumption but inappropriate to attempt to 'do something' about the ways in which women and ethnic minorities are perceived? Why are attempts to represent disabled people in wide-ranging rather than narrowly stereotypical ways perceived by some to be inappropriately political and dismissed as a form of social engineering whereas the mounting of a history exhibition which dispels myths about some aspect of the past or an art exhibition which reinterprets artworks in the light of new thinking and research are deemed to be standard elements of museum practice?

Opponents of the concept of the socially engaged museum have often built their arguments around objections to the instrumentalisation of culture – the use of museums by governmental agencies, to achieve social and political ends (Appleton 2001; Munira 2006). My contention that museums might play a part in countering prejudice is not, however, based on their appropriation by external agencies. Rather I suggest that, irrespective of the demands and expectations imposed on them by governments, museums are inevitably implicated in the construction of cultural narratives which shape conceptions of difference. The findings from my audience research suggest that the question practitioners face is not, in fact, whether museums *should* be engaged in attempts to shape the ways in which difference is viewed but rather *how* they can most appropriately do so. The particular and unique ways in which audiences view and make use of exhibitions mean that, *regardless of intent*, museums construct ways of seeing which have social and political effects.

I do not conclude from this that all museums should adopt goals and develop specific programmes that attempt to ameliorate prejudice. It is difficult to imagine a more bland and tedious vision of museums than one which is characterised by a uniformity of purpose. Rather I would argue that, in the pursuit of their diverse missions, museums of all kinds should deploy reflexive practices which acknowledge their part in privileging particular ways of understanding and viewing difference. There is no neutral position and exhibition-makers face choices concerning the ways in which they develop narratives. The interpretations they construct and offer to audiences can reflect hierarchical notions of superiority and inferiority, they can perpetuate negative and demeaning stereotypes and they can marginalise and exclude through omission. Alternatively, there are opportunities to develop exhibitions with an acknowledgement of their potential to serve as resources which expand visitors' capacities for mutual understanding, which challenge, complicate and begin to unravel prevalent negative stereotypes, and which offer ways of understanding difference which reflect adherence to principles of social justice and equity.

This approach will inevitably raise concerns over impartiality and suggests a degree of didacticism with which many are uncomfortable. As Robert Sullivan has argued:

> To propose that museums be purposefully involved in moral education can cause great anxiety among museum professionals. The anxiety emanates from a fear of accusations of sectarianism or values indoctrination; a belief that museums can and should be non-moral and value-neutral in their behaviours; a confusion over the difference between moral education (based on concepts

of justice) and religious education (based on theological concepts); and a general ambivalence about the power and role of the museum as an educational and social change agent.

(1985: 12–13)

In many situations, I would argue, these concerns about impartiality are used as an excuse to avoid engaging with social issues and acknowledging that museums of all kinds – including those that make the strongest claims to neutrality – embody particular moral standpoints. Adopting and seeking to engender support for a particular vision of the good society, one that draws on concepts of justice and equal human rights, need not preclude the accommodation of different perspectives and the deployment of interpretive techniques designed to elicit and value visitors' diverse opinions. There are ways of constructing exhibitions which avoid moralising didacticism, which open up rather than close off possibilities for debate but which nevertheless offer ethical parameters within which conversations about difference can take place.

By acknowledging that their portrayals of difference have real effects, museums can provide opportunities for debating the challenging questions which are an inevitable consequence of inequitable and increasingly diverse societies. This acknowledgment of social agency requires not only that practitioners reflect upon the messages, unconscious as well as conscious, that are embodied within and communicated by the exhibitions they construct but also that they make explicit to audiences the values which the museum stands for. Rather than aiming for objectivity or neutrality, museums might more usefully aim to adopt a position of fairness – in relation to the objects' various meanings, to the many possible points of view that audiences will bring to the exhibition encounter and, most importantly, fairness to those whose human rights are at issue.

As the approaches developed by St Mungo's, the Anne Frank House and the examples I have used throughout this book demonstrate, exhibitions constructed with an acknowledgement of their potential to frame society's conversations about difference do not, as many might fear, offer didactic, univocal, simplistic, sanitised and saccharine interpretations of cultural difference. Exhibitions that privilege non-prejudiced ways of seeing offer interpretations, though shaped by an underlying, non-negotiable, institutional commitment to the importance of equality for all and a due respect for difference, that can be as complex, multifaceted and challenging as any other.

APPENDIX 1

Investigating visitor responses: notes on methodology, research design and data sources

A qualitative approach

An investigation of the ways in which audiences respond to museum exhibitions intended to counter prejudice could potentially be approached via either of the two main research traditions in the social sciences – positivism and interpretivism. Positivism 'forms the theoretical basis for the hard sciences in suggesting that the world has a fixed, observable structure which can be measured via the correct methodologies' (Mason 1996: 5). A positivist approach to the topic might therefore suggest a quantitative, experimental design in which pre- and post-exhibition visit tests seek to measure changes in visitors' attitudes. This approach was deemed to be ontologically inconsistent with the theoretical frameworks for understanding both prejudice practices as well as media–audience relations that were developed for this study. Rather, a qualitative approach located within the interpretivist sociological tradition was considered most appropriate.

Qualitative research has a number of characteristics which suggest its suitability for this study. Firstly, it is based on an interpretivist philosophical position 'in the sense that it is concerned with how the social world is interpreted, understood, experienced or produced' (Mason 1996: 4). Secondly, in contrast to the highly structured and firmly standardized methods employed by quantitative approaches, qualitative research utilises methods of data generation which are both flexible and responsive to the social context in which the investigation takes place. Finally, qualitative research is 'based on methods of analysis and explanation building which involve understandings of complexity, detail and context' (ibid.: 4). Rather than using data to establish directly causal relationships between, for example, a museum exhibition and the reactions of the audience, a qualitative approach will generate rich, dense and deep data which can be analysed and interpreted in a holistic way and which may offer contextual-ised, nuanced and multi-layered interpretations.

Research methods and data sources

Case study research is characterised by the use of both multiple sources of data and multiple methods of data collection and generation. At both the St Mungo Museum of Religious Life and Art and the Anne Frank House, observation, in-depth interviews and visitors' written comments were all used to investigate and develop an understanding of audience responses.

Observation

I visited both the Anne Frank House and St Mungo's prior to their selection as case studies. During these visits I carried out observation of visitors to gain a sense of the practical issues that might affect the use of these museums as sites for investigation. Additional observation of the ways in which visi-tors utilised the museums' exhibitions was also undertaken at different times of the day throughout the period subsequently spent at each site. During these times I was able to undertake participant observation; rather than attempting to be entirely detached from the situation being observed (systematic observation), I remained visible and immersed within the exhi-bition space. Most of the time I took on the role of the museum visitor in an attempt to observe 'natural' behaviours and environmental conditions. However, I also undertook observation when recruiting participants for interview and, at these times, the use of an identification badge suggested my role in an official capacity. These periods of observation informed the subsequent process of data gathering through interviews and contributed to the ongoing process of data analysis. For example, observation enabled me to get a sense of the different amounts of time visitors spent in different parts of each museum, which exhibits seemed to provoke most interest or discus-sion and which were often passed by. Observation also gave me a sense of the extent to which comments made by interviewees might be typical or atypical of visitor responses in general.

Interviews

Sixty-two in-depth interviews with a total of 122 English-speaking indi-viduals and small groups of adults (sometimes with accompanying children) were carried out at St Mungo's during May/June 2003 and at the Anne Frank House during August 2003. Consistent with exploratory qualitative studies of this kind, variability within the research population was sought in terms of age, gender, ethnicity and place of residence although visitors were not selected according to rigid sampling criteria. Most interviews lasted around half an hour with the longest being eighty-four minutes and the shortest twelve. Often, but not always, the richest strands of data were generated by interviews with more than one person where participants engaged in lively debate with their partner or with others in their group.

Interviews were carried out in accordance with the British Sociological Association's statement of ethical practice. Participants were informed that the purpose of the interview was to find out about their experience of the visit, their reasons for visiting and their views on and feelings about the exhibitions they had seen. Significantly, they were not told that the study was especially concerned with issues relating to prejudice as it was felt that this would unhelpfully bias responses. Participants were assured of anonymity and confidentiality. Indeed, although basic socio-demographic information was collected, no names or addresses were sought or recorded. (Pseudonyms have been used throughout the book.)

Visitors were approached towards the end of their visit. All interviews were conducted in private rooms provided by the museums and each was tape recorded in full with the participants' permission. On average between two and three interviews were conducted each day allowing time for reflection, preliminary analysis and the addition of field notes to support the taped accounts. Open-ended and loosely-structured interview protocols (see below) were designed to allow for the generation of rich and unexpected data. The use of open questions has been found to be most useful within the interview process as a means of generating visitors' accounts and perceptions of their visit (Macdonald 2002). The purpose of open-ended interviewing is to enable participants themselves to lead in shaping the research agenda. Rather than focusing from the outset on issues relating to prejudice and cultural difference the interviews therefore allowed the subjects to decide for themselves the most salient aspects of their visit (Ruddock 2001). In terms of interview design, this involved the process of 'funnelling', where the interviewer begins with general questions before moving on to more specific ones that link more directly to the original goals of the study. As Ruddock suggests, 'This allows the researcher both to pursue the initial question and also to see how relevant that question is to actual audience experience' (2001: 135).

Interview protocols were piloted at both case study sites resulting in refinements in the phrasing and sequencing of the questions. This process highlighted questions that were insufficiently clear or were too repetitive in relation to other questions posed. One or two questions proved superfluous and were subsequently removed, for example, 'Do you have a particular interest in the subject matter and how do you pursue it?' This question generated either responses which appeared to be irrelevant or material which naturally emerged in response to related questions.

Visitors' written comments

A selection of visitors' written comments made between 2000 and 2003 were also reviewed. These comments came from visitor books at the Anne Frank House and from the database that maintains a record of visitors' comments cards at the St Mungo Museum of Religious Life and Art. These were reviewed to identify comments that were especially relevant to my research questions and which could contextualise the data generated through in-depth interviews.

Data analysis and interpretation

The research design allowed for analysis to begin in the field and to take place simultaneously with data generation. After each interview was completed I listened to the tape recording at least once and captured my thoughts on what was especially interesting or significant in a field journal. This is a distinctive characteristic of qualitative research and helps the researcher to capture the meanings bound within the specific context being investigated. Analysis then is seen as an iterative, ongoing process. All visitor interviews were later transcribed and subsequently coded and analysed with the assistance of qualitative data analysis software. The use of this software supported the management and interrogation of the data set and facilitated flexibility in coding and recoding the interview transcripts. Alongside the process of coding, a journal of spontaneous thoughts, interpretations and emerging themes was also maintained through the software – a facility which helps to enrich and refine the process of data analysis and interpretation over time.

Visitor interview protocols

Introduction

Hello – I am from Sheffield University and I am doing a study about people's experiences of visiting St Mungo's/the Anne Frank House. Could I please ask you a few questions?

A. General

1. Where have you come from today? Is that where you live?

2. Who are you visiting with today?

B. Motivation/Expectations

3. What prompted you to visit today?

4. Have you visited before?

    If yes – When did you last visit?

    If no   – How does your experience today compare with what you expected?

C. The visit/experience

5. What part or parts of the museum did you like most or find most interesting? Why?

6. Were there any parts of the museum you didn't like or found least interesting? Why?

7. Were there any particular parts of the museum that prompted you to pause for discussion or to share your thoughts (with your friends/family/companion/ or with museum staff?) For example, was there any part of the museum that you found especially provocative?

If yes – What kinds of things did you talk about?

D. *The 'message'*

8. Do you feel the museum is trying to communicate any particular message?

      If yes – What would you say this message is?

          – Where in particular do you think this comes across most strongly?

          – Who do you think the museum is aiming this message at?

          – Were there any aspects of this message that you especially agreed or disagreed with? Why?

9. What do you feel you will take away from your visit? (For example, is there anything you feel differently about or know more about as a result of your visit?)

E. *The Museum*

10. What do you think is the overall purpose of this museum?

11. The topics and issues covered in this museum might also be addressed by other media, for example television or newspapers. How do you think the museum's approach to this topic is different from these other sources of information?

12. Do you think people respond differently to the museum than they do to these other sources? How?

F. Visitor background

13. Can I ask approximately how old you are?

14. What is your occupation? (If unemployed or retired, please give previous job if applicable.)

15. Are there any aspects of your identity – such as religion or life experience – that makes your visit/this museum especially meaningful to you?

16. Do you visit museums often?

17. When was the last time you visited a museum and which was it?

18. What other museums have you visited in the last year?

Thank you very much for your time.

APPENDIX 2

Buried in the Footnotes: the representation of disabled people in museum and gallery collections

Self-completion questionnaire to curators

The first phase of the research into the material held within UK collections that relates to disability involved a self-completion questionnaire (below) sent to 224 curators across a sample of museums and galleries selected to achieve variation in geographical distribution, mode of governance, size and collection type.

Buried in the Footnotes: the representation of disabled people in museum and gallery collections

Introduction

This project, initiated by RCMG and funded through the AHRB's Innovation Awards scheme, aims to identify the evidence that exists within museums' and galleries' collections that can attest to the historical lives of disabled people. It also aims to explore the factors that potentially influence the way in which this material is recorded and presented within museums.

Our earliest research in this field was undertaken in 1996. We believe that all of us know more about disability than we did in 1996, and will see connections that we did not see then. Please forgive us, therefore, if you think you have already been asked these questions. We do still need the answers again.

This survey is being distributed to over 200 curators within UK museums and galleries. The data gathered from this phase will help us to establish a broad context for the project. We will also use it to help us to select a small number of case studies for more in-depth qualitative research during the next stage of the project.

We would be very grateful if you could help us by filling in the questionnaire answering the questions as they relate to the collection(s) for which you are responsible. If you feel that the questionnaire may also be of interest to other curatorial colleagues within your organisation please pass them a copy.

A note on definitions of disability

Contemporary ideas about disability are different from historic ones. Our aim is to find disability wherever it is, so we encourage you to search under words which would not be comfortably used today – freak, cripple or deaf-mute, for example. To guide your research, we are looking for:

- People who are physically disabled – who walk with aids, cannot walk, have lost limbs or have deformities.

- People who are blind, Deaf or have lesser sensory impairments (loss of sight or hearing).

- People who have disfigurements of the face or body caused by disease, mutilation, war or work injury.

- People who have learning difficulties – who may, in the past, have been described as 'idiots' or characterised as children when they are adult.

- People who experienced mental illnesses such as depression or mania – look for words like 'lunatic', 'madman' or 'possessed'.

- Local characters or freaks – giants, dwarves or people with identified disfigurements.

If you are not sure about something you have found, please do include it. We would rather find something we haven't thought of than risk missing something.

We also want to be clear that no judgement is attached by us to words that you may use to describe an item, to the way it is displayed or to the level of information that exists about it. We are looking for information, and the way that objects are described on their labels or accession details is part of that information.

Part 1 – About your organisation

Name of museum or gallery:

Address:

E-mail:

Questionnaire completed by (please provide name and position):

Type of collection(s) for which you have curatorial responsibility:

Part 2 – About the museum's displays/collections

2.a Displays and exhibitions

2.1 As far as you are aware, do your displays currently include any representation, of real disabled people, their artwork or possessions, or of images/artefacts portraying disabled people (fictional or unknown characters)?

Yes/No

(If yes, please could you identify the items which are displayed in your answers to question 2.b below).

2.2 Within the past five years, have you organised or hosted any exhibition which featured disabled people or their work – either as a main topic or as part of a wider project?

Yes/No

If yes, please give us the title, date and a brief description of content:

2.b Specific items/collections

2.3 Are you aware of any material in your collections which relates to disability and/or the lives of disabled people?

This might be:

• *Objects, clothing or personal items used or owned by disabled people*

• *Works of art or objects which portray disability as a feature or central topic*

• *Art works or objects created by artists/makers who had a disability*

Yes/No

If yes, please either identify specific objects (please list below) or – if you feel there are relevant collections – please summarise their content:

2.4 What kinds of information do you have, related to these objects or collections, which explains the connection to a disabled person or gives detail about their life? Please include a copy if possible.

2.5 How could a member of the public get access to this information?

2.6 Are any of these items / collections on display at the moment?

Yes/No

If no, when was the item last on display?

If yes, please enclose the label text below:

Part 3 – Participating in this research

Museums and galleries who agree to participate in the next stage of our research and are subsequently selected as case studies will be asked to host our researchers for a one or two day review (browsing collections and associated information, interviews with curators). You may also be asked to undertake some more in-depth searches into your own collections, using guidance from the researchers.

3.1 Would your organisation be willing to participate as a case study in this research?

Yes/No

3.2 If yes, who should we approach to secure agreement and make arrangements?

Name:

Position within organisation:

Contact information:

Telephone:

E-mail:

3.3 Please use this space to tell us about any other department in your organisation, or other organisation, which you feel would be relevant to our research.

Thank you for taking the time to complete this survey.

NOTES

1 MUSEUMS AND THE GOOD SOCIETY

1 Whilst these museums can be understood to share a common concern for combating prejudice and promoting human rights, they nevertheless couch their goals and purposes in variable ways. For example, the mission of the Lower East Side Tenement Museum is 'to promote tolerance and historical perspective through the presentation and interpretation of the variety of immigrant and migrant experiences on Manhattan's Lower East Side, a gateway to America' (Abram 2002). The Japanese American National Museum states: 'We share the story of Japanese Americans because we honor our nation's diversity. We believe in the importance of remembering our history to better guard against the prejudice that threatens liberty and equality in a democratic society. We strive as a world-class museum to provide a voice for Japanese Americans and a forum that enables all people to explore their own heritage and culture' (JANM 2005).

2 This statement appeared in a press release, dated April 2005, announcing the theme of International Museums Day as 'Museums Bridging Cultures'.

3 I borrow the term 'society's conversation' from Goldhagen 1996.

4 See, for example, Lynda Kelly and Phil Gordon's account of initiatives designed to promote reconciliation with Indigenous peoples at the Australian Museum in Sydney, Australia.

5 See, for example, Littler (2005) and Young (2002).

6 See, for example, O'Neill (2004) and Sandell (2005).

7 I use the term sexual minorities here since it is a more inclusive term than gay or lesbian, 'being open to any group (previously, now, or in the future) stigmatized or despised as a result of sexual orientation, identity, or behaviour' including gay men, lesbians, bisexuals and transgendered people (Donnelly 2003: 229).

8 I use both the terms 'heterosexism' and 'homophobia' throughout the book to refer to prejudice directed at sexual minorities. Although less widely used than 'homophobia', heterosexism is rather more satisfactory for the purposes of this project since it reflects the discursive rather than individualist understanding of prejudice which I have adopted for my investigations. This is developed in detail in chapter 2. As Kath Weston explains, 'With its allusion to psychiatric diagnostic categories, homophobia not only implies a pathological and exceptional condition, but lays responsibility at the foot of the individual. Heterosexism, in contrast, acknowledges that gay and lesbian oppression is socially structured and multiply determined' (1991: 223).

209

9 The study was commissioned by the Japan Society, undertaken by the Bureau of Social Science Research at the American University in Washington DC, and funded through a grant from John D. Rockefeller.

10 The Research Centre for Museums and Galleries (RCMG) is part of the Department of Museum Studies at the University of Leicester, England. The research project I draw on was undertaken collaboratively by a team comprising Jocelyn Dodd, Richard Sandell, Annie Delin, Jackie Gay and Ceri Jones.

2 ON PREJUDICE

1 Concerning racial prejudice in particular, Duckitt states that, 'During the nineteenth century and even the early decades of the twentieth, negative and derogatory racial attitudes were seen as basically natural responses by advanced Western peoples to backward colonial peoples. It was only in the aftermath of the First World War that the concept of prejudice became widely adopted to express what had only then come to be seen as profoundly unfair and irrational negative attitudes to culturally different people and national minorities' (2001: 253).

2 Much of the research has taken place within the context of often fierce debates since investigations have been closely linked with attempts to understand and resolve politically sensitive and contested issues around, for example, racism, racial discrimination and other specific forms of social conflict. Although my study is not concerned specifically with racism, but rather more broadly with the concept of prejudice against diverse groups perceived as different, as 'other' and inferior, it is useful to acknowledge the political context within which much of the existing research on the topic has taken place.

3 See, for example, Augoustinos and Reynolds 2001.

4 See, for example, Philomena Essed's (1991) influential study of everyday contemporary racism in the United States and the Netherlands.

5 In support of Essed's theory of everyday racism, van Dijk states that 'racism does not consist of only white supremacist ideologies of race, or only of aggressive, overt or blatantly discriminatory acts, the forms of racism as it is currently understood in informal conversations, in the media, or in much of the social sciences. Racism also involves the everyday, mundane, negative opinions, attitudes and ideologies and the seemingly subtle acts and conditions of discrimination against minorities, namely, those social cognitions and social acts, processes, structures, or institutions that directly or indirectly contribute to the dominance of the white group and the subordinate position of minorities' (1993: 5).

6 For the purposes of readability, I have followed anthropological tradition and given pseudonyms to some visitors where extracts from their interviews are used. To ensure anonymity, the names of individual visitors were not gathered as part of the interview process.

7 The occupations are as visitors themselves described them.

8 These strategically deployed linguistic accomplishments might be seen to echo the strategies of positive self-presentation that van Dijk and Wetherell and Potter found in their research into racism (cited in LeCouteur and Augoustinos 2001) although it should be noted that, in those instances, these strategies were deployed purposefully to enable the individual to deflect accusations of racism whilst still making discriminatory comments.

9 van Dijk uses the term 'elites' to denote groups in society that have special power resources. 'Depending on the societal domain or field in which they wield power, we may speak of, for example, political, state, corporate, scientific, military, or

social elites ... The power resources of elites may be multiple and include property, income, decision control, knowledge, expertise, position, rank, as well as social and ideological resources such as status, prestige, fame, influence, respect and similar resources ascribed to them by groups, institutions, or society at large' (1993: 44). This definition can readily be applied to a notion of 'cultural elites' as those with the power and resources to control museums and other forms of cultural production.

10 Although van Dijk acknowledges the agency of non-elites, arguing that 'popular racism' can also influence, from the bottom up, the actions of the elites, he states that 'much of the motivation and many of the prejudiced arguments that seem to inspire popular racism are "prepared" by elites' (1993: 10).

11 Essed, for example, acknowledges that 'Racism not only operates through culture, it is also the expression of structural conflict. Individuals are actors in a power structure. Power can be used to reproduce racism, but it can also be used to combat racism' (1991: viii).

3 PURPOSE, MEDIA AND MESSAGE

1 The 'One Scotland: no place for racism' website quotes Jack McConnell, head of the devolved Scottish government: 'This campaign promotes a Scotland of many cultures. It highlights the need for all of us to examine critically our attitudes. It urges us to challenge racism, whatever form it takes' (Scottish Executive 2005).

2 See, for example, Essed 1991.

3 It might be argued that visitors to museums which more overtly convey their social purpose and their moral position to potential audiences prior to arrival through their title, publicity materials and reputation (for example, peace museums, tolerance museums and human rights museums) might, in doing so, filter out those audiences who feel that these kinds of places are 'not for them'. In contrast, the Anne Frank House, St Mungo's and many other museums with social missions which are not necessarily evident prior to visiting might, to a greater or lesser extent, 'catch visitors unawares' and may therefore reach some of those who might otherwise self-exclude.

4 In 2006, the painting was relocated to Kelvingrove Museum and Art Gallery, part of Glasgow Museums, where it had previously been on display before St Mungo's was created.

4 THE VISITOR–EXHIBITION ENCOUNTER

1 This approach is typified by the work of Adorno (1991).

2 See, for example, Appleton 2001.

3 See, for example, McQuail (1997), Moores (1993), Alasuutari (1999), Ruddock (2001).

4 For a fuller discussion of these shifts, see Silverstone (1994) and Macdonald (2002).

5 Some have highlighted the dangers of conflating the criticism of a religion with racism. See, for example, Toynbee (2004).

6 Anas Altikriti (2004), for example, states, 'The ferocity of recent attacks on Muslims and Islam in the mainstream British media has led many to question what is driving these attempts to incite hatred and fear of our community ... The attempt to force the overwhelming majority of moderate Muslims into the tiny space occupied by the minority extremist element is nothing short of wicked.

These latest media attacks appear to be part of a concerted attempt not only to do that, but also to tarnish the remarkable history of Muslims in this country and the role they have played in the shaping of our nation.' For an in-depth analysis of the British media's role in producing and reproducing anti-Muslim racism and prejudice, see Richardson (2004).

5 MUSEUMS IN THE MEDIASCAPE

1 For further discussion of the ways in which museums often exaggerate distance between viewer and subject, see Riegel (1996).
2 Although the person writing this card authored their comments by giving their full name I have nevertheless chosen to use a pseudonym in line with the approach used for interviewees.
3 See, for example, Duncan (1995), Riegel (1996), Karp and Kratz (2000).
4 For further discussion of the museum's authority, see, for example, Duncan (1995) (on art museums, in particular) and Handler and Gable's (1997) account of history making at Colonial Williamsburg.
5 Analysis of an exhibition at a university art gallery in Nottingham, England, in 1999, which explored the lives of refugees from Bosnia-Herzegovina, hints at the potential role which museums might play as sites for disseminating non-prejudiced resources. Maggie O'Neill et al. state that, '"Global Refugees: The Bosnians in Nottingham – Past, Present and Future" was accessed by a relatively wide audience in the Bonington Gallery, Nottingham, and also discussed in local newspaper articles. The latter served to re-present the Bosnian community in ways that challenged negative stereotypes of "refugees" and presented their stories of resistance, loss and exile in creative, informative ways' (2002: 86).

6 DISPLAYING DIFFERENCE

1 Hall defines the practice of trans-coding as 'taking an existing meaning and re-appropriating it for new meanings' (1997: 270).
2 The study was funded through an Innovation Award from the Arts and Humanities Research Board. The project team comprised Jocelyn Dodd, Richard Sandell, Annie Delin and Jackie Gay.
3 The researchers report that, 'Cultural and national differences within the category Asian – be it Sikh, Muslim, Hindu, Pakistani or Indian – were not recognised' by respondents in their study.
4 John Richardson, in his study of the ways in which British broadsheet newspapers are implicated in the production and promulgation of anti-Muslim prejudice similarly highlights the fluidity of racism. He states, 'Of course racism is not a fixed concept – to the degree that it may be more appropriate to talk of racisms. This point is illustrated by the manner in which racism has changed, shifted and re-emerged in different guises over the last 300 years or so, and the way it *continues* to re-emerge, creating new positions on racial hierarchies and warranting new forms of social control to police these new racisms' (2004: xiv).
5 More recently, Hevey curated an exhibition, *Giants: Disabled People Reaching for Equality*, which was created to celebrate the European Year of Disabled People and which was shown at the City Hall, London in 2003. The exhibition represents a purposive attempt to counter the negative perceptions of disabled people he had earlier written about.

6 Rosalinda Hardiman (1990), for example, has highlighted the lack of attention given by museums to issues related to the employment of disabled staff.

7 In an article on the under-representation of disabled people in British museum displays, Peter Berridge, Director of Colchester Museums offered a similar viewpoint. 'If you walked down a street in Roman Colchester you'd see people of different races and you'd see disabled people, whether they were beggars or soldiers injured in the war … If we don't display them' he argued, 'then it means we're editing them out' (Nightingale 2004: 29).

8 The selected case studies were Snibston Discovery Park, Leicestershire; Manx Museum, Isle of Man; National Museum of Scotland, Edinburgh; Royal Pump Room, Leamington Spa Art Gallery and Museum; Whitby Museum, Yorkshire; Royal London Hospital Museum and Archives; The Walker Art Gallery, Liverpool; Birmingham Museum and Art Gallery; National Maritime Museum, Greenwich and Colchester Museums.

9 Interestingly, a senior museum professional participating in the colloquium suggested that some of these questions concerning definition were so pedantic as to constitute forms of evasion and reflected an entrenched unwillingness on the part of some curators to engage with the broader issues raised by the research.

10 For further discussion of the controversy surrounding the new addition to the FDR memorial, see Garland Thomson (2001).

11 Hall (1997) similarly highlights this danger in relation to interventions designed to contest racialised regimes of representation.

12 Interestingly – especially given the UK context for the empirical element of *Buried in the Footnotes* – Laura Peers has highlighted differences in approaches to exhibition development between museums in the UK and those in other contexts. Although focusing on the field of ethnographic curation, her observations nevertheless suggests that the prevailing approach to curatorship in the UK is one in which the habit of consulting stakeholders about issues of representation is less fully formed than it is elsewhere. 'Museums in North America, Australia and other areas where local indigenous populations have pressed for change to museum practice,' she argues, 'are now working in a very different manner from many of those in the UK and Europe, where physical and political distance permits another set of approaches to museum display and representation … North American museums dealing with Native materials have shifted away from a model of exhibition development which is controlled from within the institution and in which the curator is the ultimate authority … Source community members have also become integral to the entire process of curation and exhibition development … While not all exhibitions on Native people developed at North American museums work this way, the climate of curation has shifted significantly on that continent, to make collaboration and co-management the model for such work' (2000: 8–10).

7 (RE)FRAMING CONVERSATIONS

1 Today 'The Museum's primary mission is to advance and disseminate knowledge about this unprecedented tragedy; to preserve the memory of those who suffered; and to encourage its visitors to reflect upon the moral and spiritual questions raised by the events of the Holocaust as well as their own responsibilities as citizens of a democracy'. This enhancement of purpose and expansion of goals, which grew out of the strategic review process, resulted in the establishment within the museum of the National Institute for Holocaust Education which focuses on engaging a range of audiences in exploring the contemporary

implications of the Holocaust. For example, the Center has developed a series of partnerships which offer training programmes for personnel from a number of professions – in particular law enforcement and national security, health and medicine and teaching – to utilise the museum and its resources as a platform from which to reflect on trends, challenges and ethical concerns arising in their own professional practice (Ogilvie 2006).

2 For example, Timothy Kaiser, Director of Interpretive Resources, explained that some visitors take a copy of each of the museum's brochures that focus attention on 'the other victims' of the Holocaust – Poles, Sinti and Roma, Jehovah's witnesses and so on – but decline (or sometimes more actively refuse) the one that deals with the Nazi's treatment of homosexuals.

3 The panel reads, 'In Buffalo, New York, Dr. Barnett Slepian was assassinated in his home by an extreme opponent of abortion. His family and fellow doctors mourned, and Americans feared the escalation of ideological differences into violence and terrorism. Prior to his murder, Dr Slepian's name appeared on an Internet web page that threatens abortion clinic doctors. The Internet is increasingly used to incite hate crimes.'

4 For reflections on the controversy surrounding the opening of the National Museum of Australia see Casey (2001).

5 In an article entitled 'Rabbis Attack Gay Inclusion in Shoah Museum' the *Jewish News Weekly of Northern California* reported on comments made by 'right-of-center' groups of Orthodox rabbis who were threatening to boycott the museum as long as it included material about homosexual victims of the Holocaust. The article also reported on angry responses from 'more mainstream' Orthodox rabbis, both at a national and regional level, who were appalled by the attack and called the boycott inappropriate and inexcusable (Nussbaum et al. 1997).

BIBLIOGRAPHY

Abercrombie, N. and Longhurst, B. (1998) *Audiences: A Sociological Theory of Performance and Imagination*, London, Thousand Oaks, New Delhi: Sage.

Abram, R. (2002) 'Harnessing the Power of History', in R. Sandell (ed.) *Museums, Society, Inequality*, London and New York: Routledge.

—(2005) 'History is as History Does: The Evolution of a Mission-Driven Museum', in R. R. Janes and G. T. Conarty (eds) *Looking Reality in the Eye: Museums and Social Responsibility*, Calgary: University of Calgary Press.

Adorno, T. W. (1991) *The Culture Industry*, London: Routledge.

Alasuutari, P. (1999) 'Introduction: Three Phases of Reception Studies', in P. Alasuutari (ed.) *Rethinking the Media Audience*, London, Thousand Oaks, New Delhi: Sage.

Altikriti, A. (2004) 'No, We Don't Want to Conquer the World', *The Guardian*, 5 August 2004.

American Association of Museums (1992) *Excellence and Equity: Education and the Public Dimension of Museums*, Washington DC: American Association of Museums.

Ames, M. (1992) *Cannibal Tours and Glass Boxes: The Anthropology of Museums*, Vancouver: University of British Columbia Press.

Ang, I. (1985) *Watching Dallas: Soap Opera and the Melodramatic Imagination*, London: Methuen.

Anne Frank House (2000) 'The Anne Frank House: More than a Museum', *Anne Frank Magazine*, 24–27.

—(2004) *Anne Frank House Annual Report 2003*, Amsterdam: Anne Frank Stichting.

—(2005) *Activities: Anne Frank House*, Amsterdam: Anne Frank Stichting. Online. Available HTTP: <http://www.annefrank.org> Accessed 5 October 2005.

Appleton, J. (ed) (2001) *Museums for 'The People': Conversations in Print*, London: Institute of Ideas.

Arnold, K. (1998) '*Birth and Breeding*: Politics on Display at the Wellcome Institute for the History of Medicine', in S. Macdonald (ed.) *The Politics of Display: Museums, Science, Culture*, London and New York: Routledge.

Artley, A. (1993) 'Many Mansions', *The Spectator*, 15 May 1993: 48–51.

Augoustinos, M. and Reynolds, K. J. (2001) 'Prejudice, Racism and Social Psychology', in M. Augoustinos and K. J. Reynolds (eds) *Understanding Prejudice, Racism and Social Conflict*, London, Thousand Oaks, New Delhi: Sage.

215

Bagnall, G. (2003) 'Performance and Performativity at Heritage Sites', *Museum and Society*, vol. 1, no. 2: 87–103.

Barnes, C. (1992) *Disabling Imagery and the Media: An Exploration of Principles for Media Representation of Disabled People*, (BCODP) British Council of Organisations of Disabled People, Halifax: Ryburn Publishing.

Bennett, S. (1997) *Theatre Audiences: A Theory of Production and Reception*, 2nd edn, London: Routledge.

Bennett, T. (1988) 'The Exhibitionary Complex', *New Formations*, no. 4: 73–102.

—(1998) 'Speaking to the Eyes: Museums, Legibility and the Social Order', in S. Macdonald (ed.) *The Politics of Display: Museums, Science, Culture*, London and New York, Routledge.

—(2003) 'Representation and Exhibition?', *The Journal of Education in Museums*, no. 24: 3–8.

—(2005) 'Civic Laboratories: Museums, Cultural Objecthood, and the Governance of the Social', *CRESC Working Paper Series*, no. 2, University of Manchester and the Open University.

—(2006) 'Civic Seeing: Museums and the Organisation of Vision', in S. Macdonald (ed.) *A Companion to Museum Studies*, Massachusetts and Oxford: Blackwell Publishing.

Bourne, G. (1996) 'The Last Taboo?', *Museum Journal*, vol. 96, no. 11: 28–29.

Bower, R. T. and Sharp, L. M. (1956) 'The Use of Art in International Communication: A Case Study', *The Public Opinion Quarterly*, vol. 20, no. 1: 221–229.

Brooker, W. (2001) 'Living on Dawson's Creek: Teen Viewers, Cultural Convergence and Television Overflow', *International Journal of Cultural Studies*, vol. 4, no. 4.

Brooker, W. and Jermyn, D. (2003) 'Paradigm Shift: from "Effects" to "Uses and Gratifications"', in W. Brooker and D. Jermyn (eds) *The Audience Studies Reader*, London and New York: Routledge.

Brown, R. (1995) *Prejudice: Its Social Psychology*, Oxford: Blackwell.

Cameron, D. F. (1972) 'The Museum, a Temple or the Forum', *Journal of World History*, vol. 14, no. 1: 189–199.

Casey, D. (2001) 'Museums as Agents for Social and Political Change', *Curator*, vol. 44, no. 3: 230–237.

Cooper, E. and Dinerman, H. (1951) 'Analysis of the Film *Don't Be A Sucker*, A Study in Communication', in W. Brooker and D. Jermyn (eds) *The Audience Studies Reader*, London and New York: Routledge: 27–36.

Corner, J., Schlesinger, P. and Silverstone, R. (eds) (1997) *International Media Research: A Critical Survey*, London and New York: Routledge.

Cowan, J. K., Dembour, M. and Wilson, R. A. (eds) (2001) *Culture and Rights: Anthropological Perspectives*, Cambridge: Cambridge University Press.

Da Breo, H. (1990) 'Into the Heart of Africa'. Exhibition Review in *Culture*, vol. 10, no. 1: 104–105.

Delin, A. (2002) 'Buried in the Footnotes: The Absence of Disabled People in the Collective Imagery of our Past', in R. Sandell (ed.) *Museums, Society, Inequality*, London and New York: Routledge: 84–97.

Department for Culture, Media and Sport (DCMS) (2000) *Centres for Social Change: Museums, Galleries and Archives for All: Policy Guidance on Social Inclusion for*

DCMS Funded and Local Authority Museums, Galleries and Archives in England, London: DCMS.

—(2005) *Understanding the Future: Museums and 21st Century Life, the Value of Museums*, London: DCMS.

Dodd, J. (2002) 'Museums and the Health of the Community', in R. Sandell (ed.) *Museums, Society, Inequality*, London and New York: Routledge.

Donnelly, J. (2003) *Universal Human Rights in Theory and Practice*, 2nd edn, Ithaca and London: Cornell University Press.

Duckitt, J. (2001) 'Reducing Prejudice: An Historical and Multi-Level Approach', in M. Augoustinos and K. J. Reynolds (eds) (2001) *Understanding Prejudice, Racism and Social Conflict*, London, Thousand Oaks, New Delhi: Sage.

Duncan, C. (1991) 'Art Museums and the Ritual of Citizenship', in I. Karp and S. D. Lavine (eds) *Exhibiting Cultures: The Poetics and Politics of Museum Display*, Washington and London: Smithsonian Institution Press: 88–103.

—(1995) *Civilizing Rituals: Inside Public Art Museums*, London and New York: Routledge.

Dunlop, H. (2002) 'Faith Under the Spotlight', *Interpretation: Journal of the Association of Heritage Interpretation*, vol. 7, no. 2: 8–9.

—(2003) Interview with the Author, 23 May 2003.

Dyer, R. (1993) *The Matter of Images: Essays on Representation*, 2nd edn, London and New York: Routledge.

Essed, P. (1991) *Understanding Everyday Racism*, Newbury Park, London, New Delhi: Sage.

Evans, J. (1999) 'Introduction: Nation and Representation', in D. Boswell and J. Evans (eds) *Representing the Nation: A Reader*, London and New York: Routledge.

Fraser, J. (2005) 'Museums, Drama, Ritual and Power: A Theory of the Museum Experience' unpublished thesis, University of Leicester.

Garland Thomson, R. (1997) *Extraordinary Bodies: Figuring Physical Disability in American Culture and Literature*, New York: Columbia University Press.

—(2001) 'The FDR Memorial: Who Speaks from the Wheelchair', *Chronicle of Higher Education*, 26 January 2001.

—(2002) 'The Politics of Staring: Visual Rhetorics of Disability in Popular Photography', in S. L. Snyder, B. J. Brueggemann and R. Garland Thomson (eds) *Disability Studies: Enabling the Humanities*, New York: The Modern Language Association of America: 56–75.

—(2005) 'Staring at the Other', *Disability Studies Quarterly*, vol. 25, no. 4.

Geft, L. (2005) Interview with the Author, 20 June 2005.

Gerber, D. A. (1996) 'The "Careers" of People Exhibited in Freak Shows: The Problem of Volition and Valorization', in R. Garland Thomson (ed) *Freakery: Cultural Spectacles of the Extraordinary Body*, New York: New York University Press: 38–54.

Glasgow City Council (2001) *Best Value Review Final Report*, July 2001, Museums, Heritage and Visual Arts, Online. Available HTTP: <http://www.glasgowmuseums.com/reports.cfm> Accessed 5 October 2005.

Gledhill, R. (1993) 'From Mungo to the Muslims; St Mungo Museum, Glasgow', *The Times*, 31 March: 29.

Goldhagen, D. J. (1996) *Hitler's Willing Executioners: Ordinary Germans and the Holocaust*. London: Abacus/Little Brown and Co.

Gourevitch, P. (1995) 'What They Saw at the Holocaust Museum', *New York Sunday Times Magazine*, February 2: 44–45.

Hall, S. (1982) 'The Rediscovery of "Ideology": Return of the Repressed in Media Studies', in M. Gurevitch, T. Bennett, J. Curran and J. Woollacott (eds) *Culture, Society and the Media*, London: Methuen.

—(1990a) *Culture, Media, Language*, London: Unwin Hyman.

—(1990b) 'Encoding, Decoding', in S. During (ed.) *The Cultural Studies Reader*, 2nd edn, London and New York: Routledge.

—(ed.) (1997) *Representation: Cultural Representations and Signifying Practices*, London, Thousand Oaks, New Delhi: Sage.

Handler, R. and Gable, E. (1997) *The New History in an Old Museum: Creating the Past at Colonial Williamsburg*, Durham, NC and London: Duke University Press.

Hardiman, R. (1990) 'Some More Equal than Others', *Museums Journal*, November 1990: 28–30.

HBO (2002) 'Six Feet Under Bulletin Board'. Online. Available HTTP: <http://www/hbo.com/sixfeetunder/wisteria/comingout> Accessed 5 March 2002.

Hein, G. E. (1998) *Learning in the Museum*, London and New York: Routledge.

Hevey, D. (1992) *The Creatures that Time Forgot: Photography and Disability Imagery*, London: Routledge.

Hirano, I. (2002) 'A Public Service Responsibility', in *Mastering Civic Engagement: A Challenge to Museums*, Washington DC: American Association of Museums.

Holden, L. (1991) *Forms of Deformity*, Sheffield: JSOT Press.

Hooper-Greenhill, E. (2000) *Museums and the Interpretation of Visual Culture*, London and New York: Routledge.

Horton, D. and Wohl, R. (1956) 'Mass Communications and Para-Social Interaction', *Psychiatry*, vol. 19, 215–229.

International Council of Museums (2005) 'International Museum Day – Bridging Cultures', Paris: International Council of Museums. Online. Available HTTP: <http://icom.museum/release.bridging.html> Accessed 5 October 2005.

Janes, R. R. and Conarty, G. T. (eds) (2005) *Looking Reality in the Eye: Museums and Social Responsibility*, Calgary: University of Calgary Press.

JANM (2005) *Museum Information*, Los Angeles: Japanese American National Museum. Online. Available HTTP: <http://www.janm.org> Accessed 7 October 2005.

Karp, I. and Kratz, C. A. (2000) 'Reflections on the Fate of Tippoo's Tiger: Defining Cultures through Public Display', in E. Hallam and B. V. Street (eds) *Cultural Encounters: Representing 'Otherness'*, London and New York: Routledge.

Karp, I. and Lavine, S. D. (eds) (1995) *Exhibiting Cultures: The Poetics and Politics of Museum Display*, Washington and London: Smithsonian Institution Press.

Katz, E., Blumler, J. G. and Gurevitch, M. (1974) 'Utilization of Mass Communication by the Individual', in J. G. Blumler and E. Katz (eds) *The Uses of Mass Communication*, London: Sage.

Kratz, C. A. (2002) *The Ones that are Wanted: Communication and the Politics of Representation in a Photographic Exhibition*, Berkeley, Los Angeles, London: University of California Press.

Kriegel, L. (1987) 'The Cripple in Literature', in A. Gartner and T. Joe (eds) *Images of the Disabled, Disabling Images*. New York: Praeger.

Kudlick, C. J. (2003) 'Disability History: Why We Need Another "Other"', *American Historical Review*, vol. 108, no. 3: 763–793.

—(2005) 'The Local History Museum, so Near and yet so Far', *The Public Historian*, vol. 27, no. 2: 75–81.

LeCouteur A. and Augoustinos, M. (2001) 'The Language of Prejudice and Racism', in M. Augoustinos and K. J. Reynolds (eds) *Understanding Prejudice, Racism and Social Conflict*, London, Thousand Oaks, New Delhi: Sage.

Laurence, A. (1994) *Women in England 1500–1760: A Social History*, London: Weidenfeld and Nicolson/Orion.

Leinhardt, G. and Knutson, K. (2004) *Listening in on Museum Conversations*, Walnut Creek, CA and Oxford: Altamira Press.

Liddiard, M. (2004) 'Changing Histories: Museums, Sexuality and the Future of the Past', *Museum and Society*, vol. 2, no. 1: 15–29.

Littler, J. (2005) 'Introduction: British Heritage and the Legacies of "Race"', in J. Littler and R. Naidoo (eds) *The Politics of Heritage: The Legacies of 'Race'*, Abingdon and New York: Routledge.

Luke, T. W. (2002) *Museum Politics: Power Plays at the Exhibition*, Minneapolis and London: University of Minnesota Press.

Macdonald, S. (1998) 'Exhibitions of Power and Powers of Exhibition: An Introduction to the Politics of Display', in S. Macdonald (ed.) *The Politics of Display: Museums, Science, Culture*, London and New York: Routledge.

—(2002) *Behind the Scenes at the Science Museum*, Oxford and New York: Berg.

—(2003) 'Museums, National, Postnational and Transcultural Identities', *Museum and Society*, vol. 1, no. 1: 1–16.

—(2005) 'Accessing Audiences: Visiting Visitor Books', *Museum and Society*, vol. 3, no. 3: 119–136.

Macdonald, S. and Silverstone, R. (1990) 'Rewriting the Museum's Fictions: Taxonomies, Stories and Readers', *Cultural Studies*, vol. 4, no. 2: 176–191.

Majewski, J. and Bunch, L. (1998) 'The Expanding Definition of Diversity: Accessibility and Disability Culture Issues in Museum Exhibitions', *Curator*, vol. 41, no. 3: 153–161.

Marstine, J. (2005) *New Museum Theory and Practice: An Introduction*, Massachusetts and Oxford: Blackwell Publishing.

Mason, J. (1996) *Qualitative Researching*, London: Sage.

Mason, R. (2006) 'Cultural Theory and Museum Studies', in S. Macdonald (ed.) *A Companion to Museum Studies*, Massachusetts and Oxford: Blackwell Publishing.

McLean, K. (1999) 'Museum Exhibitions and the Dynamics of Dialogue', *Daedalus*, vol. 28, no. 3: 83–108.

McQuail, D. (1997) *Audience Analysis*, Thousand Oaks, London, New Delhi: Sage.

Mead, M. (1970) 'Museums in a Media-Saturated World', *Museum News*, September 1970.

Miller, P., Parker, S. and Gillinson, S. (2004) *Disablism: How to Tackle the Last Prejudice*, London: DEMOS.

Moores, S. (1993) *Interpreting Audiences: The Ethnography of Media Consumption*, London, Thousand Oaks, New Delhi: Sage.

Morley, D. (1980) *The Nationwide Audience*, London: BFI.

Müller, K. (2001) 'Invisible Visitors: Museums and the Gay and Lesbian Community', *Museum News*, September/October: 34–39 and 67–69.

Munira, M. (ed.) (2006) *Culture Vultures: Is UK Arts Policy Damaging the Arts?*, London: Policy Exchange.

Namaste, V. (2000) *Invisible Lives: The Erasure of Transsexual and Transgendered People*, Chicago: University of Chicago Press.

Nightingale, J. (2004) 'Hidden History', *Museums Journal*, vol. 104, no. 9: 26–29.

Nussbaum Cohen, D. and Katz, L. (1997) 'Rabbis Attack Gay Inclusion in Shoah Museum', *The Jewish News Weekly of Northern California*. Online. Available HTTP: <http://www.jewishsf.com> Accessed 15 October 2005.

Ogilvie, S. (2005) Interview with the Author, 3 August 2005.

—(2006) E-mail, 21 March 2006.

Okihiro, G. Y. (2005) *Educational Framework: Fighting for Democracy*, Los Angeles: National Center for the Preservation of Democracy, an affiliate of the Japanese American National Museum.

O'Neill, M. (1993) 'The St Mungo Museum of Religious Life and Art', *Scottish Museum News*, Edinburgh: Scottish Museums Council: 10–11.

—(1994) 'Serious Earth', *Museums Journal*, February 1994, Museums Association: 28–31.

—(1995) 'Exploring the Meaning of Life: The St Mungo Museum of Religious Life and Art', *Museum International*, No. 185 (Vol. 47, No. 1) UNESCO, Paris: Blackwell Publishers: 50–53.

—(2004) 'Enlightenment Museums: Universal or Merely Global?', *Museum and Society*, vol. 2, no. 3: 190–202.

O'Neill, M. (in association with Giddens, S., Breatnach, P., Bagley, C., Bourne, D. and Judge, T.) (2002) 'Renewed Methodologies for Social Research: Ethno-Mimesis as Performative Praxis', *The Sociological Review*, vol. 50, no. 1: 69–88.

Ott, K. (2005a) 'Disability and the Practice of Public History: An Introduction', *The Public Historian*, vol. 27, no. 2: 11–24.

—(2005) Interview with the Author, 8 June 2005.

Peers, L. (2000) 'Native Americans in Museums: A Review of the Chase Manhattan Gallery of North America', *Anthropology Today*, vol. 16, no. 6: 8–13.

Phillips, E. (2005) Interview with the Author, 30 June 2005.

Potter, J. and Wetherell, M. (1987) *Discourse and Social Psychology: Beyond Attitudes and Behaviour*, London: Sage.

Preziosi, D. and Farago, C. (eds) (2004) *Grasping the World: The Idea of the Museum*, Burlington, VT: Ashgate.

Radway, J. (1984, reprinted 1991) *Reading the Romance: Women, Patriarchy and Popular Literature*, Chapel Hill, NC: University of North Carolina Press.

Rapley, M. (2001) '"How to Do X without Doing Y": Accomplishing Discrimination Without "Being Racist" – "Doing Equity"', in M. Augoustinos and K. J. Reynolds (eds) *Understanding Prejudice, Racism, and Social Conflict*, London, Thousand Oaks, New Delhi: Sage.

Richardson, J. E. (2004) *(Mis)representing Islam: The Racism and Rhetoric of British Broadsheet Newspapers*, Amsterdam and Philadelphia: John Benjamins Publishing.

Richardson, M. (2002) 'Hearing Things: The Scandal of Speech in Deaf Performance', in S. L. Snyder, B. J. Brueggemann, and R. Garland Thomson (eds) *Disability Studies: Enabling the Humanities*, New York: The Modern Language Association of America: 76–87.

Riegel, H. (1996) 'Into the Heart of Irony: Ethnographic Exhibitions and the Politics of Difference', in S. Macdonald and G. Fyfe (eds) *Theorizing Museums: Representing Identity and Diversity in a Changing World*, Oxford: Blackwell Publishers.

Ruddock, A. (2001) *Understanding Audiences: Theory and Method*, London, Thousand Oaks, New Delhi: Sage.

Runnymede Trust (1997) *Islamophobia, A Challenge for Us All: A Report of The Runnymede Trust Commission on British Muslims and Islamophobia*, London: Runnymede Trust.

Sandell, R. (1998) 'Museums as Agents of Social Inclusion', *Museum Management and Curatorship*, vol. 17, no. 4: 401–418.

—(2002a) 'Museums and the Combating of Social Inequality: Roles, Responsibilities, Resistance', in R. Sandell (ed.) *Museums, Society, Inequality*, London and New York: Routledge.

—(2002b) *Museums, Society, Inequality*, London and New York: Routledge.

—(2005) 'Constructing and Communicating Equality: The Social Agency of Museum Space', in S. Macleod (ed.) *Reshaping Museum Space: Architecture, Design, Exhibitions*, London and New York: Routledge.

Scott, C. (2002) 'Measuring Social Value', in R. Sandell (ed.) *Museums, Society, Inequality*, London and New York: Routledge.

Scottish Executive (2005) *One Scotland: No Place for Racism*, Online. Available HTTP: <http://www.onescotland.com> Accessed 5 October 2005.

Scottish Museums Council (2000) *Museums and Social Justice*, Edinburgh: Scottish Museums Council.

Silverman, L. (2002) 'The Therapeutic Potential of Museums as Pathways to Inclusion', in R. Sandell (ed.) *Museums, Society, Inequality*, London and New York: Routledge.

Silverstone, R. (1988) 'Museums and the Media: A Theoretical and Methodological Exploration', *The International Journal of Museum Management and Curatorship*, vol. 7, no. 3: 231–241.

—(1994) *Television and Everyday Life*, London and New York: Routledge.

Snyder, S. L., Brueggemann, B. J. and Garland Thomson, R. (eds) *Disability Studies: Enabling the Humanities*, New York: The Modern Language Association of America.

Sullivan, R. (1985) 'The Museum as Moral Artefact', *Moral Education Forum*, 10th Anniversary Issue, The Sociomoral Dimension of Museum Design, vol. 10, nos 3 and 4, Hunter College, City University of New York: 2–18 and 61.

Sze, L. (2006) E-mail, 9 August 2005.

Szekeres, V. (2002) 'Representing Diversity and Challenging Racism: The Migration Museum', in R. Sandell (ed.) *Museums, Society, Inequality*, London and New York: Routledge.

Taylor, L. and Mullan, B. (1986) *Uninvited Guests*, London: Chatto and Windus.

Toynbee, P. (2004) 'We Must Be Free to Criticise Without Being Called Racist', *The Guardian*, 18 August 2004.

Turner, V. (1982) *From Ritual to Theatre*, New York: PAJ Publications.

Usherwood, B., Wilson, K. and Bryson, J. (2005) *Relevant Repositories of Public Knowledge? Perceptions of Archives, Libraries and Museums in Modern Britain*, The Centre for the Public Library and Information in Society, Department of Information Studies, the University of Sheffield. Online. Available HTTP: <http://cplis.shef.ac.uk/publications.htm> Accessed 6 October 2005.

Valentine, G. and McDonald, I. (2004) *Understanding Prejudice: Attitudes Towards Minorities*, London: Stonewall.

Vallely, P. (2002) 'Who is the Real Anne Frank?', *The Independent Review*, Friday 14 June 2002: 4–6.

van der Wal, B. (1985) 'The Anne Frank Center: The Evolution of a Holocaust Memorial into an Educational Institution', *Moral Education Forum*, 10th Anniversary Issue, 'The Sociomoral Dimension of Museum Design', vol. 10, nos 3 and 4, Hunter College, City University of New York: 54–61.

van Dijk, T. (1993) *Elite Discourse and Racism*, Newbury Park, London, New Delhi: Sage.

Vanegas, A. (2002) 'Representing Lesbians and Gay Men in British Social History Museums', in R. Sandell (ed.) *Museums, Society, Inequality*, London and New York: Routledge: 98–109.

van Kooten, J. (2003) Interview with the Author, 4 August 2003.

vom Lehn, D., Heath, C. and Hindmarsh, J. (2001) 'Exhibiting Interaction: Conduct and Collaboration in Museums and Galleries', *Symbolic Interaction*, vol. 24, no. 2: 189–216.

Walker, I. (2001) 'The Changing Nature of Racism: From Old to New?', in M. Augoustinos and K. J. Reynolds (eds) *Understanding Prejudice, Racism and Social Conflict*, London, Thousand Oaks, New Delhi: Sage.

Walzer, M. (1997) *On Toleration*, New Haven and London: Yale University Press.

Weil, S. E. (1996) 'The Distinctive Numerator', in S. Weil (2002), *Making Museums Matter*, Washington and London: Smithsonian Institution Press.

—(1999) 'From Being *about* Something to Being *for* Somebody: The Ongoing Transformation of the American Museum', *Daedalus*, vol. 128, no. 3: 229–258.

Weinberg, J. (1994) Paper Presented at American Association of Museums Conference on the United States Holocaust Memorial Museum, Seattle, April 1994.

Weston, K. (1991) *Families we Choose: Lesbians, Gays, Kinship*, New York and Oxford: Columbia University Press.

Wetherell, M. and Potter, J. (1992) *Mapping the Language of Racism: Discourse and the Legitimation of Exploitation.* London: Harvester Wheatsheaf.

Yin, R. K. (1994) *Case Study Research; Design and Methods*, 2nd edn, Thousand Oaks, CA: Sage.

Young, I. M. (1990) *Justice and the Politics of Difference*, Princeton, NJ and Chichester: Princeton University Press.

Young, L. (2002) 'Rethinking Heritage: Cultural Policy and Inclusion', in R. Sandell (ed.) *Museums, Society, Inequality*, London and New York: Routledge.

Ziebarth, E. (2005) Interview with the Author, 8 June 2005.

INDEX